the ORIGIN of VALUES

the ORIGIN *of* VALUES

Sociology and Philosophy of Beliefs

Raymond Boudon

Transaction Publishers
New Brunswick (U.S.A.) and London (U.K.)

Library of Congress Catalog Number: 00-053259
ISBN: 0-7658-0043-8 (alk. paper)
Printed in the United States of America

Library of Congress Cataloging-in-Publication Data

Boudon, Raymond.
    The orgin of values : essays in the sociology and philosophy of beliefs / Raymond Boudon.
        p. cm.
    Includes bibliographical references and index.
    ISBN 0-7658-0043-8 (alk. paper)
    1. Values. I. Title.

BD232. B66 2000
121' .8—dc21   00-053259

Contents

Introduction

Explaining Values and Valuation:
A Major Question for the Social Sciences
and Philosophy

We spend a good deal of time wondering whether or stating that "X is good, fair, legitimate . . . " or rather "bad, unfair, illegitimate": These value statements, these axiological beliefs regulate our social life. They are a basic ingredient of our personal identity.

For this reason, values have always been a central topic of philosophy and of the social sciences, even before the word *value* itself was popularized in this sense, under Nietzsche's influence notably. *Why do such and such people think that "X is fair, good, etc . . . "?* is a recurrent question, which raises metaquestions. I, as an observer, see that such and such people believe that "X is fair," while I see it as unfair. Thus, some people think that polygamy is an acceptable institution, or that *apartheid* was a good thing. How, as a social scientist, should I explain this difference? Should I assume without discussion that I am right and that they are wrong? Should I ignore this question of validity and content myself with trying to identify the causes of their beliefs? But then to which register or registers of causes should I pay attention?

Some social scientists and philosophers, as Nietzsche, Max Weber or Pareto, have raised these questions directly. They are responsible for what may be called a theory of values and of valuation. Thus, Nietzsche has supported the seminal view that values should be held to a large extent as illusions: I believe that "X is good" and I am convinced that I believe that "X is good" because X *is* actually good.

1

In fact, there are in many cases no ways of showing that something is good or bad, so that X would be in such cases, suggests Nietzsche, neither good nor bad. My belief would be a "rationalization," as Freud would have said later. I believe that "X is good," because believing so serves my psychological interests. Max Scheler writes rightly in 1912 that we can easily find illustrations of La Fontaine's fable, *The Fox and the Sour Grapes* (Max Scheler, 1978 [1912]: 29–30): when we try to please somebody and find out we are repeatedly rejected by him or her, we will soon "discover" his or her many defects. This will likely produce a feeling of psychological appeasement. This effect, more exactly the fact that we are unconsciously trying to produce this effect, is the *real cause* of our value statement, in other words of our axiological belief that "this (wo)man is narrowminded, coldhearted, etc . . . ." That such psychological mechanisms do exist is beyond doubt. The question, however, already raised by Max Weber, is whether we are entitled to give such mechanisms the status of a general theory of values. The question has to be raised, for "postmodernist" thinking on values often precisely takes for granted that Nietzsche's insights provide the ultimate truth on values and can be held as general. Freud's work contributed to reinforcing Nietzsche's influence. To Freud also, normative beliefs–the endorsement by social subjects of such and such value statements—have their causes mainly in the psychological effects they produce or more precisely in the unconscious anticipation of these effects.

So Nietzsche has proposed a theory of value beliefs which was to become very influential, where values are explained by their *psychological functions*. With Marx, values were also held as illusions in the sense that while people tend to think the values they believe in are objectively grounded ("I believe that 'X is good' because X *is* actually good"), they are not. As Nietzsche, Marx offered before him a functional theory of values: people endorse such and such value because of their (unconsciously) anticipated effects. But the effects are, to Marx, sociological rather than psychological: I think I believe that X is good because X is actually good, while in fact I believe that X is good *because* it serves my class interests. Neo-Nietzscheans and neo-Marxians would add a complementary assumption, belonging also to the "functional" register: the subjects should not see that their beliefs are illusory, otherwise they would have some doubts as to whether their beliefs were actually objectively grounded or not. In a word, the illusion would then not operate properly. Freud's "unconscious" and Mehring's "false consciousness" are essential ingredients of these functional theories.

Nietzsche's, Freud's, and Marx's views on values have been very influential on modern writers on values. As rightly noted by acute observers of the French intellectual scene, the French intellectuals, who were christened the "68–Thinkers," take their inspiration from them, without always recognizing it, and add little to their models, except that they write in an unmistakably obscure style of their own: Foucault's work can be characterized as the work of a "French Nietzsche," while Lacan would be a "French Freud," Derrida a "French Heidegger," and P. Bourdieu a "French Marx" (Ferry, Renaut, 1985). Most of the 68–Thinkers have developed one variant or another of the so-called "postmodernist" relativistic theory of values: beyond their differences, they have in common the viewpoint of seeing values as illusions.

This latter theory is the best known *today*, essentially because it is congruent with the relativistic *Zeitgeist* prevailing in the Western world. But many other theories have been produced in the past and others are being produced currently. As we tend to pay exclusive attention to the theories that are fashionable here and there, though, we tend not to perceive this diversity. Thus, Max Scheler's already mentioned essay on resentment remains popular today because it follows, though in a critical fashion, the theory of values proposed by Nietzsche. But few people today pay attention to the fact that the same Scheler is responsible for a much more ambitious work, where he develops a theory of values of his own, in which Nietzsche's ideas play a very limited role, and where he tries rather to develop insights inspired by phenomenology. I am not saying that this theory is the ultimate truth on values, by far it is not. What I am saying is that this theory, although not negligible, has disappeared from the field of attention because it does not follow today's favorite relativistic theories of values.

Because of this effect, which Anthony Downs has happily called the "cycles of attention" (Downs, 1972), I felt it necessary, once I became interested in the problem of the explanation of values and valuation, to try to develop a general overview of the theories concerned with this problem. This is the main aim of one of the chapters in this volume ("Explaining Values and Valuation: A Question That Has Inspired Many Theories"). The task was not easy, not only because of the "cycles of attention" effect, but also because, while some authors are recognized as having developed a theory of values, others have rather developed indirectly interesting explanatory schemes on this subject, without having properly proposed a full-fledged theory. The case of Rawls's *Theory of Justice* (Rawls, 1971) illustrates this point: Rawls proposes among other things a theory as to whether people consider the inequality in the distribution of primary goods legitimate or not. While Rawls is not considered a theorist of values, he is, in fact, one since his book contains what may be considered an ingenious explanation of the feelings of people confronted with a given level of inequalities in the distribution of primary goods. Moreover, beyond this explanation, a more general explanatory scheme can be detected in his theory: people tend to consider X as good, if and only if they tend to consider X as good in the case where they would be able to make an entire abstraction of their interests, in a word, where they would consider X as good once placed under the "veil of ignorance." Rawls's scheme is powerful, which is undoubtedly a major reason for his success. But it is hardly noted that Rawls's "veil of ignorance" has its roots in an earlier and today underestimated idea, such as Adam Smith's notion of the "impartial spectator" as opposed to the "partial actor," as we would say, or as Kant's notion of "practical reason."

A first task for anyone interested in the theory of values and valuation is to acquire an overview of all the explicit and implicit, forgotten or popular, theories on the subject produced by the classical and modern social scientists and philosophers.

The "cycles of attention" effect is also responsible for the fact that some theories are commonly misread. Such is the case of Durkheim's. Durkheim is currently read with the glasses of the neo-Durkeimians: a given individual in a society would believe that "X is good," because everybody around him believes so; the content of the "collective consciousness" would be the ultimate cause of the content of any individual consciousness. Many anthropologists among others endorse this type of explanation. Thus, to the prominent American anthropologist Clifford Geertz, all cultures have their idiosyncratic values; people normally endorse them simply because those around them endorse the same values (Geertz, 1984). As Geertz rightly recalls, Montaigne had already noted that values vary from one society to another, and contended that values should for this reason be considered as arbitrary, and that people endorse them under the mere effect of "socialization," as we would say. That this is true in some circumstances is beyond doubt. We believe a number of things because others think so. But whether this is always true is questionable. "We believe a million things on the faith of others," wrote Tocqueville. By this he meant that, if I am not, say, a biologist myself, I would tend to draw my convictions on biological matters from biologists. In this case, I know that I believe that "X is true" on the faith of others, and I perceive clearly why I follow the opinions of other people. Geertz, however, draws from Montaigne much more than these simple ideas: to him, *all* our beliefs would be individual projections, so to speak, of collective beliefs.

Durkheim does not use the word *value* in the sense Nietzsche gave it, since it was not current in France in Durkheim's time, but he developed a well articulated theory of values. Whether his main point on the subject was, as often contended by neo-Durkheimians, to develop in his own words basically the same views as Montaigne is highly questionable. The careful reader of *The Elementary Forms of Religious Life* is impressed, on the contrary, by the fact that Durkheim insists repeatedly on the point that beliefs should not be analyzed as illusions (Boudon, 1999a). Even a cat, he writes, can easily distinguish between a ball of string and a mouse. The cat will for a while play with the ball of string, because it *believes* it is a mouse. But it will soon see that the ball *is not* a mouse and lose interest in it. A child talks to his puppet, giving an observer the impression he believes his puppet is a living being. But he would be surprised if his puppet should suddenly punch him in the nose. Should all these people who believe in all kinds of things in which we do not believe ourselves, asks Durkheim ironically, be considered as being more easily the victims of illusion than a child or a cat? We normally hold something as true in a first stage, writes Durkheim, because everybody around us believes so; but in a second stage, we need to know it is actually true. A belief is held by a given individual as true in a first stage because it is collective; in a second stage, it becomes collective because it is true.[1] To Durkheim, while values vary from one society to another, they should in other words not be analyzed as illusions. They vary from one society to another because the context, the cognitive resources, the level of information of people on such and such subjects and many other factors vary. But they are far from being mere illusions injected into people's minds by obscure social forces. This does not lead to the conclusion that all societies should have the same values. Firstly, because some values may be functional in one society, but not in another; secondly, because different values may be equally legitimate in the eyes of social actors; thirdly, because values are often expressed in an indirect way, through symbols, metaphors, myths or more or less opaque concepts, and because there are obviously many ways to symbolize verbally a value. Thus, the notion of "person," the concept of "soul," the notion of "equality" all point to the value of the equal dignity of all. In a word, Durkheim's theory is much more complex and also much more acceptable than many of the more modern theories, even though they state that they lean on Durkheim's work.

The same effect of the "attention cycles" can be illustrated in the case of Max Weber. Most interpretations of Weber describe his theory as close to "postmodernist" views on values: values would be ultimately ungrounded; they would be the effect of "free" decisions. This view is currently characterized as the "decisionist" theory of values. As existentialist philosophers argued, if man is free, he should be able to act, behave, or believe without being determined by any reasons or causes. Whether Weber endorsed a decisionist theory of values is more than debatable. This interpretation of Weber was originally offered by theorists such as Leo Strauss and Carl Schmitt. As they were themselves men of strong convictions, they perceived Weber as a relativist and maintained that his relativism was grounded in his supposedly decisionist theory of values. On the basis of this interpretation, Leo Strauss described Weber as one the intellectuals responsible for the crisis of values characterizing the modern Western world. The same analysis was conducted by Erich Voegelin (1952) and by Allan Bloom (1987). Ironically, postmodernist writers follow lazily the same interpretation, but draw from it an opposite conclusion. They see Max Weber as a forerunner of "postmodernism" and praise him for his supposed decisionist-relativist theory of values.[2]

What Weber actually says is very different. Yes, he states, some ultimate values cannot be demonstrated as acceptable. It is impossible for instance to show that it is interesting to try to describe reality as it is. This postulate, which is the ground principle on which the whole construction of science is built, is effectively a *postulate* or a *principle*, as such undemonstrable, as the very words *postulate* and *prin-*

ciple clearly indicate. In the same way, it cannot be shown that respecting the dignity of all is a good thing. Once the postulate was proposed by the apostle Paul, however, writes Max Weber, it was not to be forgotten again and started impregnating the history of the Western world for the next two thousand years (Weber, 1978 [1921]: 40). And so, there are ultimate principles proposed on the market of ideas by innovators. According to the interest they arouse in the audience and to their fruitfulness, they are then selected or rejected. In the eighteenth century, aesthetics were institutionalized as a discipline of their own, says Weber, because the postulate which grounded the new discipline, that the greatness of art works, the interest they are able to arouse, in a word—their value—is the product of some features of the works themselves, was launched on the market of ideas and selected because it appeared as fruitful. Of course, while, according to Weber, moral life is characterized by a "diffuse rationalization" (*Durchration-alisierung*), this rationalization process can be thwarted or slowed down by "historical forces." Equality, democracy are basic values; they have been irreversibly selected. This does not say, though, that democracy will never be threatened, nor that the principle of the equality of all will not be damaged. Still, one cannot doubt the irreversibility of some values. While slavery is still present in many parts of the world, no one would dare any more to contend that it is a good thing. Aristotle, by contrast, thought, as most of his fellow men, that slavery was an indispensable social institution.

Weber's theory of values is thus far from Nietzsche's. Weber insists heavily on the role of rationality in moral life and history. When someone thinks that "X is good," he has good reasons for thinking so, and he thinks so *because* of these reasons. When the Roman civil servants felt powerfully attracted by Mithraïsm, they had good reasons of preferring it to the old polytheistic Roman religion. Human beliefs, prescriptive or descriptive, should be considered as "understandable." This is a basic principle of "comprehensive" sociology in Weber's sense. How can this idea, central in Weber's work, that beliefs and actions should be considered as understandable, be held as compatible with a "decisionist" view of values according to which, as values cannot be demonstrated true or false, they should be endorsed without reasons? In other words, the current neo-Nietzschean interpretation of Weber's theory of values misses its complexity, and is radically incompatible with the very idea of a "comprehensive" sociology. But it tends to be treated today as common knowledge, essentially because, if Weber, beside Nietzsche, can be read as one of the forerunners of the postmodernist theory of values, it tends to confirm that this theory represents the ultimate truth on the subject.

The dominant contemporary relativistic view of values can, more precisely, be characterized by two statements, easy to formulate (I leave aside here a crucial question raised by the brutal and hence questionable distinction introduced below between norms and values):

1. *Norms* and the endorsement of norms (valuation) can be analyzed in a basically "utilitarian" way. I tend to endorse the statement, "The norm X is good" as soon as I can consider that X produces positive effects. I believe that traffic lights are a good thing, because I see that without them, driving a car would be even more difficult and slower.

2. As to *values*, they should be distinguished from norms precisely by the fact that they cannot be justified merely by their effects. Why should they then be endorsed? The most current answer to this question is that they would be endorsed either under the effect of an ungrounded decision or under the effect of psychological, sociological, or biological forces. Why do some people believe, for instance, that polygamy is a good thing here and now? Perhaps because it had been functional at one point in the history of their society, had been selected then, had become positively perceived and remains positively perceived, under the effect of the "weight" of tradition.

The influence of this theory, according to which the endorsement of norms would be rational, while the endorsement of values would be irrational, raises two questions. The first question belongs to the sociology of knowledge: why this influence? The second can be formulated: is this "postmodernist" theory the ultimate truth the social sciences and philosophy have to propose on this crucial question of values and valuation?

That the answer to the second question should be negative is one of the main points developed in the following chapters. But I must stress now the fact that the "postmodernist" view of values has already inspired many reactions and counterproposals. Thus, a number of writers, such as James Wilson (1993), have proposed a return to the old

Aristotelian tradition, and sustained that our sense of values derives from our human nature. How far can we go on this path? Given the present state of the art on value explanation, it is certainly important to raise this question. Other theorists, such as J. Rawls or J. Habermas, should also be held as serious opponents to the dominant relativistic theory of values in the sense that they propose rather a rational theory of values. As often stressed, Habermas's theory is purely procedural, however: X can be considered good if a freely discussing assembly would reach the conclusion that X is good. This might be a simple objection, but the scientific community is the closest illustration of such a community. Now, as Pareto has rightly stressed, the scientific community produces normally false theories and statements, in addition to true ones. Free discussion is, in other words, neither a sufficient nor a necessary condition of the production of scientific truths: it simply makes truth more easily and quickly accessible. Supposing, as Habermas seems to suppose, that there is a moral truth, it follows that the procedures defining his "communicational rationality" are neither a necessary nor a sufficient condition of the production of moral truth. The fairness of the procedure constitutes as such no guarantee of the truth of the collective beliefs produced by a freely discussing assembly. A free discussion assembly in ancient Greece would have sincerely and, in the eyes of most of its members, convincingly argued that slavery is a good institution. This objection to Habermas is so obvious, that one understands easily why the average historian, sociologist, or anthropologist will likely endorse Montaigne's view on values as seen by C. Geertz, rather than Habermas's. Habermas's theoretical model does not work, because scientific truth (not to speak of moral truth, if there is one) is determined by a complex selection process developing in the long term, with the consequence that freely discussing assemblies are likely to conclude at some point in time that "X is true" or that "Y is good," and at some later time that "X is false" or that "Y is bad." As with Rawls, he, too, offers a general procedure thanks to which it could be determined whether "X is good, bad, etc.," and correlatively explains why people feel that "X is good, bad, etc." But his theory itself offers exclusively an explanation of a few basic values (basic liberties, equality of opportunity, the constraint that inequalities should be "functional"). Neither Habermas's nor Rawls's theories are able to account for the historicity of values. I mention these theories because they are the theories belonging to the category of "rational" theories that have, more than others, drawn the attention of the public in the recent years. Their success is the symptom of a demand. However, whether the supply meets the demand is questionable. If it would, the influence of the irrational relativistic theories of values would likely be weaker.

Another reason why it is interesting to go back to the question of the explanation of values is that, while postmodernist views are dominant on the subject, many interesting proposals are currently being presented by social scientists and philosophers that are worth discussion, although, as in the cases of the powerful theories developed by J. Rawls, J. Habermas, or J. Wilson, major flaws can easily be detected at first glance. Again, if the currently available rational theories of values were sufficiently convincing, they would eliminate or at least arouse serious doubts about the dominant irrational postmodernist views.

The question of the origin of values is both crucial and complex, and has been the center of my intellectual interests for years. For intrinsic reasons the notion of a "crisis of values" in our societies has become common talk. The idea that in modern societies individuals should and would "choose" their values freely has become an accepted idea. But I am motivated by another type of consideration. As Durkheim, Simmel, Weber, Mead and other classical sociologists have suggested, I can have the feeling that "X is good" only if I have the feeling simultaneously that the other man should feel and think in the same way. I cannot feel that an object is beautiful, contends Simmel, if I do not sense that my feeling is caused by some features in the object itself, so that I necessarily have then the feeling that other people should think and feel the same way as I do about the object. In other words, to Simmel as to Durkheim, Weber, or Tocqueville, value feelings are not perceived by the social subject as subjective and are effectively not merely subjective, with the exception of "tastes." But tastes are perceived as tastes and recognized as such: I have no problem accepting the idea that many Germans do not like raw oysters, while many Frenchmen like them. Now, leading contemporary theories of values see values, to put it in simple terms, as a matter of "taste." The contradiction of this view with hard facts appears immediately: who would consider seriously statements such as "liquidating *apartheid* was a good thing," "polygamy is a good thing" as reflecting mere *tastes*?

I have tried to develop and synthesize a number of intuitions pro-

need to feel values objective

posed notably by classical sociology into what I call here a "judicatory" theory of values. I call it sometimes "cognitivist," sometimes
"judicatory," having come recently to this latter qualification, when,
at on occasion of a colloquium, I was given the duty of presenting
Max Scheler's views on values. I read carefully his main work on the
subject for this occasion, and realized that he had written very insight-
ful pages on Adam Smith's theory of values. Although he concludes
his presentation of Smith's theory by stating his deep disagreement
with it, he identifies rightly its core postulates and qualifies adequately
Smith's theory as *urteilsartig*. I translated this German word to
judicatoire in French and propose now to translate it to *judicatory* in
English. Although the theory I propose in the following chapters is
much more complex than Smith's, the same word adequately characterizes its core.

Instead of presenting this theory in a linear manner, I have chosen
to show that it offers an adequate answer to a number of precise
questions. With a method that derives both from intrinsic and opportunistic reasons. From intrinsic reasons: the matter is so complex that a
linear treatment would have likely been inappropriate. From opportunistic reasons: I had the privilege in the last few years of being invited
to various congresses, seminars, colloquia in Britain, Germany, and
France notably, where this subject of the explanation of norms and
values was discussed. Also, I was invited by the *American Journal of
Sociology* to treat the scope of an influential theoretical orientation,
the so-called "Rational Choice Model," and a German association
requested I write on Weber's "axiological rationality." These papers
have an idiosyncratic side, deriving from the constraints imposed by
the context in which they were written. But, they were inspired by a
common basic methodological and/or theoretical question (may I say
incidentally that, to me, "theory," "method" or "criticism" in the sense
established by Kant are almost equivalent notions): how should values
and valuation be explained, if we want the explanation to satisfy the
usual criteria according to that by which scientific theories are normally appreciated? Consequently, the contingencies in the history of
the papers should not break their basic unity. The history of the papers
is also responsible for the fact that some points or examples are evoked
in more than one paper. I intentionally kept these (few) repetitions, not
only because *bis repetita placent*, but also because it was the only way
of keeping the self-contained character of each of the papers. More-

over, it is not easy to find illuminating examples on the questions raised here. The reader will easily note that many of my examples are drawn from classical sociologists, possibly because they were convinced that a main objective of the social sciences would be to explain puzzling social phenomena. As the contents should immediately make clear, the papers are ranked in a definite order, and go from the presentation of the various available theories of values, to a discussion of some particularly important and influential theories, then to a presentation of the "judicatory" theory I advocate, and finally to applications of this theory to two empirical fields. While the reader can follow this order, as the chapters are self-contained, he can also read them in the order of his choice.

Other papers, exclusively available in French at the present time, could also have been included in the present volume, such as a paper on Durkheim's *Elementary Forms of Religious Life*, or the unpublished paper on Max Scheler's theory of values I mentioned earlier (Boudon, 1999b). But, while they would have been complementary to the chapters included in this book, they are not indispensable, in the sense that the latter give a precise account of the available theories of values, a listing of the main strengths and weaknesses of the most important ones, a precise idea of the synthetic theory developed under the qualification of a "judicatory theory" of values, as well as empirical applications of the theory.

I mention at this point that I have methodically examined a frequent objection to this judicatory theory in a paper listed in the references (Boudon, 1997c), the objection being that I do not offer criteria as to what makes a system of reasons "strong." I deal with this problem here (chapter 6) in a lapidary fashion, starting from a crucial point raised by Kant and ignored by Popper, possibly because it goes against received ideas, that there are no such criteria as far as the systems of arguments constituting scientific theories are concerned, so that the question as to what such criteria would look like in the case of prescriptive systems of reasons appears as a naïve one.

I hope that this volume will not be perceived by philosophers as containing too many empirical examples, while it would present too few in the eyes of social scientists. But on a subject such as the explanation of values, which is a central topic both of the social sciences and of philosophy, I did not see how I could avoid addressing the two types of corporations, being well aware of the fact that in recent decades divergent traditions as to how questions should be raised and dealt with have been developed. And so, I have deliberately decided to sit between two chairs, with the idea in the back of my mind that both philosophy and the social sciences would be more effective as far as our understanding of values is concerned, if they saw the "anomic" effects that the division of labor may sometimes generate. M. Hechter goes perhaps a bit too far when he contends that the theory of values has not made any progress since Max Weber (Hechter, 1992). But there is something true in this remark. Possibly one reason for the relative sterility of modern social sciences and philosophy on the subject of values resides in the already mentioned anomic character of the division of labor between the two disciplines. Among modern writers, those such as Habermas, J. Wilson, or Rawls who have presented interesting views on values, have in common that they succeeded in transcending this division of labor. The effectiveness, fruitfulness, and insightfulness of A. Smith's, Tocqueville's, Durkheim's, Simmel's or Weber's views on values–and on other subjects as well—derive probably in part from the fact that they cared little about the question of whether they wrote as philosophers or social scientists, for the simple reason that the distinction did not exist socially then.

I would add that the "anomic" effects of the division of labor are possibly more harmful on the chapter of values than on others. Sociologists and anthropologists start often from the implicit principle that their function, as defined by the invisible constitution regulating their discipline, would consist in describing the variation of values over time and space and eventually explaining why some type of behavior or state of affairs is treated *hic et nunc* as fine, while it was collectively rejected in some other time or is presently rejected in some other society. Philosophers for their part would have to show, according to their own implicit constitution, why some type of behavior or state of affairs is treated as universally good or bad, legitimate or not, etc., unless, if they feel close to relativism, they prefer to show that the ultimate and universal truth on values is that there are no universal values. To simplify, philosophers would deal with the universal side of values, while sociologists and other social scientists would be in charge of their particularistic-contextual side. As the latter corporations communicate too little with the former, this division of labor generates a situation which can be compared to the situation where the right hand would strike with a hammer on a nail held by the left hand, each of the two hands ignoring what the other one is doing. I insist on this point, because my main aim in the chapters comprising this volume has not been empirical. It has not been in other words to explain why values are different here from what they are there, nor less to guess what values will characterize the societies of tomorrow nor to speculate, say, about the effects of globalization on values, but rather to raise a problem which seems to me essential, whether it is called methodological or theoretical, that is, how can values and valuation be explained in a scientifically satisfactory way, and to suggest that a good theory of values should produce a coherent synthesis between various powerful insights derived from the sociological and the philosophical literature, classical and modern, on the subject. The diversity, the heterogeneity and the partially contradictory character of these insights suggest that the task is both crucial and difficult. My objective was, in other words, to defend and illustrate the principle that the universal and contextual sides of values cannot be theorized independently from one another. To use an analogy which seems to me able to describe concretely this interdependence, values can be compared to the solutions of a system of equations. The *same* equations produce different solutions with *different* numerical values for the parameters, so that reciprocally explaining the difference in the solutions is possible only provided one sees that the equations are the *same* and the parameters *different*.

A few words can now introduce each of the following chapters and essentially stress the way they are related to the questions described above. Chapter 1 is devoted to a classification of the main theories of values. Chapters 2 and 3 are mainly concerned with the criticism of some particularly influential theories. The last four chapters develop in a sequence of progressive steps the judicatory theory of values that synthesizes in my mind a number of intuitions developed earlier, notably by classical sociologists, and propose applications of this theory.

More precisely, the main purpose of the chapter 1, "Explaining Values and Valuation: A Question That Has Inspired Many Theories," is to bring some order to the numerous theories of values and valuation proposed by social scientists and philosophers. A good way to generate this order is to show that the theories can fill the cells of a typology, a prior constraint being to identify the relevant dimensions, the combination of which produces the cells of the typology. I hope I have succeeded, not only producing a valid typology, but also in showing that its cells identify intellectual constants, so to say, in the sense that it can be shown that theories belonging to each of these cells have been constantly produced, from the classical to the modern age of both the social sciences and philosophy. Given the typological objective of the chapter, the theories evoked here are neither presented nor discussed in detail.

Chapter 2, "Rational Theories: Limits of the 'Rational Choice Model,'" deals with one of the major "rational" theories used today to explain norms and values: the so-called "Rational Choice Model" (RCM). The uninformed reader, at this point, should be made aware of the fact that in the expression "Rational Choice Model" the word *rational* is used in an indigenous fashion, as an equivalent of "instrumentally rational." An action is "rational" in this sense if it can be held as representing objectively a good way of reaching the goal the subject is following. The chapter deals with the RCM generally, trying to make the point that, while its supporters see it as a potentially universally valid theory, in other words as the only one actually able to explain indistinctly all social phenomena, and notably norms and values, this claim seems ungrounded. The model is very effective in explaining many social phenomena, and among them some categories of norms and values, but definitely not all. The chapter tries to explain why.

Chapter 3, "Relativistic vs. Naturalistic Theories: Their Interest and Limits," deals with what I have qualified above as the dominant theory of values, the "postmodernist" one, according to which values should be considered as the emanation of singular cultures and, for this reason, vary from one culture to another. As I said before, this model raises two questions: Why is this theory dominant today? Is it acceptable? In this paper I consider exclusively one of the variants of the "postmodernist" theory of values: the "culturalist" variant. There are also other variants, such as the previously mentioned neo-Nietzschean or neo-Marxian theory of values. These variants have in common with the culturalist version that they defend a relativistic view of values and treat the perception people have of the reasons as to why they endorse such and such values as illusory. These latter neo-Marxian or neo-Freudian theories, however, have become more parochial and also less influential than the culturalist variant. While they were dominant in the sixties and seventies, they are now dominated, as far as the register of the relativistic theories of values is concerned, by the *culturalist* variant. For this reason I have chosen to concentrate rather on this latter variant. Some opponents of the relativistic theories have proposed to develop instead a *naturalistic* theory of values. This chapter presents a discussion of Wilson's work on the moral sense, an illustration of this category. But, through this discussion of a particular theory, my objective was to raise a general question and to check how far a naturalistic theory of values can bring us in the understanding of value endorsement. Wilson's theory is certainly one of the most interesting ones in the category of modern naturalistic theories. It takes its inspiration, in a flexible and creative way, from the Aristotelian tradition, but also from sociobiology. It draws and uses in a creative fashion impressive empirical material from experimental sociology as well as history. While I do not treat the question explicitly, it should also be noted that the objections raised here against the naturalistic model could also be raised against intuitionist theories, such as Scheler's.

The first three chapters deal in a word critically with some major theoretical orientations, all being very prominent, in classical and modern social sciences and philosophy.

Chapter 4, "A Seminal and Difficult Notion: 'Axiological Rationality,'" is the first of a sequence of constructive rather than critical chapters. It tries to disentangle the meaning of Weber's notion of "axiological rationality" (*Wertrationalität*), starting from an undefeatable remark: Weber's distinction between *axiological rationality* and *instrumental rationality* means that he thought it necessary to introduce the notion of a *non-instrumental* type of rationality. This raises the question as to what this category means, a difficult and much debated question. One point at least is clear in this respect: as "instrumental rationality" (*Zweckrationalität*) deals with the relations between means and ends, the notion of axiological rationality introduces the idea of a *non-consequential* type of rationality. My purpose in the chapter was less to guess what Weber actually had in mind when he introduced this difficult notion than to explore the potential fruitfulness of the idea of a non-consequential type of rationality. In other words, the chapter should be read as presenting a sketch of a new theory of values starting from Weber's notion of a non-consequential type of rationality, rather than an interpretation proper of his notion of "axiological rationality." As far as the explanation of axiological feelings is concerned, the interpretation I propose of his "axiological rationality" is (this is at least my hope) more promising than the trivial frequently endorsed one, which sees this notion as describing merely the cases where social actors act in conformity with their values. I do not see how it would be possible to show in an irrefutable way that this trivial interpretation was the one Weber actually had in mind, and it should be clear that I am well aware that what I say here about "axiological rationality" goes much further than what Weber actually wrote. For the readers interested in the question as to what Weber actually had in mind, I suggest in the chapter that the non-trivial interpretation of this notion appears much more compatible with other Weberian key notions. But again, although the circumstances in which the paper was written incited me to present it as a discussion of Weber, my latent aim was rather to discuss the notion of a non-consequential type of rationality.

Chapter 5, "Generalizing the 'Rational Choice Model' into a Cognitivist Model," starts from the idea that the notion of rationality, a complex one, has two very different meanings, illustrated respectively by the sense of the concept in economics and the philosophy of science. Can this distinction be considered as overlapping the distinction introduced notably by Max Weber, when he distinguishes between an instrumental and a non-instrumental form of rationality, alternatively a consequential and a non-consequential form of rationality? The answer to the question, far from having a mere conceptual and speculative interest, has, on the contrary, a powerful heuristic virtue: it shows that many observational data drawn from various disciplines and generally interpreted as implying on the part of the subject some form of irrationality can, on the contrary, be interpreted rationally, provided the notion of rationality is adequately defined. An attempt is made in this chapter to develop this reformed version of the idea of rationality, in other words to develop the "judicatory" or "cognitivist" theory of rationality that I mentioned earlier, and to apply it in an illustrative fashion to some empirical data dealing with descriptive and normative beliefs that are currently interpreted as demonstrating the existence of a "magical" way of thinking from the part of the observed subjects. Also, the theory suggests that ordinary and scientific knowledge on the one hand, positive and normative thinking on the other follow the same mechanisms.

Chapter 6, "The Cognitivist Model Applied to the Analysis of the Feelings of Justice," is an attempt to apply the judicatory theory of values to a well-circumscribed field: the feelings of justice. Given the importance of social justice in our societies, much empirical and theoretical research has been conducted in this area. This is one of the reasons, besides the intrinsic interest of the subject, that I have chosen this field of application. Philosophers, as Rawls, propose implicitly, as I mentioned earlier, a theory as to what people mean when they perceive a distribution of goods as fair or unfair. Sociologists and social psychologists have conducted numerous observations and experiments on the feelings of justice on samples of people in such and such natural or experimental situations. Empirical research, though very fruitful and leading to a host of illuminating findings, raises more problems than it solves, however, in the sense that the complexity of the findings it has produced gives the impression that the theories of the feelings of justice proposed by social scientists as well as by philosophers have definitely not been able to give account of this complexity. People appear as strictly "Rawlsian" in some situations, while they appear as resolutely "anti-Rawlsian" in others. They are in some circumstances Kantian (that is, they tend to follow principles of universal value), while they are rather in other circumstances utilitarian (that is, they tend to follow their interest and hold principles as valid provided they can consider them as serving their interest). Concepts as "local justice" or "bounded justice" appear here and there in the literature. They are concerned with building a bridge between empirical research and theory on the feelings of justice.[3] But the question can be raised as to whether these concepts offer more than a sign of recognition of the difficulty opposed to the building of this bridge. I attempt to show in this chapter that, with the judicatory theory in mind, it is possible to reconstruct the processes in the mind of people that generate the complex findings observed by empirical research, in other words to link efficiently the micro mechanisms of valuation to the aggregate data observed at the macro level.

Chapter 7, "The Cognitivist Model Applied to the Analysis of Public Opinion," presents an essential piece in this judicatory theory. While the first chapter in this book, "Explaining Values and Valuation: A Question That Has Inspired Many Theories," conveys the impression that the numerous theories of values and valuation are deeply heterogeneous, some being rational and some irrational, some seeing values as the mere effect of social inculcation, others the effect of emotional factors, as resentment, some attempting to derive values from self-interest, others from the constraints imposed by society on individuals, etc., this last chapter attempts to show that theories can at least partly be synthesized. When, in social life, I have to know whether or not I endorse or not the value statement "X is good, bad, legitimate, etc.," the question creates a situation which can belong to one of several types: if my answer to the question whether "X is good, etc.," can have a potential effect on my psychological or class interests, it can certainly be affected by these interests. If, on the other hand, my social position is such that my interests, individual and collective, are in no way concerned with and cannot in any way be dependent upon the question, they will unlikely be the cause of my answer. This distinction was introduced by Adam Smith, when he created the notion of the "impartial spectator." It reappears in Rawls's "veil of ignorance." As such, the distinction is crucial: it is sufficient to show that the mechanisms of value endorsement theorized by Marx, Nietzsche, Freud and their followers, as well as by followers of the Benthamian tradition (as supporters of the Rational Choice Model) cannot be general. Moreover, once it has been realized that the opinions, beliefs, and values of people, as they are observed for instance in surveys and polls, are in most cases a mixture (in proportions depending notably on the nature of the question, but on other parameters as well) of answers given by partial actors and impartial spectators, the meaning to be given to a statement such as "a majority of people is for (or against) X" depends evidently on the proportions of people belonging respectively to the two categories. Of course, a careful account should be taken of the fact that, on many subjects, we can be simultaneously "impartial spectators" and "partial actors": be biased and still see that we should not be guided by our biases. This last piece of the judiciary theory should lead moreover to a much more adequate interpretation of the distribution of opinions and beliefs as they appear notably in polls and surveys, and to a better understanding of this essential piece in the political life of democratic societies: public opinion.

As Durkheim once said, explaining collective beliefs and notably accounting for the states of public opinion are the major tasks of the social sciences.[4]

Notes

1. "The concept that is initially held as true because it is collective tends to become collective exclusively under the condition that it is held as true: it has to produce its certificate before we believe in its validity" ["Le concept qui, primitivement, est tenu pour vrai parce qu'il est collectif tend à ne devenir collectif qu'à condition d'être tenu pour vrai: nous lui demandons ses titres avant de lui accorder notre créance," (Durkheim, 1979 [1912]: 624)].
2. "Many commentators have contended . . . that Strauss completely misunderstood Max Weber; but this seems never to have disturbed him or his followers," writes rightly Lewis Coser (Coser, 1984).
3. See Elster, 1992 ; Schmidt, 1994.
4. "Taking collective opinions as an object of investigation and building a scientific theory of opinion is the main objective of sociology" [. . . on peut prendre l'opinion comme objet d'étude et en faire la science; c'est en cela que consiste principalement la sociologie" (Durkheim, 1979 [1912], 626)] ; "Collective beliefs are states of public opinion" ["les croyances . . . sont des états de l'opinion" (Ibid., 50)].

1

Explaining Values and Valuation: A Question That Has Inspired Many Theories

1.1 The Diversity and Empirical Inefficiency of Value Theories

We spend a great part of our time formulating value statements: "X is good, bad, legitimate, illegitimate, etc." In most cases, we express these statements because we endorse them. Why? Why do we believe in value statements? This is a difficult question as soon as we recognize that the validity of values cannot be checked as easily as the reality of facts. Value statements are more problematic than factual statements.

This question is so important that all human sciences, psychology as well as sociology and, before them, philosophy, have raised it. What are their answers? How can they be classified? Are some of them more acceptable, more valid, than others? Can they be unified? Here are some of the points on which I would like to present some reflections.

My interest in these questions was originally stimulated by the fact that the answers proposed by human sciences to the question as to where values come from are extraordinarily diverse. "X–for instance, a given distribution of good—is fair (or unfair)" states a majority of respondents in a sociological inquiry. Do the respondents plainly observe that the distribution is effectively fair (or unfair)? If so, in what sense is it fair or unfair, what are the criteria leading to one of the opposite conclusions? Is the answer rather the effect of the individual or collective interests of the respondents? Does it result from the application by the respondents of principles they would hold as intuitively valid? Or from the application of arbitrary principles they would have endorsed? Of principles the respondents would simply have been socialized to? Or is the answer strategic? Is it the effect of passions, such as envy? Of resentment? These questions have occupied a good part of the work of several classical and modern philosophers (Nietzsche, but also Max Scheler or John Rawls for instance) and several classical and modern sociologists (Simmel, Durkheim, Piaget, functionalists, rational choice theorists, etc.) Are all these theories equally valid? Is one of them better? Are they all valid but in diverse circumstances?

Another observation has attracted my attention for a long time: as soon as one considers certain subjects, like the feelings of justice, on which empirical investigations by sociologists, social psychologists, and psychologists have been particularly numerous, one gets the impression that no theory is able to explain in a satisfactory fashion the reactions of people as they are empirically observed. Hence, the impression that empirical research and theory are unable to converge. Thus, in some observations, people seem to have sentiments of justice congruent with Rawls's theory, while in others they appear as non-Rawlsians. Roughly, they want that inequalities are minimum in the sense where they should not be higher than the level required to optimize the production of goods, while in other situations people seem not to care on this point. How are these contradictions to be explained?

1.2 Münchhausen's Trilemma

A primary reason for this complexity possibly has something to do with a basic theorem formulated, after others, by the German philosopher and sociologist Hans Albert, a theorem which he has proposed to label "Münchhausen's trilemma." It is as follows: "Any given theory (a moral as well as an astronomical or physical theory, etc.) is grounded on principles: either these principles are treated as true though they are ungrounded, or they are grounded on other principles and these other principles still on other principles *ad infinitum*, or they are treated as grounded on their consequences, in a circular fashion." In other words, moral or scientific certainty evokes the story of Münchhausen, the legendary baron who succeeded in extracting himself from the pond where he had fallen by drawing his own hairs.

What conclusions should be drawn from this theorem? That certainty–moral as well as scientific—is an illusion? That one cannot legitimately assume the knowledge–moral as well as scientific—is grounded on absolute principles? That moral certainties are purely subjective matter? That they derive from an ungrounded decision? This question was raised repeatedly by the human sciences. One can even maintain that it represents one of their most crucial questions. One of the reasons why Marx, Nietzsche, Freud or Pareto claimed that what subjects perceive as truths are really illusions, is that they had the impression that no knowledge can be considered as grounded on undefeatable principles.

1.3 Münchhausen's Trilemma and Scientific Knowledge

Before I consider the conclusions to be derived from Münchhausen's trilemma regarding the question, namely why we endorse values, I will consider the consequences to be drawn from this theorem regarding scientific theories.

If we choose the first of the three solutions proposed by the trilemma, we get what I would call a *fideist* theory of knowledge: in that case, I recognize that any given scientific theory rests upon undemonstrated and undemonstrable principles, but I consider these principles solid and valid. I hold the consequences drawn from theses principles as true, as valid, because I *believe* in the principles on which they are grounded.

But we can also of course draw from Münchhausen's trilemma a *skeptical* theory of scientific knowledge: as any theory rests upon ungrounded principles, nothing is sure.[1]

This skeptical theory appears at first view as the most credible. It is true that any theory, even of the most familiar type, rests upon ungrounded principles. Thus, a statement of the form "X is cause of Y" (as "this fertilizer is effective") rests upon the assumption that the notion of "cause" is clear, while it is not, since many philosophers or scientists, as Bertrand Russell, have proposed to get rid of it.[2]

But on the other hand, we normally have the feeling that the two conclusions I have just evoked, the fideist and the skeptical, make us deeply uncomfortable. We can easily accept neither the view that scientific theories are grounded on principles which we would accept by an ungrounded act of faith, nor the view that they would be ultimately ungrounded. We can easily accept neither the Cartesian view that there are ultimate self-evident principles on which scientific theories would be grounded, nor the conventionalist view, according to which they would be grounded on principles on which we would agree, but which would be neither evident nor grounded. We have some trouble accepting the idea, supported by modern conventionalists, as the German philosopher Hübner (1985), that myths would be representations of the world that we should consider as valid as scientific theories. We have, on the contrary, the impression that science produces more reliable representations than myths and we are reluctant toward the idea that this impression would be a mere illusion.

The Good Solution

More generally, the fideist and skeptical conclusions that are often derived from Münchhausen's trilemma makes it difficult to understand that certain scientific statements are considered as definitely true, or that magical practices are less efficient than scientific ones. In other words, the two possible, most acceptable conclusions that can be derived from Münchhausen's trilemma appear as contradictory with evidence.

To get out from beneath these difficulties and contradictions, we must accept the idea that scientific knowledge is gained by a dynamic move going from principles to consequences and, in turn, from the consequences to the principles. A scientific theory is normally grounded on undemonstrated principles. If the theory appears wrong and if it seems difficult to reconcile it with data, after a while, a normal step will be to put the principles into question and possibly to replace them by other principles. If, by contrast, some principles appear as capable of being indefinitely maintained because a flow of adequate scientific theories can be produced, then scientists will accept them and not put them into question any more, provided no difficulties appear which would cause scientists again to question their principles. What I have presented here in a few words is the core of Popperian theory of knowledge: principles are conjectures. They can become truths when it does not appear relevant to put them into question. But they can always be in principle criticized and put into question. We can summarize this philosophy by saying that it endorses the third solution of

Münchhausen's trilemma: knowledge is "circular" in the sense that it rests on a basic procedure whereby principles give birth to theories and explanations, the latter giving birth to consequences that can be accepted or not; if not, this can lead to a revision of the principles. Of course, the word "circular" should be put in quotes, because it is not circular in the strict logical sense.

This theory of knowledge, to me the most acceptable, was defended before Popper (1976), by Simmel (1892). It is rejected, though, by those who do not want knowledge to be circular and either endorse a fideist or a skeptical vision (Albert, 1990). Incidentally, as I have shown elsewhere, accepting the idea that knowledge consists of conjectures and refutations does not lead to accepting Popper's falsification theory (Boudon, 1994b).

Example: The Theory of Turmoils

I am referring here to a famous discussion among Middle Ages physicists. They started from the principle that any move must have a cause. This is typically a statement that does not derive directly from observation, but that is confirmed though by an indefinite number of observations. This leaf of paper moves because I make it move. Otherwise, it would stay at rest. But the principle led to questions which appeared as difficult to answer. If any move has a cause, which cause keeps the boat moving when the wind has suddenly completely fallen? Which cause keeps the arrow moving once it has left the bow? Physicists of the Middle Ages started from the principle that *any* move has a cause. They devised answers that appear to us now easily ridiculous: the boat would provoke an invisible turmoil that would push it and keep it moving after the wind has fallen. If so, said a physicist, if such a turmoil does actually operate, a heap of corn should fly in different directions depending on whether it is located in the front or at the back of the boat's deck. Progressively, the theory of turmoils appeared on the whole to create more questions than it solved. But again, how can it be explained that the boat or the arrow keep moving? The solution to this puzzle was found once the weakness of the principle "every move has a cause" was discovered, and once it was understood that it should be completed and reformulated: "no object at rest will move without a cause making it move, and no object in move will come to rest without a cause bringing it to rest." From this new principle, the revolutionary consequence could be drawn that no cause makes the boat or the arrow move. This new principle, the Newtonian principle of inertia, was from that moment definitely accepted. It seems unlikely that it would be put into question.

This example of the principle of inertia is probably one of the most spectacular the history of science provides of the back-and-forth process between principles and consequences characterizing the production of knowledge. Many others of course could be offered. To mention just another equally instructive one, the Greeks drew from the fact that the ratio S/D of the side S of a square of length one to its diagonal D should be both even and odd the conclusion that S/D was not a "number" but a "growth" ("*grandeur*"). In other words, they postulated the existence of two types of quantities. It took centuries before it was realized that the notion of number should not be restricted to natural and relative numbers (that is, of type A/B where A and B are integers) but should include "ir-*ratio*-nal" numbers as well, in other words, numbers which cannot be expressed as the *ratio* of two integers. The principle, here the definition as to what numbers are, was reformed because by so doing, it was possible to eliminate the obscure notion of a "growth," which would not be possible to measure by a number.

Finally, we believe in a scientific truth; we believe that "X is true," because X appears to us as grounded on a system of reasons, which appear to us as strong, given the state of the discussion at a given time. Before the principle of inertia was elaborated, the physicists had reasons to believe in the theory of turmoils: they could perceive it as strong. Once the principle of inertia was formulated, the reasons supporting the earlier theory of turmoils were weakened. So, we believe in a theory when it appears to us as supported by stronger reasons than any alternative theories. We believe the theory that "the earth is round rather than flat," because it is grounded on stronger reasons than the theory "the earth is flat." Our belief is grounded on the fact that we see that all the arguments supporting the theory "the earth is flat" would be definitely weaker.

1.4 Münchhausen's Trilemma and the Explanation of Norms and Values

This "circular" or "back and forth" theory of knowledge makes clear why Münchhausen's trilemma never convinced anyone that scientific theories would be ungrounded. Although, as the Sokal's affair shows, the so-called "postmodernist" sociologists of science have tried to develop a skeptical and "constructivist" view of science, according to which scientific theories would not be more objective than mythical representations of the world. However, using Münchhausen's trilemma implicitly as the basis of their argument, they were unable to succeed in convincing people, because the skeptical interpretation of Münchhausen's trilemma is only one among many. Another theory is that, in essence, knowledge is obtained by a back and forth procedure.

By contrast, Münchhausen's trilemma seems to have been taken more literally by theoreticians of norms and values. Even if they do not refer explicitly to it, many theoreticians of norms and values draw from it the conclusion that axiological beliefs can rest exclusively either on faith or on sand. Other writers, starting from the idea that axiological beliefs cannot be grounded, attempt to find the causes which would be responsible for them, while still others attempt to show that they are grounded on ultimate principles, the truth of which would be intuitive.

This classification can be refined. A first class of theories of normative beliefs would include the *fideist* theories, those that attempt to show that axiological beliefs are grounded on principles of absolute value. A second class of theories would include the skeptical theories, for which axiological beliefs cannot be grounded. Those who endorse this skeptical view can, in turn, be sorted into two categories. *Decisionist* theories start from the viewpoint that axiological beliefs are based on principles freely endorsed by the subjects. *Causalist* theories start from the viewpoint that they are implanted in the minds of people under the effect of psychic, social, or biological mechanisms operating without the subjects being aware of them, but which can be inferred with the help of scientific procedures. The latter can be included in the skeptical category, for they start from the principle that normative beliefs cannot be treated as grounded: to them, they should be considered as states of mind resulting from the action of causes, not as conclusions deriving from reasons.[3]

Finally, a number of theories can be called *rational*. They cannot be included into the skeptical nor the fideist theories. But it may be noted that they respect Münchhausen's trilemma in their own way, since, in most cases, they attempt to derive moral convictions from procedures to which they grant an absolute value, as in the cases of Kant or today,

J. Rawls. In that sense, they can be qualified not only as rational but as *absolutist*.

On the whole, it is not exaggerated to say that a good part of the theories of norms and values appear as dominated by the objective of solving Münchhausen's trilemma, as though the theorists of norms and values had more or less clearly seen this theorem, and as though they had picked up the various interpretations given to it.

I will not attempt to present exhaustively these theories, nor to criticize them. My objective is rather, on the one hand, to support the conjecture according to which Münchhausen's trilemma has oriented the construction of value theories by evoking some influential theories of axiological beliefs, and, on the other hand, to show that Münchhausen's trilemma can be solved by a better theory than the fideist, the skeptical theory (either in its decisionist or in its causalist form), or the absolutist rational theory.

1.5 "Fideist" Theories

"Fideist" theories start from the assumption that norms and values can be grounded on principles of absolute validity, in other words, on principles the validity of which need not be demonstrated.

The phenomenological theory of values developed by Max Scheler belongs to this category. It is certainly one of its most interesting illustrations (Scheler, 1954 [1916]).[4] According to Scheler, we become aware of values thanks to a sense of values that would be comparable to our sense of colors. Values have to him an intuitive character that phenomenological analysis can, accordingly, reveal. Of course, this sense of value can be mistaken. But our sense of colors can also be mistaken, for instance, under the effect of some diseases, for example, jaundice.

The main weakness of this theory can easily be identified: the existence of a "sense of values" cannot be identified as easily as the existence of a sense of colors. The intuitionist conception of values defended by Scheler rests on the observation that some values appear as universally endorsed. It is true that a heap of garbage is universally seen as negative. It is true also that value statements are often conceived by social subjects as being objectively grounded. When I state that "X is good, legitimate, beautiful," I have often the feeling that I state so because X is actually, that is, objectively, good, legitimate or beautiful. For this reason, I have the impression that other people should also be convinced of the validity of the statement. Simmel says that we cannot find an object beautiful unless we have the feeling that our impression is provoked by some attributes of the object itself (Simmel, 1989).

These two observations, namely that some value statements appear as universal and that others are normally felt by a subject as "objective" are probably responsible for Scheler's theory according to which we would have a sense of values comparable to our sense of colors.

Many value statements cannot, however, be related to this conjectural sense of values. Supposing we accept its existence, a value statement such as "this policy, which aims at reducing unemployment, is good (or bad)" is certainly not its mere effect. Or assuming we have a general sense of justice or of fairness, evoking this sense cannot explain why we consider such and such distribution of goods as just or fair, unjust or unfair.

Although I do not want to discuss further Scheler's theory, it must be recognized that it has a unique feature: it attempts to combine the idea of the "objectivity" of values (values would be essences which phenomenological analysis would be able to identify) with their historical and social variability. For this reason, Scheler began as a philosopher but ended as the grounder of the so-called "sociology of knowledge." But while he raised important questions, the answers he gave them are debatable.

The important point for our discussion is that the Schelerian theory of values illustrates the theories that give the Münchhausen trilemma a fideist solution: it attempts to show that value statements rest upon intuitively evident normative data. In the same way that our sense of colors make us sure that the leaves of trees are green, our sense of values would tell us that such and such behavior or state of affairs is good or bad, acceptable or not, etc.

Incidentally, I can note a point which would be worth further development, namely that the notion of religious revelation introduces also the idea that axiological truths, as they would have been revealed, would have no need of demonstration. Scheler himself considered reciprocally that revealed religions express symbolically the notion of a sense of values which phenomenological analysis could detect. Before Scheler, Benjamin Constant and Tocqueville also defended the idea that religions express in a symbolic fashion axiological truths, which social subjects perceive in a confused fashion. Durkheim in his *Formes élémentaires* and Simmel in his writings on the sociology of religion defend the same idea: that religions express symbolically moral truths intuitively given to social subjects.

1.6 Skeptical Theories

I turn now to skeptical theories. They can be classified, as I noted before, into two categories: *decisionist* theories according to which value statements would be neither grounded on reasons nor produced by causes, but would derive from a free decision, and *causalist* theories, according to which axiological beliefs would be produced in the mind of social subjects by biological, psychological, or social causes rather than by reasons, in other words, by irrational causes.

Decisionist Theories

Generally, a theory is qualified as "decisionist" when it includes the three following statements: (1) it recognizes that social subjects endorse values, believe in values statements, etc.; (2) it assumes that values can be grounded neither on revelation, nor on intuition, nor, as an application of Münchhausen's trilemma, on reason; (3) it rejects the idea of analyzing value endorsement as the mere effects of psychological, biological, or social causes.

Sartre's existentialism illustrates this type of theory. The "choice" between such and such value is "absurd," according to Sartre, meaning by this expression that such a choice could not be justified (Münchhausen's trilemma) without contradiction.

A current interpretation of German sociologist Max Weber contends that the theory of values he has sketched in many of his writings would belong to the decisionist type. In his lecture, *Wissenschaft als Beruf*, Weber has used two influential metaphors "value polytheism" and "the war between gods." They suggest that values can be incompatible with one another, that, in some cases, it is impossible to show that one should choose one value rather than another, that social subjects often cannot justify their axiological choices, that is, explain why they endorse such and such value statements.

In fact, the theory of values developed by Max Weber is complex: it is scattered in many writings, not always compatible with one another. One point is certain, at any rate: if this theory could be reduced to the decisionist type, one would hardly understand why Weber created the notion of "axiological rationality" (*Wertrationalität*), nor how he could have made the idea of *Verstehen* a basic point of his methodology. Understanding why people do what they do, believe what they believe, is a crucial task for the sociologist, he contends. This means that, to Weber, actions and beliefs, far from being "absurd," unmotivated, are grounded in the eyes of actors themselves. He never analyzes beliefs and actions either as absurd or as illusory. In several circumstances, he criticizes Marx's or Nietzsche's theories according to which normative beliefs would be illusions, as when I believe that "X is good," while X is merely congruent with my psychological interests or with my class interests. Generally, Weber assumes that people's beliefs are grounded. The causes of the beliefs are their meaning to the actor, in other words, the reasons which they have to endorse them. As to the expression "axiological rationality," it evidently evokes the Kantian notion of "practical reason."

It can be noted incidentally that this decisionist interpretation of Weber is mainly due to the influence of Leo Strauss (1953). By fighting Weber's supposedly decisionist theory, Strauss tried to reinforce his own "naturalistic" theory. For the same kind of reason, E. Voegelin has been negative about Weber: he would have developed a decisionist theory of values detrimental to the only acceptable theory, the naturalistic one; he would be the father of modern relativism. Allan Bloom (1987), a disciple of Strauss, has even contended that Weber would have corrupted by his ideas on values New York taxi drivers and converted them to nihilism.[5]

In France, Raymond Aron, who has attracted attention to the importance of Weber, has interpreted Weber's lecture, given at the end of 1918, *Wissenschaft als Beruf*, as a tragic message, insisting on the mutual incompatibility of values. The tone of the lecture was quiet and peaceful. It can be read now rather as a message of tolerance: cultures, notably national cultures, such as the French and the German, bear various values; one should recognize that it is often not easy to determine which are better. It seems to me unlikely that, at the end of 1918, Weber could really have delivered a tragic message insisting on the struggle between values. Moreover, this conference cannot be considered as containing an exposition of Weber's theory of values, which is rather contained in his essays in the sociology of religion.

Moreover, one need only look at the examples of value conflicts presented by Weber in this lecture to see that he did not intend to present these conflicts as tragic. English physics is different in style from continental physics, he writes, for instance. While British physicists seem primarily concerned with the technical applications their theories are able to produce, continental physicists would be more interested in offering an explanation of the physical world. The former would be more oriented toward the applications of physics, the latter toward the explanation of the physical world. Now, it is impossible to prove that one of these orientations would be better than the other. This example illustrates the notion of "value polytheism" and of the "war between gods." But one does not derive from this remark the idea that, to Weber, continental and British physicists would be opposed to one another in a fratricide war, nor, of course, that because their work is inspired by different and undemonstrable values, they would produce different physical truths. Weber's "value polytheism" entails no relativism. The British and the continental physicists are all effective: they produce valid physical theories. So, their basic orientations, though divergent with regard to one another, are good. And Weber considered certainly that this competition and divergence had on the whole positive effects on the overall development of physics.

In summary, to Weber, values can be undemonstrable. But this implies no relativism, nor that the choice of such and such value would be "absurd," in other words irrational.

Causalist Theories

"Causalist" theories represent another solution out of Münchhausen's trilemma. According to these theories, the ultimate principles on which beliefs, and particularly normative beliefs, rest are generated by "material" causes.

According to these theories, I believe in such and such statement because biological, psychological, or sociological processes produce this belief in me, in a fashion analogous to the physiological processes to which I am subjected. These theories see beliefs, not as *grounded*, but as *caused*. Axiological beliefs notably would be endorsed by social subjects, not because they are considered by them as the consequences of principles, but because they are the effects of natural causes. While these theories, in their fashion, "solve" Münchhausen's trilemma, they do so at a high price.

Social subjects, state these theories, see their convictions as grounded on reasons. As a consequence of Münchhausen's trilemma, these convictions cannot be considered as effectively grounded. It follows that they are actually brought about rather by some causes social actors are not aware of, and that their beliefs are grounded on reasons is an illusion. The question then is: why this illusion? What are the causes of this illusion?

In other words, all the theories that start from the principle that beliefs are caused rather than grounded, while subjects themselves see them as grounded, introduce necessarily the assumption christened in the Marxist tradition, since F. Mehring, "false consciousness."

Intermezzo on the Notion of "False Consciousness"

The notion of "false consciousness" can, when properly used, describe well-defined psychological processes. It happens that social subjects are mistaken on the reasons or motivations moving them: I believe that what my friend says is true, but I am actually blinded by my friendship toward him. If the notion of "false consciousness" is used in such a context, it does not raise any difficulty, since it describes in this case a set of states of consciousness well identifiable thanks to empirical indices: any observer can note that what my friend says is false, that I do not see it, although I am generally more critical, that I support him using controversial arguments, but that I give the impression of being sincere, etc. The notion of "false consciousness" can still be used validly in other circumstances: for instance, to describe the cases where a subject subsumes a situation which is new to him with the help of inadequate categories or theories, simply because adequate categories or theories are not available to him. Of course, these two cases do not exhaust the list of situations where the notion of "false consciousness" can be used in a perfectly acceptable fashion to describe well-defined states of consciousness.

But to suppose that consciousness is normally false, that beliefs normally perceived by subjects are grounded on reasons that are always illusory, as the theories I evoke presently do, introduces a much heavier and less acceptable assumption. An objection can immediately be raised against this view: why is the observer immunized against "false consciousness"?

Indirectly, as a consequence of the causalist approach that characterizes their theories, Marx, Freud, Durkheim, Pareto and others have contributed to making the notion of "false consciousness" in this meta-physical sense a current one, which was to be used in an uncritical fashion, as though the notion could go without saying. Under their influence, an entirely new "psychology" appeared on the market, as rightly noted by R. Nisbet (1966). To this must be added, that while a Marx or a Freud or a Durkheim introduced the notion (or its equiva-lents) in a very careful fashion, this was not always the case with their followers. Thus, Durkheim makes the point that religious beliefs are symbolic and more or less confuse expressions of realities well per-ceived but ill identified by social subjects. He introduces here the notion (the notion not the word of course) of "false consciousness" in the second of the meanings I have identified above. But Durkheim's followers have often translated his ideas into the assumption that so-cial structures can mechanically introduce into the mind of people beliefs which people see as grounded while they are not. Possibly, the importance of the new "causalist" psychology has not been well real-ized.

Affective Causes

Pareto and Freud are probably the most important writers among those who attribute affective causes to axiological beliefs.

For the two of them, feelings of value are distorted expressions of affective causes. I believe that X is good because an instinct pushes me to feel so. But, as I do not want to see myself as moved by instincts, I cover my belief with what Pareto calls a "logical varnish" ("un vernis logique"): I construct arguments (Pareto's "derivations") to "demonstrate" that X is good and justify my belief to my own eyes. Alternatively, I can also look for theories available on the market that would justify my feeling, and endorse them. Example: I am poor and suffer from this situation, so I will endorse easily theories supporting the idea that personal merits play a limited role in the determination of social status, that birth, social relations, and social manipulation are the basic determinants of status, etc. I am rich: I will endorse rather easily the idea that status is basically determined by personal merits. Where Pareto talks of "vernis logique," Freud talks of "rationaliza-tion."

Such processes of course do exist and are easily observable. But the idea that all normative beliefs should be explained in this fashion cannot be accepted.

It should be noted that Pareto's work is ambiguous in this respect. On the one hand, he proposes to consider that the arguments which we use to justify our beliefs are not the causes of these beliefs, but rather their effect. On the other hand, the most important, developed, and probably the most remarkable part of his *Traité de sociologie générale*, the part where he develops his *"théorie des dérivations"* starts from the basic idea that we cannot convince and be convinced by any type of argument. On the contrary, invalid arguments must look like valid ones. This seems to imply that, in contradiction with Pareto's exoteric theory, axiological beliefs are the effects of reasons rather than of irrational causes.

Nietzsche has been a main source of inspiration for the causalist theories of moral sentiments. His theory of resentment proposes to consider that a subject endorses a belief when it satisfies some of his instincts or psychological needs. Thus, lower-class people would have a tendency to find that society is unfair. Believing that in a future life "the first ones will be the last ones" generates a psychological appeasement. Unfortunately, Weber took his inspiration from Nietzsche when he contended that Indian Untouchables accepted their situation because they were convinced that in a future reincarnation they would be better off and that their present situation was the consequence of some misbehavior in a previous reincarnation. All studies show, however, that Untouchables do not effectively accept their situation (Deliège, 1993). Still, the Nietzschean hypothesis of resentment can in some instances be worthwhile. Some beliefs can, to some extent, be explained by the positive psychological effects they generate. As Weber rightly contends though, it should not be generalized. Moreover, the psychological interest for the subject of a theory has the effect rather of drawing his attention toward the theory, eventually of pushing him to perceive the theory with sympathy. But more is needed to explain that the subject is convinced of the truth of the theory.

Above all, it is unacceptable to explain generally moral and axiological feelings by their supposed psychological effects, as some neo-Nietzscheans (Foucault) have tried to do.

Socio-Functional Causes

According to Marx, normative beliefs would be a distorted expression of class interests. This theory belongs to the class of functional theories. According to this theory, beliefs are namely, as in the Nietzschean theory, explained by their function: in this case, the promotion of the social interests of those who endorse them.

Such a theory raises several questions, however: why do I have the impression that the ideas in which I believe are fair or valid, and not that they serve my class interests? Where does this "false consciousness" come from? The answer generally given to this question by functionalist theories belongs to the same functionalist register: by eliminating any doubt from the mind of the subject, his "false consciousness" would have the function of reinforcing his faith in beliefs that are useful to him.

Several objections can be raised against these functionalist theories: how can one be sure of the existence of the hidden forces responsible for the generation of beliefs? Pareto's "sentiments," Nietzsche's "resentment" are mere constructs, that can be tested with difficulty. Why should a particular cause, as the social position of subjects, be the ultimate cause of normative beliefs (as P. Bourdieu contends, see Schweisguth, Grunberg, 1996)? Why should the functional causes be the only ones worth being considered? Why should we so easily accept that the consciousness of social actors is "false" and that this "falsity" derives from its functional value?

These classical objections, already opposed by Max Weber to Marx, are sufficient to reveal that these "functional" theories should be used with caution. They do not meet the criteria normally used in the evaluation of scientific theories. At any rate, they cannot be considered as general theories of beliefs. Why have they become so influential? Probably because the social sciences are not sufficiently guided by scientific criteria.

Biological and Generally "Natural" Causes

Other theories attempt to make values an effect of biological processes. Thus, the sociobiologist M. Ruse proposes to apply to the genealogy of morals the principles of the neo-Darwinian theory of evolution (Ruse, 1993): he introduces the conjecture that moral sense is a necessary effect of natural selection. Mankind cannot survive without social and moral rules. A nonsocial human being could not have possibly survived, nor reproduce himself: he would have been discarded by social evolution. So natural evolution has made men social and moral. It would ultimately be responsible for the essence of man as the "social living being" (the *zoon politikon*) of Aristotle.

Other writers, as A. MacIntyre, ground their naturalistic theory of normative beliefs on a neo-Aristotelian viewpoint (MacIntyre, 1981).

Some other theories of moral feelings, such as J. Wilson's, take their inspiration both from Aristotle and from sociobiology. According to Wilson, social psychology, sociobiology, and the Aristotelian philosophical tradition would converge and demonstrate the existence of a moral sense that would be a fundamental characteristic of the essence of human beings (Wilson, 1993). This theory can be objected: (1) that it is easy to produce an indefinite number of examples of normative beliefs, of which it would be difficult to assume that they are the product of a conjectural moral sense (for instance: "it is not a good idea for a government to aim at making the standard deviation of the distribution of incomes as low as possible"); (2) that the Aristotelian theory of moral sentiments is not explanatory but descriptive: it says what moral sentiments are; it does not say where the moral sentiments come from. For this reason, Wilson has tried, carefully, to combine Aristotle with sociobiology, since biology provides conjectures as to the origin of moral feelings.

As the Marxian variant of functionalism, the evolutionary version of sociobiological inspiration is twice functionalist: not only does it propose to explain moral feelings by their function, moreover, it develops further a functional theory of the supposed "false consciousness" of social subjects. People, contends Ruse, are not conscious of the sociobiological function of moral feelings. They believe on the contrary that their axiological beliefs are objectively valid. But this "false consciousness" has a function: namely, to consolidate the moral beliefs of social subjects.

It is interesting to note that, formally, the theory follows exactly the footsteps of the Marxian and the Nietzschean versions of functionalism. While they all display essentially the same scientific weaknesses, Marxian or Nietzschean functionalists would strongly reject it.

Social Causes

Finally, a word on the last variant of causalist theories, the "culturalist" theories, that is, the theories for which normative beliefs are a mere product of the various "cultures." As to the social subjects, they would, according to this type of theories, believe that "X is right" or that "Y is wrong," etc., because they would tend to see as right and wrong what is generally considered as such in their culture: as they endorse the values of their culture, these values would reproduce themselves from one generation to the next.

Montaigne had already drawn from his observation of the diversity of values through cultures the conclusion that values must be seen as customs that people would consider as good, simply because they have been taught by the various socialization agents that they are good. The eminent anthropologist C. Geertz interprets Montaigne in this fashion, at least, and suggests that the social sciences should follow him in this respect.

This type of theory, however, explains certain facts, but ignores others. By reducing values to customs, it erases a crucial distinction. Some values appear as "culturally" variable, but others, on the contrary, as universally valid: notions such as the notions of responsibility, duty, politeness, etc., are universal. It is true that the ways of expressing politeness appear as variable from one society or culture to the next. The French shake hands, the Englishmen do not. But politeness is a value independent of the ways it is expressed. Another argument can be raised against this reductionism: if values were really embedded in cultures without any universal dimension, why would we feel that we are entitled to judge other cultures? Of course, "culturalists" would object that social subjects tend to be "sociocentric," namely that they tend to make their society the measure of all things. That can be true. But such mechanisms cannot be held as general. That in some cultures *sauerkraut* is preferred to steak frites or mussels is one thing. That people can tend to be sociocentric on such issues is true. But does sociocentrism really explain that we feel *apartheid* as a bad institution? The reduction of values to customs does not only erase evident distinctions, it appears also as contradictory with observations: even if we prefer sauerkraut, even if we think sauerkraut is objectively better than steak frites, we will be easily convinced that objectively it is not, that this is a matter of taste, etc. But we would not be as easily convinced that our repulsion against apartheid is merely the effect of the fact that we have been educated in the respect of values that are contradictory with apartheid. We would normally insist that apartheid *is* bad. These distinctions deal with states of consciousness. Although such facts are subjective, a careful scientific analysis should take care of them.

"Culturalist" theories are fashionable and influent, though. First, because they start from uncontroversial data: it is true that customs appear as variable from one society to another. The influence of culturalism derives also from the scientific legitimization which anthropology has conferred to it. To C. Geertz, anthropology would have definitely demonstrated the truth of relativism, that is, the truth of the idea according to which there would be no objective truth, neither in the scientific nor in the axiological, neither in the descriptive nor in the prescriptive domains (Geertz, 1984).[6] A third factor explaining the influence of "culturalist" theories: the development of "communautarianism," a movement according to which each community must be entitled to live with the norms and values to which it is attached. Communautarianism in the ideological and political domain and culturalism in the scientific domain reinforce and make each other legitimate.

Münchhausen's Trilemma, Causalist Explanations and Positivism

An important point is worth being stressed. "Causalist" theories, that is, the theories that make value statements, axiological beliefs, moral feelings, etc., illusions, are not only numerous, popular, and influent because they solve in their own way Münchhausen's trilemma, they are also often wholeheartedly endorsed by social scientists because they have the characteristic of attributing material causes to psychological states of mind. In the positivist tradition, material causes are by principle the only causes that a scientist should look for and take care of. Therefore, the congruence of "causalist" theories with the basic principles of positivism, more precisely of the scientistic version of positivism, is possibly also responsible for the development and influence of these theories in the social sciences.

All the classical writers whom I have evoked, as Freud, Marx, Pareto, etc., and all their followers were deeply influenced by positivism, and had consequently the impression that they could not accept the idea that beliefs would be caused by reasons, or, in other words, that mental states could be caused by mental states; they had the impression, on the contrary, that mental states should be explained by non-mental causes, and consequently that, when the social actors have the impression that their beliefs are the effect of reasons, this impression would necessarily be illusory. Among the other difficulties generated by these diffuse positivistic ideas, one is worth being evoked: they produce a dual version of the mind in the sense that the "causalist" theories of beliefs view scientific beliefs as produced by reasons and ordinary beliefs by irrational causes. Durkheim, here again, appears as transcending this difficulty: to him, ordinary beliefs, as well as philosophical or religious beliefs, are generated by the same processes as scientific beliefs. True: the latter are clearer and more precise, while the former are more confused. But all categories of beliefs have to be grounded on reasons in the mind of actors. Otherwise, actors would not endorse them except temporarily. Still, these complexities of Durkheim's thinking were less retained by his followers than the assumption that society is able to structure the contents of the minds of social actors. Generally, Freud, Marx or Durkheim owe much of their influence to the fact that they are currently perceived as having been able to identify the "material" (biological, psychological, or sociological) causes of the mental states of social actors.

The influence of positivism reappears today in the attempts made by the so-called "cognitive sciences" to explain mental states by their supposed biological, emotional, or neurological infrastructure (see Sperber, 1996).

1.7 Rational Theories

Beside what I have called the fideist and the skeptical theories of normative and axiological beliefs, another category of theories can be identified: the rational theories. Some have been proposed by sociologists, others by philosophers, others by psychologists. But they all have a feature in common: they suppose that subjects endorse axiological and normative beliefs because they have strong reasons of doing so. Moreover, these reasons are not private. They are, on the contrary, public, in the sense that as soon as an actor has the feeling that his beliefs are grounded on strong reasons, he has also the feeling that other people should accept these reasons as strong. In other words, the processes generating axiological convictions would not be basically different from the processes generating scientific convictions.

Crucial also to our discussion is the fact that most of these rational theories attempt to solve Münchhausen's trilemma by assuming that axiological beliefs are grounded on absolutely valid ultimate principles. As I said before, they are for the most part, not only "rationalist" but "absolutist."

Utilitarian Theories

Utilitarian theories of normative beliefs represent a first and important illustration of these rational theories of normative beliefs. The utilitarian tradition has indeed given birth to a number of works with a common denominator: they propose to explain norms by their interest to the actors: according to these theories, I would approve or disapprove such and such norms because I have strong reasons for doing so, these reasons dealing with my interests. The Archimedes' point, in other words the ultimate principle on which normative beliefs would be grounded, would be the utility of social actors.

Several theorists have tried to push the idea that the utilitarian theory of normative beliefs (and of the generation and evolution of norms) would be the only theory that could legitimately claim a vocation to being universal.[7] They argue that, when people seem to adopt a value in consideration of reasons that would have nothing to do with the actors' interests, this would be a superficial interpretation that should be replaced by a utilitarian explanation. Thus, social psychologists have observed that, when two subjects are directed to part a divisible good between them, they would in most cases propose an egalitarian distribution: 50 percent to A and 50 percent to B. The commonsense interpretation generally given to such observations is that social subjects are not exclusively moved by their interest as they see it. But, contend the utilitarians (or in more modern parlance the "rational choice theorists") by the voice of Harsanyi (1961, 1977), A and B each know that neither himself nor the other would accept being treated unfairly in the distribution of goods. The simplest solution for each of them, if they want to maximize their gains under the constraint that the other will also want to maximize his gain, is for each of them to propose an equal distribution. One draws from this analysis an important consequence: that the domain of validity of the "rational choice theory," of the utilitarian analysis of normative beliefs, is much wider than it would seem at first sight, since it suggests that apparent altruism can be analyzed as deriving from an enlightened consideration of one's interests. Politeness, for instance, can be analyzed in such terms. More generally, the norms governing the impersonal relations within dyads can be analyzed along this line. I keep the promise I have made to Alter, because, if I would not do so, Alter would not keep his promises to me. Rousseau had already demonstrated that the citizens of democratic societies consider as legitimate the basic political norms and constraints that are imposed on them because they can be analyzed as serving the interests of all, such as transforming structures with suboptimal outcomes into cooperative games turning to the benefit of all (to use the language of game theory). Thus, traffic lights impose constraints on individuals, but serve the interests of all, since they make traffic more fluid. This type of analysis can be classified under the label utilitarianism, but also under the labels functionalism and contractualism. I will come back to functionalism in a moment.

For the time being, one point must be stressed: that many observations show that it is impossible to consider that value and norms endorsement can in all cases be explained by theories belonging to the utilitarian category.

Probably because he has seen this point clearly, Max Weber has proposed to distinguish what he calls "axiological rationality" from "instrumental rationality" and to consider the two categories as equally important, and as complementary, though distinct from one another. Now, instrumental rationality is a gender of which utilitarian rationality is a species. Instrumental rationality labels the procedure aiming at choosing the best means to satisfy a given goal. Utilitarian rationality (the type of rationality at work in the Rational Choice Model) is nothing other than instrumental rationality when the goal is to satisfy one's interest. Axiological rationality labels the type of rationality at work when subjects do not follow any goal, but aim at behaving in a way congruent with principles they consider worth following.

My classification, that makes utilitarian theories of norms and values a gender of the family of rational theories, can perhaps be criticized. Utilitarian theories start from the axiom that social subjects are dominated by their interests (alternatively by their "preferences," in modern vocabulary, or by their "passions" in eighteenth-century vocabulary). But the interests of the actors are treated by utilitarian theorists as parameters which they observe without attempting to explain them. The essence of these theories consists in attributing to the social actor a capacity of calculating rationally the best means to satisfy his preferences. For this reason, I classify utilitarian theories in the category of rational theory.

Functional Theories

Another important illustration of the category of rational theories of norms and values is functionalism (in the sociological sense of the word). It has nothing to do with the "functional" explanations inspired by Marx and Nietzsche that I mentioned earlier, nor with the sociobiological theory of morals.

Functional sociological theories represent an important contribution to the rational theories of norms and values. The basic intuition on which sociological functional theories rest is that actors have an interest in the way the system and subsystems they are embedded in operate. If an institution makes a system operate more satisfactorily, they will consider the institution good. Thus, the selection of new members would be considered good in any "club," that is, in any organization aiming at reaching definite goals. Taken in this sense, churches, universities, academies are examples of clubs. Since clubs are defined by their objectives, selecting members is a "good" thing. Otherwise, members could be admitted to the club who would have no motivation in contributing to the objectives followed by the club. As for the outside observer, he would easily understand and approve the fact that clubs are normally selective.

Cognitivist Theories

Utilitarian and functionalist theories start from an assumption on the ultimate principles responsible for human behavior. To the former, axiological beliefs have to be explained by the interests of the actors; to the latter, they have to be explained by the interest of the actors for the fact that the social system and subsystems in which they are embedded operate in a satisfactory fashion.

Cognitivist (they are also called "cognitive") theories start from the idea that values and norms derive from procedures that the social actors should consider as acceptable. They solve Münchhausen's trilemma by introducing absolutely valid procedures. The difference with the earlier evoked fideist theories is that not principles but procedures are the fixed point thanks to which the trilemma can be solved. The words "cognitive," "cognitivist" have here a meaning different from the meaning they have in the expression "cognitive sciences."

Kant

Kant's theory is certainly the most famous illustration of this category of theories of norms and values. To summarize it briefly, Kant sees the origin of normative beliefs in "practical reason." As speculative reason imposes on the subject the categories of time, space, or cause, practical reason imposes on the subject the idea, for instance, that he cannot do to Alter what he would not accept Alter doing to him. Durkheim has determined well that Kant's theory should be considered seriously by sociologists: it suggests that moral feelings are rational in the sense that they make social interaction possible. Durkheim has observed that Kant was right to use the term "reason" in his expression "the practical reason" in order to stress the fact that moral feelings derive from rational principles. Also, Kant's theory is important because it suggests that utilitarian theories cannot explain moral feelings. Moral rules should be accepted by all. So, they can only be accepted by a given social subject if he sees them as applicable to all. In other words, a moral rule is a rule that an individual would accept if he would be able to make an entire abstraction of his own interests. In some cases, it would be interesting for me to do to the other man something which I would not like to suffer myself from him. I would like to steal from him, but would not like to be stolen from. As stealing cannot be universalized, it cannot be morally accepted. Kant inspired not only Durkheim but also Max Weber, when the latter coined his famous distinction between "axiological" and "instrumental" rationality. Weber, as Durkheim, recognized clearly that utilitarian theories cannot really aim at explaining general moral feelings. Also, Kant's theory can be considered as prefiguring Rawls's notion of the "veil of ignorance."

Objections were raised very early against Kant's theory. Thus, Benjamin Constant had already noted that lying, in some circumstances, can be morally recommended, while generally it cannot. Kant's theory does not provide any path to explain such data.

Kant's theory has not only a normative or philosophical value. While it is presented as a normative theory, it can also, as well noted by Durkheim or Weber, be considered as a positive theory, in other words as a theory explaining why people generally consider some actions morally good or bad. Not only is it prescriptive, but it can also be held as descriptive and explanatory.

Rawls

Rawls's theory is possibly the most famous contemporary illustration of cognitive theories of axiological beliefs. It has been well received by professionals of law, as well as by political philosophers, who saw it rightly as a theory providing criteria, thanks to which the validity of some institutions could be appreciated. Thus, the theory provides criteria to determine whether a distribution of income can be considered fair or not.

As Kant's theory, Rawls's theory can also be considered as providing an explanation of the *feelings* of fairness or unfairness experienced by people, notably when they are informed that goods are distributed in such and such a fashion.

Thus, a number of empirical studies show that, in an organization, people tend to have an implicit "functional" theory of the distribution of rewards. They appreciate that the organization operates as effectively as possible. They understand that to reach this objective, actors must be motivated and consequently rewarded differentially, depending on their level of competence and responsibility. At the same time, they want the differences to be minimal: that they do not exceed the level corresponding to these functional requirements. In other words, in the studies I am referring to here, the subjects appear effectively as Rawlsian (see Boudon, 1994a). The "difference principle" is effectively the criterion implicitly used by actors when they evaluate a given distribution of rewards in an organization. This example shows that Rawls's theory is not only a normative theory: it may also suggest explanations of data collected by sociological empirical studies.

At any rate, the theories of Kant yesterday, of Rawls today, or the rational theories proposed by sociologists ("rational choice theory," sociological functionalism, exchange theory, contractualism) show that the normative convictions of the social subjects can, as with their descriptive convictions, be analyzed as grounded on reasons. The nega-

Table 1.1
Typology of the Theories of Moral Feelings

1. Irrational theories	1.1. Decisionist (Sartre, Weber's war of gods seen by Leo Strauss)	
	1.2. Fideist (Scheler, intuitionnism)	
	1.3 Causalist	1.3.1 Psychic causes (Pareto, Nietzsche, psychological cognitivism, behaviorism)
		1.3.2 Social causes (Marx, Durkheim, Nietzsche, post-modernism, neo-Marxism)
		1.3.3 Biological causes (Ruse, Wilson)
2. Rational theories	2.1.Absolutist	2.1.1. Universal (Kant, utilitari anism)
		2.1.2. Partial (Rawls, sociologi cal functionalism)
	2.2. Contextualist (Weber's axiological rationality, neo-Weberianism, moral cognitivism)	

tive valorization of stealing in Kant's theory, the positive or negative appreciation of the distribution of goods in Rawls's theory are analyzed as grounded by the social subjects on reasons perceived by them as strong.

The attached table presents synoptically the different types of solutions given by the theories of axiological feelings to Münchhausen's trilemma.

1.8. Normative and Positive Beliefs

As Positive Theories, Axiological Theories are "Circular"

The objections that have been raised against the cognitivist theories which I have just evoked show that none of them is able to explain axiological feelings as they are observed. The utilitarian theories are able to explain *some* observed feelings, while Rawls's or Kant's theories explain others. But counterexamples can easily be opposed to each of the theories. These failures bring us back to Münchhausen's trilemma: they suggest that it is useless to look for ultimate principles from which it would be possible to explain all moral feelings as expressed by social actors. The counterexamples which can be opposed to each of the theories, to Kant's, Rawls's theory, to functionalist or utilitarian theories, show in summary that the network of prescriptive truths is as complex as the network of descriptive truths. Scientific truths, even in a given scientific field, cannot be described as deriving from ultimate principles. Why should axiological truths be?

Axiological beliefs can be collective because they rest on reasons perceived by people as strong, exactly as positive beliefs. But these reasons do not derive from ultimate principles. As factual beliefs, axiological beliefs are grounded on complex systems of arguments.

In other words, if we follow here Weber's ideas, as I perceive them, or rather as I elaborate on them since Weber's developments on "axiological rationality" are very sketchy, we generate a special cognitivist theory, according to which social subjects would judge that "X is good" if, in a given context, a system of arguments, firstly leads to the conclusion "X is good," and secondly has no serious competitor which would lead to the opposite conclusion.

This amounts to saying that the selection of normative ideas and generally of axiological ideas follows the same principles as the selection of "positive" ideas. I believe in the Newtonian principle of inertia because I have strong reasons for believing in it and because there is no known system of arguments that would lead to its refutation.

In the same fashion, I believe that lying is bad in general; but, in certain circumstances, it can be a good thing (one can think here of the classical example of the man who resists the Gestapo officer who asks him to give the names of his companions of arms). A system of arguments satisfying the two above conditions will ground in his mind the beliefs that lying in such a case is a good thing. At the same time, the system of arguments grounding his belief in his mind will confer to his belief a character of "objectivity," or, as Durkheim would have said, of "universality" or of "necessity," in the sense that he would normally expect that any observer would normally approve his behavior. Empirical observations show abundantly that this is effectively the case.

An objection to this theory is sometimes raised: reasons can be perceived as strong without being good. Thus, the Germans who, during the Weimar republic, voted for the national-socialist party had strong reasons for doing so, but the reasons were invalid.

As the history of science shows, this situation occurs as well in the case of positive beliefs. Scientists have believed in all kinds of false ideas on the basis of reasons perceived as strong and which were perceived later as weak. Descartes had strong reasons to believe that nature does not like emptiness, as Newton had strong reasons to believe in alchemy: to us, however, their reasons were invalid. They appeared as invalid when new arguments were developed that made them weak. Thus, Toricelli and Pascal disqualified Descartes's view, that the part of a tube filled with quicksilver that appeared to remain empty was in fact filled by a subtle matter because nature abhorred emptiness, when they showed that this apparently empty part was higher on the top than at the bottom of a mountain. Should nature abhor emptiness more at the bottom than on the top of mountains? asked Pascal. The powerful argument hidden behind this joke discredited Descartes's "subtle matter."

It is easy to cite examples where the devaluation or reevaluation of axiological arguments follows the process of innovation and selection that characterize the crystallization or devaluation of positive beliefs. Thus, Kant's statements according to which paid work would always be a kind of prostitution (Kant, 1785) or his thesis that lying would always be bad, does not appear to us as less absurd than Descartes's "subtle matter" that would fill the higher part of a tube of quicksilver or than the "turmoils" that, according to physicists of the Middle Ages, would explain how ships keep moving even after the wind has stopped. Kant's beliefs on paid work or on lying are irreversibly dead. Even neo-Kantians would not support them today. Why? Because the interests of the workers are protected by unions, an institution which Kant could hardly anticipate, and by an effective body of legislation; because they can legitimately use powerful social weapons, such as the strike, speaking of paid work as a prostitution is to us meaningless. When he developed this viewpoint, Kant did not anticipate at all this evolution in labor relations. He did not anticipate either the cruelties which we have experienced in the twentieth century, nor imagined situations where, to struggle against an absolute evil, lying would be a duty. Such processes are in no way different from the processes I have just evoked, through which positive beliefs were disqualified. In all of these cases, people believe that "X is good, bad, legitimate, etc.," because they have strong reasons to believe so. Descartes' beliefs are neither more nor less absurd than the beliefs of the German voter in 1933. Unless I can be shown in which respects the two types of beliefs are different from one another, I will endorse the *Verstehen* postulate, which is, when people believe that something is true, fair, legitimate, etc., the cause of their belief resides in the meaning of the belief to them, in other words, in the reasons they perceive the belief as strong.

Tocqueville uses the *Verstehen* postulate when he states that the "most profound geniuses of Rome and Greece" never came to the idea that slavery could be abolished:

> The most profound and broadest geniuses of Rome and Greece have never been able to come to this so general, but at the same time so simple idea, of the similarity of men and of the equal right to liberty that each of them bears in being born; and they have spent energy to prove that slavery was in the nature of things, and that it would always exist. Furthermore, the available evidence shows that those in Antiquity who had been slaves before becoming free citizens, and of whom several have left us significant writings, had the same viewpoint on the institution of slavery.[8]

Why? Because, answers Tocqueville, in a society officially hierarchized as were these societies, people had easily the impression, not only that they belonged to their class, but that each social class constituted a kind of natural species, and that mankind as such was an abstract gender composed of a set of concrete species:

> When the social conditions are very unequal and when inequalities are everlasting, individuals become progressively so dissimilar, that one would think that there are as many different types of mankind as there are social classes; one discovers them separately and, losing sight of the general link that gathers them all in the vast category of mankind, one pays attention to certain men, but not to man. [9]

This parallelism between positive and normative beliefs explains why no normative theory starting from simple ultimate principles, as Kant's yesterday or Rawls's today, can generate the complex networks of arguments which give birth to axiological collective beliefs. The world of axiological beliefs is as complex as the world of positive beliefs. Until the end of the nineteenth century, the belief was spread that physical knowledge could be unified. No one still endorses this belief. Physicists do not dream anymore of a unified physics; as to biologists, they still believe less in the unification of their disciplines. Each piece of knowledge is grounded on strong reasons, but it is impossible to identify ultimate principles which would be at the root of these more or less closely related pieces of knowledge.

Why should the situation be different in the case of normative beliefs? Technical and institutional innovations create continuously new situations (see the case of bioethics). Why should they not modify our systems of arguments and our beliefs? If Kant had anticipated the evolution of the rights of workers, he would never have come to the idea that paid work can be assimilated to a form of prostitution. [10]

Rawls's theory provides another illustration of the impossibility of deducing from ultimate principles even very limited sets of axiological feelings, like the feelings generated by the distribution of goods. His "principle of difference" aims at providing a general criterion by which it would be possible to determine whether such and such distribution of goods is legitimate or not. At the same time, the theory offers a conjectural explanation as to why people would have a feeling of fairness or unfairness when they are confronted with such and such distribution of goods, namely the famous "difference principle." In-equalities, says this principle, should never be higher than the threshold below which the situation of the worse off would deteriorate. The "difference principle" can be considered an adequate theory able to reproduce and explain the feelings of fairness and unfairness really experienced by people in a transparent organization. In this case, people accept inequalities provided they are functional, provided they optimize the situation of all. If they were higher, if the higher paid would be paid beyond the functional level, the morale in the organization would deteriorate and the situation of the worse off would consequently become worse. In other words, in such circumstances, people are effectively Rawlsians.

But it is readily checked that the same "difference principle" cannot provide a general theory of the feelings of fairness or unfairness generated by distributions of goods.

In the case of a global society, it is impossible to evaluate the fairness of income distribution thanks to the difference principle. Why? Because in this case, it is impossible to determine, even roughly, the "functional" level of inequality, namely the level beyond which inequalities would have no function and would create mere privileges. In other words, it is impossible to determine the theoretical level above which the level of inequality could be reduced without any negative effect on the worse off. Probably because people perceive in a more or less confused manner that, in the case of a global society, it is impossible to determine the functional level of inequalities, they appear as non-Rawlsians.

This criticism reaches Rawls's theory at its very heart. It shows that the difference principle can provide a criterion to determine the legitimate or illegitimate character of a distribution of goods in *particular*, but not in general circumstances. It invites us to leave aside the ambition of building a general rational-absolutist theory of moral feelings, and to substitute for it a new approach to axiological feelings, namely a rational-contextualist approach. The members of a transparent organization who judge that inequalities are fair or unfair endorse probably this judgment because they apply the "difference principle": they assimilate fair inequalities with functional inequalities. Respondents who are asked whether a global income distribution in a national society is fair or not are likely not to ground their answer on the same principle, because they see that in this case the functional or a-functional character of a level of inequalities cannot be determined. As an illuminating study shows, they are effectively not Rawlsian in such circumstances (Frohlich, Oppenheimer, 1992; Boudon, 1995a). Thus, depending on the parameters characterizing a context, the statement "X is good, bad, legitimate, illegitimate, etc.," can be endorsed or on the contrary be rejected with strong reasons.

This does not mean that any prediction is impossible and that one would be doomed to a "local" theory of justice feelings, where each context would be in last analysis singular. The example of Rawls shows, on the contrary, that it is possible to identify the relevant parameters of contexts, and consequently to define classes of contexts. The question as to whether the degree of functionality of inequalities can be determined or not gives a good example of these relevant parameters. It determines two classes of contexts. Depending on whether the answer is positive or negative, namely whether in the context the functional level of inequalities can be determined or not, the moral feelings aroused by the standard deviation (or any other measure of inequality), will be different.

Rawls would possibly argue that his theory is normative, that he did not aim at reconstructing the axiological feeling of people as they are actually observed, but to determine what they should be. But is it really credible that a theorist can propose a theory of moral feelings which would be unrelated to the moral feelings of people as they actually are? Can the normative philosopher have moral feelings different from the moral feelings of most people? If not, can he propose a moral theory that would have no relation with his moral feelings? To say the truth, I think that normative theories of morals are always more or less theories of moral feelings. For a simple reason: I can endorse a value statement (leaving aside statements dealing with taste) only if I have the impression the other man would also endorse it. It is impossible to have the feeling that "X is good, legitimate, etc.," without having at the same time the impression that X is effectively good, bad, etc., and consequently without expecting that the other man would also have the same feeling. For this reason, a moral theory is always a theory of moral feelings.

Not only the theory of moral feelings and more generally of axiological feelings, the feelings relative to what *should be* follow the "circular" processes characteristic of the generation of positive beliefs ; this is also true of axiological theories. In order to explain why X *is perceived as* good, legitimate, etc., but also why X *is* good, legitimate, etc., amounts to reconstructing an argumentation that is likely to appear as stronger than alternative sets of arguments leading to the opposite conclusion and of which one can suppose that it grounds the beliefs of the social actors.

That this reconstruction is submitted to Münchhausen's trilemma is not more incompatible with the objectives of certainty, truth, and objectivity in the normative field than in the descriptive field. In the two cases, the statements perceived as "valid" are grounded on a complex network of arguments.

If we accept the idea that positive theories of moral feelings have a normative dimension (and reciprocally the normative theories a positive dimension), one can see the basic reason as to why positive convictions and normative convictions or more generally axiological convictions are finally generated by similar processes.

Whether or not this parallelism may be held as one of the great intuitions of Max Weber (Boudon, 1997a), it defines an important variant of the cognitivist type of axiological theories. The core of this parallelism is that, if it is true that principles (prescriptive or descriptive), as they are principles, cannot be demonstrated without ceasing to be principles, and if it true that, in this sense, it is impossible to escape the "war of gods" and the "polytheism of values," it does not follow that these principles cannot be rationally discussed, that they cannot be rejected by reality. On the contrary, the competition between principles is exposed to processes of rational selection, generating the processes of "rationalization" of the moral life which Weber evokes repeatedly.

1.9. The Trilemma and Moral Life

This discussion contributes, at least this is my hope, not only to clarify normative theories, but also to understand more clearly normative life.

Moral life consists in endorsing moral principles appearing a priori as interesting (for instance, the principle of the equality of all in dignity) and in trying to implant them in the real world. These principles cannot be demonstrated. The vague principle, namely describe reality as it is, which lies at the foundation of scientific activity, cannot be demonstrated to be true either. In the same way, it is impossible to show that the basic postulate of aesthetics or literary criticism, according to which objective correlates to aesthetic feelings do actually exist and are worth being scientifically investigated, is valid. Being a postulate, it cannot be demonstrated. It can only be tried, and evaluated on its outcomes. But this evaluation can last a long time.

Simmel has noted rightly in his *Philosophy of Money*, that a considerable change was introduced in the history of mankind when the *Wergeld* was dropped. This institution made the value of men a function of their social status, with the result that killing somebody was punished in a more or less severe fashion depending on the status of the victim. Behind this institution (about which one can legitimately wonder whether it is really dead), a principle was hidden, namely the principle of the unequal value of individuals. Behind its obsolescence, the opposite principle of the equal value of all, or in other words the principle that individuals are "persons," is hidden. From the moment when it was formulated, this principle appeared as irreversible and took the status of a basic guideline of social life.

Thus, moral life, exactly as scientific life, includes phases of innovation, phases of creation of moral ideas, and phases of evaluation and, hence, selection of moral ideas. The principles guiding moral life are selected and rejected, as the principles used in the description of reality. As in the case of scientific ideas, new moral ideas are devised and proposed by innovators. That Socrates or Voltaire have become major figures in the history of mankind comes from the fact that they have been the vectors or moral innovations which were selected by social evolution.

Of course, this innovation and the selection processes are thwarted by passions and interests. Normative principles are more exposed than descriptive principles to the passions and interests of men because their discussion is public. For this reason, one has easily the impression that the strength of normative ideas in the social selection process results from the strength of the groups defending them. That the selection of normative ideas is associated with social-ideological conflicts and appears, as suggested by Coser (1956), as facilitated by social conflicts, is one thing. That the moral truth would be nothing else than the outcome of this struggle and would simply reflect the relative strengths of the groups in competition supporting the various viewpoints is another. "The reasons of the stronger are not always the best" against La Fontaine's aphorism, "la raison du plus fort est toujours la meilleure."

To come back to Münchhausen trilemma, it has never inhibited the production of solid descriptive ideas. The same is true of prescriptive ideas.

A last question should be raised which I cannot explore in its full extension. Is this process of rational selection of normative ideas a characteristic of democratic societies or does it apply to all societies? I would rather choose the latter answer. Weber and Durkheim have indicated, rightly, I think, that "rationality" is a fundamental feature of man. Hence, an idea which is positive from a rational viewpoint, has an intrinsic force. This explains for instance that magic remains a serious competitor of science exclusively on the issues that science has not succeeded covering. All societies and cultures recognize this point. The same is true of axiological ideas. This is one of the important points well defended by Durkheim in his *Formes élémentaires*.

In virtue of the Münchhausen's principle there are no ultimate truths, except vague and ill-determined ("respect reality, describe reality as it is" is the ultimate value that grounds science, "respect all men equally" is the ultimate value that grounds morals), but the process of rationalization characterizes all cultures.

Notes

1. This thesis is developed notably by Hübner (1985).
2. This skeptical stance is illustrated by constructivistic sociology of science, as developed notably by D. Bloor (1980).
3. As reasons can also be causes, as Davidson (1980), among others, has shown, the words "cause" and "causalist theories" are used her implicitly as shorthand notations for "causes that are not reasons," "theories evoking causes that are not reasons."
4. See my remarks on Scheler in Boudon (1994a).
5. A. dal Lago (1988) contends that, as a Catholic, Carl Schmitt interprets Weber's "value polytheism" as deriving from the radical freedom of judgement granted to individuals in the Protestant tradition.
6. Montaigne's *skepticism* must be distinguished from Geertz *relativism*. While the latter is dogmatic, the former is flexible and, moreover, strategic. See Popkin (1964).
7. See Oberschall (1994) or Opp (1983).
8. "Les génies les plus profonds et les plus vastes de Rome et de la Grèce n'ont jamais pu arriver à cette idée si générale, mais en même temps si simple, de la similitude des hommes et du droit égal que chacun d'eux apporte, en naissant, à la liberté ; et ils se sont évertués à prouver que l'esclavage était dans la nature, et qu'il existerait toujours. Bien plus, tout indique que ceux des anciens qui ont été esclaves avant de devenir libres, et dont plusieurs nous ont laissé de beaux écrits, envisageaient eux mêmes la servitude sous le même jour" (Tocqueville, 1986 [1845]: 437–438).
9. "Lorsque les conditions sont fort inégales, et que les inégalités sont permanentes, les individus deviennent peu à peu si dissemblables, qu'on dirait qu'il y a autant d'humanités différentes qu'il y a de classes ; on ne découvre jamais à la fois que l'une d'elles, et, perdant de vue le lien général qui les rassemble toutes dans le vaste sein du genre humain, on n'envisage jamais que certains hommes et non pas l'homme" (Tocqueville, 1986 [1845]: 437).
10. B. Constant had already raised this objection against Kant. (See Janicaud, 1996.)

2

Rational Theories: Limits of the "Rational Choice Model" [1]

2.1. The Attractiveness of Rational Choice Theory (RCT)

The appeal of RCT has been well explained by J. Coleman (1986): the reason why rational action has "a unique attractiveness" as a basis for theory is that it is a conception of action "that we need ask no more question about it"; Hollis (1977) has expressed the same idea in other words: "rational action is its own explanation." [2] It is true that, once we have explained that subject X has done Y rather than Y' because it was more advantageous for him to do Y, we need to know nothing more. Even if biology was able to describe adequately the chemical or electrical processes going on in the brain when a subject makes his decision, it would add nothing to the explanation as to why the subject did Y. It would merely describe the same process in a different language. But it would be unable to confirm or disconfirm the rational explanation. This "final" side of rational explanations, the fact that rational explanations do not contain any black box is probably, as suggested by Coleman, the main source of its attractiveness.

2.2. Whether RCT is General

Two questions should be raised, however, before we give RCT the status of a general theory. Being attractive does not necessarily qualify for a theory as being acceptable, valid, or true in *all* circumstances. That "rational action is its own explanation" is one thing. Whether action can always be considered rational in the very special sense RCT gives to the notion of rationality is another. If all actions and further all social phenomena could be validly explained by RCT, this would be fine. But can they? In the same way, it would be fine if I lost my keys under a public light where they would be much easier to find than in the surrounding darkness. But this does not demonstrate that I effectively dropped my keys under the public light. Thus, an important question is whether RCT is effectively general, as contended by its followers. If yes, the discussion can stop at this point. If not, the next question is whether RCT can be revised to make it more general.

Can we legitimately apply RCT to all research situations and to all problems? The answer to this latter question is "no," for a simple reason: RCT assumes that individual action is *instrumental*, namely that it has to be explained by the actor's will to reach certain goals. Now, action can be non-instrumental, as most sociologists have recognized. Schütz through his distinction between *Weil* and *Wozu Motive*, Weber through his distinction between instrumental and axiological rationality, have stressed that action is not always instrumental. If this is true, RCT cannot claim to be a general theory of action. Thus, one cannot apply RCT notably in cases where an actor does X because he believes in Z and that Z implies his doing X independently of the consequences of X. And even when action is instrumental, it can mobilize beliefs which need being explained and which normally will not be explained by RCT. Thus, French authorities for many years were more reluctant than the Dutch to accept the idea of using methadone to curb drug addiction. Why? Because the Dutch thought methadone was an adequate means while the French thought it was not. *Why* had the French and the Dutch different beliefs on this point? [3] RCT is of little help here.

Of course, these objections are not new and there are two traditional ways out of them:

1. One way of preserving the generality of RCT is to suppose that actions that are apparently non-instrumental are instrumental *at a deeper level*. This conversion from non-instrumental into instrumental is obtained by introducing the postulate that, contrary to appearances, beliefs are the product of self-interest. This assumption constitutes the core of some classical theories besides RCT. It was introduced notably by Nietzsche, by Pareto, or by Marx: I believe X, because believing X serves my psychological interests or my class interests.

2. Another way of salvaging the generality of RCT is to appeal to M. Friedman's epistemology and to treat the causes of behavior as by principle unknowable. If so, any assumption about the causes of behavior is as good as any other and it can legitimately be assumed that self-interest explains any behavior. In virtue of this "positivistic" epistemology, this assumption cannot be discussed and the only thing that matters is whether or not theories incorporating this postulate reproduce correctly observed data.

Assumptions of type 1 can be acceptable in some cases. Thus, I can believe that social inequalities are unfair because such a belief makes my poverty undeserved and thus more acceptable to me or alternatively that social inequalities are fair because I can then perceive my opulence as well deserved. It is hard though to accept the view that *all* beliefs are generated by their psychological or social function. This objection was explicitly raised by Weber (1986 [1920]: 241) against Nietzsche and Marx: "resentment" theory applies exclusively to particular cases. In the general case, psychological and/or social interests may draw my attention to a theory and eventually create in my mind a positive or negative disposition toward the theory in question. But interests alone are generally unable to explain conviction.

Assumption of type 2 rests upon a very debatable epistemology. Why such a view as Friedman's "positivism" was developed can be understood: it derives from the reluctance of the positivistic tradition toward taking into account subjective factors. But such an epistemology is ungrounded: I can check whether this man whom I see cutting wood in his yard wants his room to get warmer. If he puts the piece of wood in his chimney, my interpretation of his behavior will be confirmed. If the weather is hot or if he starts carving the piece of wood, my interpretation will be falsified. Even if I cannot perceive directly his reasons, I can reconstruct them. This reconstruction has the status of a theory which can be confronted with data. That the reasons motivating people are not directly observable does not imply that their reconstruction is doomed to be arbitrary. Now, E. Kiser and M. Hechter reject both Friedmanian positivism and also the view that determining the reasons explaining actions would be an empirical question. Instead, they see self-interest as the ultimate *real* cause of any action. But this raises a difficult question. The RCTheorist confronted by a voter who tells him that he votes because he considers voting a civic duty will reject the interpretation of the subject himself and, by application of his own RCTheory, assume that voting maximizes for the voter some cost-benefit balance. At this point, the RCTheorist should explain the "false consciousness" he attributes to the actor: why does the subject think he votes for one reason while he *really* votes for another? But how does the RCTheorist know that the consciousness of his voter is "false"? I am not saying here that what the actor himself thinks and says of his own motivation is the ultimate truth. It is rather a piece of information among others. What I am saying is (1) that the actor's statements about his motivation are *facts* which, as any fact, should be taken into consideration and explained; (2) that the Nietzschean, the Marxian, or the RCTheorist who attributes to the behavior of the observed subject causes which the latter does not endorse should explain his "false consciousness," notably if he rejects the Friedmanian epistemology. Hence, in contradiction with Coleman's main argument for RCT, RCT creates rather than eliminates black boxes in many circumstances (Boudon 1998).

On the whole, none of the strategies currently used to make instrumental non-instrumental actions appears as very convincing. They raise more questions than they solve. In other words, non-instrumental actions cannot easily be converted into instrumental actions. Consequently, RCT cannot be held as general.

Beside this basic objection, "empirical" objections can be raised against the RCT, namely that it has never succeeded in explaining satisfactorily important classes of phenomena. Voting is the best known of these classes. People vote, though any individual vote has a practically zero probability of having an effect on the outcome of an election. In this case, the anticipated consequences of individual action cannot easily be taken for the cause of the action. An enormous amount of literature has been devoted to this problem, that tries to reconcile RCT with the hard fact of voting (see for instance Overbye [1995]). Many other puzzles in the same style could be evoked: why do people appear so easily upset by political corruption and so sensitive to it? This familiar observation cannot be easily explained by RCT since political corruption has, in the case of Western democracies at least, a negligible and invisible effect on the well-being of citizens. In other words, the rejection here is implausibly the effect of the consideration by social actors of the consequences of corruption on themselves. Allais (1953) and a number of authors after him have revealed another Achilles' heel of RCT (if I may make Achilles' heels plural) and shown that people do not behave effectively according to RCT predictions: when they have to choose between lotteries, in given experimental circumstances, they do not behave as maximizers.

RCTheorists have tried to meet these objections by auxiliary assumptions. For instance, non-voting would include a high social cost because it would be socially disapproved; cognitive biases would make people overestimate the weight of a single vote; biases would have the effect that people see in an erroneous fashion the mathematical expectation of lotteries; cognitive "frames" would make people not see the world as it is. I cannot discuss these theories in detail here. I have done it in Boudon (1996, 1997b). In fact, none of the RCTheories proposed to explain why people vote is very satisfactory. As to the theories that propose to reconcile RCT with observed data by introducing the notions of "frames," "biases," etc., they appear as empty ("frame," "bias" are mere words); moreover, they pay a high price for the reconciliation with observation of H, since they lose the "unique attractiveness" of RCT. Once one has introduced the assumption that people see the world in such and such fashion because a bias or a frame affects their perception, the next question is namely: "where do these biases come from?" As RCT has no answer to this question, the explanation is no longer final; it generates on the contrary large black boxes.

The two categories of objections merge into a general objection. Some actions are purely instrumental. Among the purely instrumental actions, some are egoistic. Some actions are not purely instrumental in the sense that they include a cognitive dimension: the actor wants to reach goal G; he has the impression that M is a good way of reaching G, but the relation between M and G is not trivial. In that case, the non-instrumental cognitive dimension of action is the focus of the analysis. Some actions are not instrumental at all, as when an actor does X, not because he wants to generate some outcome, but because X is a consequence of principles he endorses. In that case, the main point in the analysis is to explain why the actor endorses the principles. Endorsing principles, endorsing a theory, a viewpoint, is also an action, but of the non-instrumental type. This diversity cannot be forgotten or reduced, except by two controversial strategies: considering the non-instrumental aspects of actions as uninteresting and being content with saying that the actors are subject to "biases," "frames," etc.; or assuming that all actions would be *at a deeper level* of a unique type: not only instrumental, but egoistic. I agree with M. Somers that such an assumption has a metaphysical flavor.

2.3. Alternative Way

Instead of trying to salvage RCT against these objections, a more fruitful move is to question the basic postulates of RCT. M. Somers says rightly that the weak side of RCT is not its individualistic approach but its definition of "rationality": intentionality, self-interest, maximization. Do we need to endorse this very special view about rationality? Do we really need to accept the idea that all actions are not only consequential but egoistic? Is this version of rationality the only one presenting the uniqueness of providing explanations without black boxes? The greatest of classical historical sociologists, Tocqueville and Weber, have implicitly answered this question. Yes, they said, action should be considered as meaningful; yes, the meaning of his action to the actor should be considered as its cause; yes, in most cases, the meaning to the actor of his action resides in the reasons he perceives as strong to adopt it: in other words, they introduced the general postulate that the causes of an action reside in the *reasons* the actor has for adopting this action. And they added that, depending on the situation the actor is involved in, these reasons can take the form of cost-benefit considerations, *but also other forms*. Thus, endorsing a theory is in most cases an action caused by the fact that one sees strong reasons of endorsing it. Priestley endorsed the phlogiston theory, not only because he had a strong interest defending it, but because he was convinced it explained better many facts than alternative theories.

These classical writers should be heard: they have solved implicitly by anticipation some of the crucial questions raised by the present discussion and indicated a path worth following today. They start from the view that (what *we* call) RCT can be useful notably in situations where the actor is invited to apply a cost-benefit analysis by the very nature of the situation. But, in other circumstances, the notion of "rationality" must be given another content. In modern words, RCT is not a general theory because it uses a much too rigid and narrow conception of rationality. To illustrate, I will mention briefly two examples from Tocqueville.

2.4. Two Examples from Tocqueville

Example Using "Methodological Individualism" and RCT

At one point in his *Old Regime* Tocqueville wonders why at the end
of the eighteenth century (Tocqueville [1856] 1955) French agriculture remains stagnant at a time when agriculture is flourishing in England. This is particularly puzzling since the physiocrats, who develop
the view that modernizing agriculture is the main path to growth, are
politically very influential in France at this time. Tocqueville's explanation: administrative centralization is the reason "civil servant" positions are more numerous and hence more easily available in France
than in England. Also, French centralization makes serving the King
in France a unique source of prestige, influence, and power; consequently, other things equal, landlords are more easily incited in France
than in England to leave their ground and buy a royal position. In
England, by contrast, being an innovative landowner can not only
produce local respect and prestige, it can also open the way to
Westminster. This macroscopic difference between England and France,
summarized by Tocqueville in his notion of "administrative centralization," explains why landlord absenteeism is much greater in France
than in England. Further, landlord absenteeism is the cause of the low
rate of innovation: since their interests are at Court, landlords themselves have little motivation to innovate; as to the farmers who run the
landownerships, they would have a motivation to innovate, but hardly
the capacity for doing so. Finally, the low rate of innovation is responsible for the stagnation.

Tocqueville uses here "methodological individualism" (MI). The
macroscopic difference between France and England is explained as
the effect of individual decisions made by the landlords. The individual decisions are analyzed as taken, not by "angels," but by men
belonging to social contexts. The parameters characterizing the French
and the British contexts are themselves the product of a long history.
This point gives me the opportunity of stressing that MI does not
imply solipsism as soon as individual decisions are analyzed, as here
by Tocqueville, as affected by the parameters characterizing the context. [4] Finally, Tocqueville uses here what we call RCT: by leaving
their land and serving the King, the landlords gain in influence, prestige, etc. In England by contrast, it is a better strategy to appear locally

as a modern and efficient landlord. The macroscopic statement, "centralization is a cause of agricultural underdevelopment," appears as entirely acceptable, because it is supported by this individualistic analysis. Though "centralization" is a complex factor, it is identified with precise "parameters" which affect the situation of decision of the actors, here the landlords. "Centralization" is a construct. But it is not a mere word. In summary, Tocqueville uses here MI. Moreover, he uses the basic behavioral axioms of RCT; the individuals are analyzed as selfish, goal-oriented, and maximizers. It can be noted incidentally that Tocqueville's path has been literally followed by Root (1994) in his illuminating book on the comparative development of the modern state in Britain and France.

Example Using implicitly MI, but Rejecting RCT

In other circumstances, Tocqueville uses MI but not RCT. Thus, he wonders, again in his *Old Regime*, why the cult of Reason became immensely popular in France at the end of the eighteenth century, but not in England. His answer is that traditional institutions and hence Tradition with a capital T were totally disqualified in France, but not in England. Thus, the British aristocracy fulfilled important social and economic roles. Consequently, its higher status was considered by people as grounded and legitimate. In France, by contrast, the gentry had no visible social and economic function except sitting in Versailles. Those members of the gentry who were not able to buy a royal position remained on their land. Poor and bitter, they clung ritualistically to their privileges. Their officially higher rank was perceived by the peasants as illegitimate. As it was the product of tradition, the peasants came to the idea that institutions deriving their strength from tradition are bad. Thus, when the "Philosophes" proposed to substitute for institutions grounded on Tradition with a capital T a society grounded on what they presented as the opposite term, namely Reason with a capital R, they had immediate success. After all, the notion translated widespread feelings. Tocqueville makes clear that this success cannot be analyzed as the product of interpersonal influence, since it was immediate. So, the macroscopic phenomenon under examination, namely the fulgurant success of the idea of Reason, is analyzed by Tocqueville as the effect of the fact that individual French peasants, lawyers, etc., accepted easily the theory that good institutions should be the effect of social engineering (in our language), be the product of Reason (in eighteenth-century parlance). This analysis follows MI, but not RCT. Here again, a social fact, in this case a difference between France and England, is analyzed as the product of reasons, but not of the RCT type. Individual peasants tend to endorse the political theory proposed by the "philosophes" because this theory appears to them as valid. Evidently, they expect from the application of his theory returns for themselves. Most of them are probably convinced that their condition would become better if the ideas of the Philosophes were applied. But this does not explain why they see "social engineering" as a good political philosophy. Tocqueville uses here implicitly a view of rationality which I have proposed to call "cognitive rationality." The peasants endorse the political theory of the Philosophes because they have strong cognitive reasons of seeing it as valid. This type of rationality is typically at work in the case of the scientist who chooses a theory T against a theory T'. "Cognitive rationality," in my language, overlaps with "rationality" in the sense where historians and philosophers of science use this word. Tocqueville's analysis provides a powerful hint here: that the type of rationality at work in the endorsement by scientists of an idea or theory is also at work in "ordinary knowledge."

2.5. "Cognitive Rationality"

Cognitive rationality should be distinguished from instrumental rationality. First, because endorsing a theory is a non-instrumental action; second, because the question the actor is confronted with here is not to maximize any cost-benefit balance, but to check whether, to the best of his knowledge, an idea is acceptable. Radnitzky (1987) has tried to reduce this cognitive rationality to RCT. When more and more facts appeared easily explainable by the theory that "the earth is spherical," it became more and more difficult to develop alternative arguments supporting the theory that "the earth is flat." Radnitzky proposes to substitute "costly" for "difficult" and makes then the point that the choice between alternative scientific theories can also be analyzed in RCT terms. But the main point is that the arguments supporting the theory, "the earth is spherical," appeared after a while much stronger than the arguments supporting the alternative theories. Little is gained by substituting "costly" for "difficult." "Cost" is namely a consequence of "difficulty." What needs to be explained is why a set of arguments appears as defensible or not defensible.

2.6. A Special Case of Utmost Relevance

Although I cannot go very far on this other important point, "axiological rationality" should be distinguished, as suggested by Weber, from "instrumental rationality." This notion has been much discussed and what Weber meant by it is not clear. My own interpretation (see Boudon,1997b) is that he wanted to introduce the idea that in some circumstances actors do X, not because they expect from doing X any desirable consequence, but because they are convinced that X is good, since grounded on strong reasons. Thus, Weber would probably never have considered voting as a paradox. It is a paradox as long as one assumes that rational action is always consequentialist, as RCT assumes. In that case, voting is a paradox, since my vote has with quasi certainty no consequence on the outcome of the election. People vote though. Why? Because they have strong reasons to believe that democracy is better than alternative regimes, they see that election is a major institution of democracy, they understand the principle, "one man, one vote," they see that this principle is an expression of a basic value, etc. In other words, they vote because one *should* vote if one believes in the value of democracy. This explanation mobilizes what, following my interpretation, Weber called "axiological rationality." I vote because I think I should vote. I think I should vote because I have strong reasons to believe in democracy, because in other words I endorse a theory concluding that democracy is a good organization of political life. Axiological rationality would then be a special case of cognitive rationality, though a special case of utmost relevance. Of course, I will have strong reasons to refrain from voting if none of the candidates convinces me, if I do not know how I should vote, etc.

As I said earlier, many efforts have been made to explain voting by RCTheories. But these theories are all unconvincing and, moreover, assume implicitly without explaining it the existence of a "false consciousness" of the voter: a huge black box.

2.7. RCT: A Particular Case of a More General Model

Finally, we come to the idea that Tocqueville and Weber among others have sketched a model, which I have proposed to call the "cognitivist model" (CM), resting on the following postulates (see Boudon, 1994b, 1996, 1998):

1. Until proof to the contrary is given, social actors should be considered as rational in the sense that they have strong reasons for believing what they believe, for doing what they do, etc.
2. In particular cases, these reasons can be realistically treated as dealing with the difference between costs and benefits of alternative lines of action. In other cases, they cannot: in particular when a decision, an action, rests upon normative or cognitive beliefs, the reasons will generally not belong exclusively to this type. This results from the fact that beliefs are unintentional, and that normative beliefs are not always consequentially grounded. Also, in many circumstances, a social actor can be personally unconcerned with an issue and have strong feelings about it (as, for example, the death penalty). This latter point is crucial: it suggests that RCT is of limited use in the analysis of public opinion.
3. In some circumstances, the core of some action is constituted by "cognitive" reasons: he did X because he believed that Z is likely true, etc., and because he had strong reasons for believing so.
4. In some circumstances, the core of some action is constituted by "axiological" reasons: he did X because he believed that Z is fair, good, unfair, etc., and had strong "non-consequential" reasons for believing so.

It follows from these postulates that RCT is a particular case of the CM ("Cognitivist Model"). When the reasons in the CM are restricted to belong to the "benefit minus cost" type, we get RCT. Reciprocally, when the restriction that reasons should belong to the "benefit minus cost" type is lifted in RCT, we get the CM. Again, RCT is a powerful model; it cannot be held as a general theory. [5]

The CM supposes that actions, decisions, and beliefs are meaningful to the actor in the sense that they are perceived by him as grounded on reasons. Even though he is unable to identify these reasons clearly, he has the intuitive impression that they are grounded on reasons.

Two important remarks can be introduced here. Although it is tautological to define "rationality" by the notion of "strong reasons," it is the only way of getting rid of the discussions as to "what rationality *really* means," where the discussants expose generally what *they* mean. As to the postulate that beliefs, actions are grounded on reasons, it is not tautological. Many traditions start, on the contrary, from the assumption that actions and beliefs are not the effect of reasons. As to finding out these reasons, reconstructing them, this can be a hard job: why were the French landlords less innovative than their British counterparts? Why did Priestley believe in the phlogiston? Why did Englishmen of the eighteenth century believe that miners should be paid more than soldiers (Smith, 1976 [1776])? Why did the people of London not try to exert pressure on political power by street gatherings as frequently as the Parisians (Root, 1994)? Why are magical beliefs more widespread in some societies than in others (Boudon, 1994b)? Why was methadone used much earlier in Holland than in France (Bergeron, 1999)? All these questions have been convincingly answered in works which use MI and an open theory of rationality rather than the special figure of rationality used by RCT. In particular it can be noted that, in his *Wealth of Nations*, Adam Smith (1976 [1776]), RCT's spiritual father, solves the above question about miners and soldiers using what I call the CM rather than RCT (Boudon, 1996, 1998).

The second remark, which I cannot develop, is that CM excludes radically solipsism: I cannot perceive as strong the reasons leading me to endorse a statement, "X is good, legitimate, right, true, etc.," without conceiving these reasons as grounded and hence as intersubjectively valid (Boudon, 1995b).

Finally, a crucial question is raised by M. Somers: what is a good theory? Sometimes, good scientific theories use mathematical language, and are derived from a general theory, etc. But such attributes are not components of a good theory generally. Otherwise, physical theories would be good, but biological theories bad, since the latter make little use of mathematics and are hardly deducted from a general theory. Celestial mechanics is not the model to be followed by all disciplines. A good scientific explanation of a phenomenon P is rather a set {S} of statements meeting three requirements: (1) that all s belonging to S are acceptable, (2) that {S}=>P, (3) that relevant facts are not arbitrarily ignored. They are satisfied for instance in Tocqueville's above examples: all statements are acceptable (simple psychological statements, empirical statements congruent with observation, no "black box" concepts in the components of the statements, etc.); moreover, {S}=>P (P=stagnation of French agriculture, enthusiasm of the peasants for the idea of Reason); finally, the theory explains not only the observed behavior but the verbal statements of actors as they have reached us.

Notes

1. Prepared for a symposium on "Historical Sociology and Rational Choice Theory" around the papers, "'We're No Angels: Realism, Rational Choice, and Rationality

in Social Science" by Margaret Somers and "The Debate on Historical Sociology: Rational Choice Theory and Its Critics" by Edgar Kiser and Michael Hechter. Published as "Limitations of Rational Choice Theory," *American Journal of Sociology,* Nov 1998, 104, 3: 817–828.
2. Quoted by Goldthorpe (1996).
3. The answer is given by Bergeron (1999), who, rather than RCT, uses the theory of rationality that I advocate here.
4. Bunge (1996) stresses rightly that MI, specifically as I have applied and defended it since Boudon (1974), has nothing to do with atomism, solipsism, and is perfectly compatible with what he calls "systemism."
5. I defended the two points already in Boudon (1982, Ch.7), but explored only later the non RCT dimensions of rationality, notably in Boudon (1994b) and later publications.

3

Relativistic vs. Naturalistic Theories:
Their Interest and Limits[1]

The notion of multiculturalism describes a vague and widespread doctrine grounded on a few interrelated principles:

1. Firstly, that national, ethnic and other social groups tend to have a distinctive culture of their own;
2. Secondly, that these cultures and subcultures include systems of values which cannot be ranked, for the reason that values cannot be grounded objectively;
3. Thirdly and consequently, that endorsing multiculturalism would imply endorsing value relativism, and reciprocally.

Whether we should accept this mutual implication between multiculturalism and relativism, between recognizing the rights of groups and notably cultural minorities and relativism, will be the question on which I would like to present some remarks with the intention of raising some issues, which appear to me essential, rather than exhausting the subject.

3.1. That Value Relativism is Widespread

Its Diffuse Influence among Intellectuals

First of all, it should be recognized that axiological relativism has become common knowledge in our societies. The idea that we would live in a world where "common values" would have disappeared, in a world irreversibly characterized by a Weberian "polytheism of values," has become a widespread belief.

Of course, it cannot be stated that this view is generally endorsed. But, still, there are many signs of its influence, diffusion, and progress, notably among intellectuals in the broad sense of the word, I mean among those who are professionally concerned with values, such as notably lawyers, teachers, media people, philosophers, and social scientists.

As far as lawyers are concerned, a prominent sociologist of law, Ann Glendon (1996), has shown recently that, in the U.S., the lawyers and judges tend to see their role, even at the level of the Supreme Court, in an entirely new way. Instead of accepting the idea that a judiciary decision should aim, in principle at least, at being grounded on impersonal reasons, they develop what she calls a "romantic" conception of their role. They seem namely convinced that the answer to the question as to what is right or wrong is of a basically subjective character and that personal conviction is the only basis on which their decisions and actions can be legitimately grounded.

As to the influence of relativism in the field of education, a movement called the "value clarification movement" has developed in the U.S. in the last years (Wilson, 1993). It starts from the principle that values are a matter of personal decision and draws from this principle the consequence that any effort to teach values and norms would be incompatible with the dignity of individuals and should consequently be banished.

There are also many signs of the diffusion of relativistic views among social scientists and philosophers. As they are supposed to be experts about values, and are often regarded as such, this is not without important consequences, not only on sociology or philosophy, but on the diffuse philosophy and sociology carried by the media, and finally on society as a whole.

An indirect sign, of special interest to us as sociologists, of this appeal of relativism among social scientists can be detected in the fact that Max Weber is becoming popular again today in some circles, essentially because he would have anticipated the success of relativism in the postmodern world. Postmodernist writers interpret namely his "polytheism of values" as meaning that, as the children of modernity, we would have definitely recognized the subjective character of our normative ideas about the world. Thus, Bryan Turner (1992: 7) writes, "the revival of interest in Nietzsche . . . for the development of

poststructuralism and postmodernism . . . has been parallel to the revival of interest in the shaping of Weberian sociology by Nietzsche."

Relativism tends also to be greatly reinforced by the corporation of
anthropologists, who commonly endorse the view that, since values
appear as variable from one culture to another, they are the product of
"cultural arbitrariness," as they sometimes state.

Thus, in an influential article entitled "anti-antirelativism," the prominent American anthropologist Clifford Geertz (1984) defends the idea
that relativism would be a final philosophical truth. Relativism was
already supported by Montaigne, he contends rightly. Then came a
long era of dogmatic philosophy which, from Descartes to Kant, Hegel,
and positivism, would have supported an illusion: that there is a moral,
more generally an axiological truth. Postmodernism, going back to
Montaigne's intuitions, would have closed the discussion: there is no
truth, there is no moral, and generally no axiological truth. Values are
contingent and rational only to the extent that they constitute a coherent totality.

Communitarianism

These relativistic-culturalist views are also at the origin of—or at
least related to—an important contemporary intellectual, philosophical, and sociological movement, namely communitarianism, which illustrates directly the relation between relativism and multiculturalism.

Communitarianism is represented by several writers, such as C.
Taylor, A. MacIntyre, M. Walzer, A. Etzioni, or R. Rorty, and has
attracted a good deal of attention, notably in the U.S. Roughly, it
states that values, far from being entitled to objectivity and eventually
universality, are embedded in concrete human communities and have
no ground other than being cultural elements endorsed by such and
such community.

This philosophy owes possibly its success notably to the fact that it
appears as congruent, at first sight at least, with facts that are both
easily observable and important.

While there are many differences between communitarian writers,
they share the common view that identity is a crucial dimension of
human beings, that personal identity develops within a cultural
context and thanks to it, and, also, that cultural contexts are incommensurable.

The need for identity exists, beyond doubt. Moreover, it is true that personal identity can only develop within a social context. As R. Hardin (1995) contends, Kurt Tucholsky probably committed suicide at the age of thirty-four because, after leaving Germany for political reasons, he emigrated to Switzerland and felt that he could not express his identity in the Swiss intellectual, social and political context, at least as he saw it.

Or to take another example, also mentioned by R. Hardin, communitarians insist on the importance of the fact that Russia and Yugoslavia exploded into a plurality of ethnical entities as soon as the communist regime they had been subjected to collapsed.

Do not such big facts demonstrate, claim communitarians, that belonging to a community is a basic human need? Do not they show that communities are totalities, that people identify themselves to these totalities? That cultures are incommensurable systems of values? That, as they are incommensurable, these values are "arbitrary"? But, while values are ungrounded, they are vital to individuals, since personalities can only develop within a definite cultural context.

3.2. Do We Need to Accept These Views as Sociologists and as People?

People Believe in Universals

While relativism, culturalism, and communitarism are widespread, all kinds of observations show that most people have on the contrary the conviction that axiological truths on all kinds of subjects do actually exist, can be formulated, and are accepted as such by most people.

Thus, most people agree (to use trivial but, I guess, uncontroversial examples) that democracy *is* a better political regime than the various forms of despotism, or that liquidating *apartheid* in South Africa was a good thing; that corruption is a bad thing, or that stealing is a bad thing, etc. In other words, on innumerable subjects, people have the impression, not less today than yesterday, that the normative statements and the values they endorse, far from being private or from being mere emanations of particular cultures, can be considered as objectively valid.

This axiological relativism is also contradicted by the fact that, as opinion polls show, as well as the literature produced by sociology, social psychology, or psychology on moral feelings, the opinions of people, far from being randomly distributed, are on the contrary highly structured on many subjects.

Thus, the discrepancy between the theory according to which values would be culturally "arbitrary" and the fact that many values are experienced as objectively grounded raises important questions. Notably: are we really ready to believe that such convictions are mere illusions?

3.3. The Naturalistic Reaction

I am (by far) not the first to raise this question. On the contrary: the discrepancy between the relativistic theories according to which values would be illusions, and the conviction of people that they are not, has produced an interesting reaction on the part of some philosophers, sociologists and anthropologists, who have proposed in recent years *naturalistic* theories of values. I cannot consider these theories in detail. But it may be useful to spend a short time on one of them in order to check the potentiality of this naturalistic orientation.

Is There a Moral Sense?

An American criminologist and political scientist, J. Wilson (1993), possibly one of the most interesting theorists in this category, proposes, in his book on *The Moral Sense*, to go back to the old notion of human nature, and to recognize that our moral sense is a crucial ingredient of it. But Wilson's version of the Aristotelian tradition is particularly interesting because it is grounded on the findings of modern social sciences, notably social psychology. More precisely, Wilson claims that the findings produced by these disciplines confirm Aristotle's views on moral sense: his general thesis can be summarized by the statement, "we have a core self, not wholly the product of culture" (Wilson, 1993:11). We owe our moral sense to our human nature.

Four Features of Human Nature

To Wilson, the reality of this moral sense can be detected by the existence of sympathy, a sense of fairness, self control and, a sense of duty. Cultural variations would develop on these basic features of human nature, but, as such, these features should be considered universal.

To ground his theory, Wilson gathers findings from psychology and social psychology and draws far-reaching conclusions from well-selected works.

Some observations are frequently brought against the notion of an instinct of sympathy, he recalls, for example that people being attacked in the subway often do not get any help from fellow passengers. But social psychology shows, he contends, that such facts should not be interpreted as they usually are. Many sociopsychological experiments show namely that the smaller the number of people present on the spot where such an aggression occurs, the higher the probability that the victim will be helped. This suggests that people are reluctant to help, not because they would not like to, but because they do not feel entitled to decide in a one-sided fashion that they should themselves enjoy the social approval which normally rewards those who help others. This social approval is of course in itself also a symptom of the instinct of sympathy.

Beside this sense of sympathy, we are led in our behavior and feelings by a sense of fairness. Here again, experiments from social psychology support Wilson's claims. In an illuminating classical experiment, subjects are proposed to play a game called the "ultimatum game": 100 Euros are available in the pocket of the experimenter. Subject A is allowed to make any proposal he wishes as to the way the 100 Euros should be shared between himself, A, and another person B. B has only the right to approve or reject A's proposal. If he rejects it, the 100 Euros remain in the experimenter's pocket. If he accepts it, he gets the sum allocated to him by A. With the "Rational Choice Model" in mind, according to which people would have no moral sense and would exclusively be concerned with maximizing net benefits, one would predict that A would make proposals of the type "70 Euros for me, A, 30 Euros for him, B." For in that case, B would not refuse the proposal and A would maximize his gains. In fact, the most frequent proposal is equal sharing.

That moral sense should not be diluted, as the utilitarian tradition proposes, into the rewards people get from their behavior can be detected at the fact that compliments make us uncomfortable rather than happy when we feel that we do not deserve them. The pupil who receives a good grade because his teacher is positively prejudiced toward him does not appreciate the compliment, as many observations from social psychology demonstrate.

I will not insist on self-control, another feature of human nature, according to Wilson. He follows again Aristotle here, who made it a main virtue.

As to the sense of duty, the last component of human nature considered by Wilson, it is true that people often behave altruistically without being forced to do so. As Adam Smith wrote, we follow the orders of "the man in the breast."

Wilson is surely right when he stresses the limits of social conditioning against the anthropologists, sociologists, and other culturalists to whom any behavior is the mere product of socialization. He rightly recalls that young children cannot be socialized indifferently to any stimulus. It is possible to induce the fear of snakes by an appropriate conditioning, not of opera glasses.

Should Moral Convictions be Explained by Moral Sense?

Should we endorse Wilson's theory that a natural "moral sense" would explain our moral reactions?

I certainly do not claim for my part that there is no moral sense, but only that this factor can explain moral and generally normative feelings only to a very limited extent. Wilson leaves us disappointed, it seems to me, in the sense that his theory is far from being general: much evidence about moral feelings cannot be explained within the framework of his theory.

For example, some redistribution policies produce the impression in the minds of social actors that they are fair, in others that they are not. Now the evaluations we bring to bear on social policies can evidently not be analyzed as a mere effect of human nature, even though they can be influenced by a sense of fairness. Another objection: how can a moral theory based on human nature explain the historical variations of our moral sensibility? Tocqueville reports, in his *Democracy in America*, that Madame de Sévigné, a classical French writer of the seventeenth century, describes in one of her letters to her daughter how she greatly enjoyed attending a public execution. Capital punishment has not been abolished everywhere, but no one today would admit enjoying it, and probably few people would have the capacity to enjoy such an event. Those with this capacity would generally be considered to have serious psychological problems, while Madame de Sévigné is rightly considered to be a normal person of her time. How can a theory based on human nature explain such changes in our moral sensibility?

Or consider Wilson's analysis of fairness. We certainly have a sense of fairness, and more generally a sense of values. But why is fairness defined in such a way in some circumstances and otherwise in others? In many cases, people are very eager to see for instance that rewards are exactly proportional to contributions and define fairness as the correspondence between contributions and rewards. In other cases, they seem not to care about this point. This discrepancy can be seen in the fact that, in some circumstances, fairness is defined by the notion of equality, while in others it is associated with the notion of equity (Boudon, 1995b; Boudon, 1999c).

A culturalist theory would provide an explanation of many of these observations more easily than a naturalistic one: we do not live in the same culture as Madame de Sévigné, hence our values are different. But such an explanation would not explain *why* our values are different.

In other words, we are facing a dilemma: Wilson's naturalistic theory fails to explain many observations, while culturalist theories provide truncated explanations.

In fact, and this will be my *first* theoretical point in this communication, it is not necessary to choose between nature and nurture. As a very simple example proposed by the great Swiss psychologist and sociologist Piaget shows, we need not evoke either a moral sense, or a cultural conditioning, to explain familiar moral reactions. When a child playing marbles cheats, he will immediately attract a negative reaction from the other children. Why? Not because they would have internalized cultural norms according to which playing marbles and following the rules of the marbles game would be good, for, without having been told that cheating at marbles is bad, any child reacts negatively to cheating,[2] nor because the rules of the marbles game would be written in our genes, which probably have nothing against cheating in marbles games. Why this reaction? Because children find the game interesting, and for this reason play it. Now, cheating destroys the game: it makes it uninteresting. So, children have strong reasons to reject cheating and, as many observations show, they are aware of these reasons at a very early age.

3.4. The Reasons for Moral Convictions

Generalizing from this example of the marbles players, I would contend that we believe that X is good or bad, when and because we have strong reasons (though we can be more or less conscious of these reasons) for believing that X is good or bad, fair or unfair, legitimate or illegitimate, etc. This assumption implies, in other words, that the processes generating moral convictions are not different in essence from the processes generating positive convictions. I believe that the square root of 2 is irrational in the mathematical sense, that it cannot be expressed as the ratio of two integers, p and q, because I have strong reasons for believing so. My claim is that we should also accept the idea that the source of moral convictions lies in strong reasons, which, of course, can be context-dependent. To use a somewhat provocative formulation, I would say that prescriptive and generally axiological beliefs become established in the same way as descriptive beliefs.

Strange as the idea may seem at first glance, it is not difficult to illustrate it. I will start from the trivial example I introduced earlier. Why is democracy considered a good thing? Because the statement that it is a good thing is grounded on solid reasons.

One needs only refer here briefly to classical theories to make this point more concrete. A good government serves the interests of the citizens rather than its own interests. For this reason, the members of a government should be exposed to the risks of elections. Electing the government does not insure that the best candidates will be elected, but limits the risk that the rulers disregard the interests of the people. Democracy does not and cannot prevent corruption. But it makes it less likely than other types of regimes. An independent press and an independent judiciary system are indispensable elements of a democracy, since, by their critical function, they can detect and break political corruption or mismanagement, etc.

My objective here is not to defend democracy (it obviously does not need me), nor to be original in matters of political philosophy, but only to suggest that there is no substantial difference between the ways in which positive and the ways in which normative statements are grounded.

If the feeling that "democracy is a good thing" were not objectively grounded, one would not observe a broad consensus on the subject in democratic societies. One would not understand that against the principles basic in international relations, which require respect for the sovereignty of foreign states, pressures on foreign governments to the effect of starting or developing democracy are generally well understood and approved by public opinion. So, theory and empirical sociology converge here. Of course, I am not saying that consensus is a proof of truth, but only that, when consensus appears, it has to be explained by making it the product of reasons likely to be perceived as objectively strong. As Durkheim explicitly writes in his *Elementary Forms of Religious Life*, moral truths are endorsed in the first stage because they are collective; then, at a further stage, they become collective because they are true, for illusions cannot last very long.

Two objections can be made against the view that our strong normative beliefs about democracy are grounded in objective reasons: namely, that democracy is not actually considered by all as a good thing and that it was certainly not always considered so.

To the first objection, it can be easily asserted that non-believers are also easily found as far as the best established scientific truths are concerned: there are certainly many people around the world that do not or would not accept the idea that tides are caused by the moon for instance.

The latter objection is less easily rejected. The consensus on democracy is recent. Before the First World War, universal voting was criticized. Pareto, for instance, saw in this right of all to vote another of the symptoms of human craziness which he liked to collect, and prophesized that it would generate social chaos. Earlier, Balzac, in his *Médecin de campagne*, a kind of treatise of political philosophy, contended that universal voting was bad, because it counts the ballots without weighing them: "il compte les voix sans les peser." The same argument reappeared repeatedly during the following decades. Does not this show that our belief that democracy is good is a product of socialization rather than of reasons and that it has little to do with our beliefs in scientific statements?

Actually, the fact that moral truths are historically variable is a deadly objection against the naturalist theories of moral feelings that propose to derive these feelings from human instincts, as Wilson's theory, but it is not contrary to a rational theory of moral feelings.

Consider scientific beliefs. To Aristotelian physicists, any physical movement was considered as produced by some force or set of forces. This sheet of paper moves because I apply a force to it. If I would not apply a force, it would not move. So, Aristotelian physicists had strong reasons to believe that any movement is the effect of some force. But they drew from this statement conclusions that appear to us ridiculous, while they appeared acceptable to them, namely that, when a ship keeps on moving after the wind has fallen, some force should be responsible for this movement. They tried therefore to figure out what this force could be, and introduced the assumption that the movement of a ship produces a turbulence which would keep it moving. After a while, however, objections were raised against this theory. But it was rejected only from the moment when physicists were able to devise a new principle, which we now consider as evident, namely the so-called Newtonian "principle of inertia," according to which a body that moves needs a force to be stopped, exactly as a body at rest needs a force to be brought into movement. The feeling of obviousness which it produces today in our mind is the product, though, of a long and complex historical process whereby ideas are proposed, evaluated, and selected.

The same kind of story could be told about normative as well as positive statements.

Thus, as noted by the great British historian George Trevelyan (1993), Voltaire believed firmly, before he came to England, that a society could not operate properly if writers were allowed to publish what they wanted. He considered the freedom of publishing as Aristotelian physicists considered the idea of a move that would be uncaused: as an idea intuitively worth being rejected. In the same fashion, ideas that political power should be concentrated, or that conflicts between political factions are evil, were long and are still in some places considered as evident. Then, the effects of the conflicts between the "Roundheads" and the "Cavaliers" during the civil war in England in the seventeenth century started being positively evaluated and the principle that institutionalized conflicts can be a good thing, as well as the principle of the separation of the executive and legislative powers, began to emerge.

On the whole, because we perceive as evident that democracy, universal voting, or the separation of powers are *good*, we tend to forget that they are the products of a long historical process during which these ideas were conceived and debated or fought over before being finally selected and considered as irreversible. And as we forget the past, we often do not see either that these selection processes are endless and that they are operating before our eyes. Bodin (1986 [1576]), an influential French political philosopher, defended at the end of the sixteenth century the idea that political decision should by its very nature come from a single ultimate source; to him, a good political society implied, in other words, a political power which would be both *sovereign* and *indivisible*.

Montesquieu discredited this theory irreversibly when he showed that a divided political power is more efficient than an undivided one. A further breakthrough will possibly be accomplished when it is recognized that a good political order not only does not imply the indivisibility of political power, but does not imply necessarily sovereignty either. This type of breakthrough appeared with Madison and the American federalists, but disappeared with the Secession war; it reappears in Europe through the so-called "subsidiarity principle," which states that the source of political decision, rather than being fixed forever, is rather an object of discussion and negotiation between national states. Possibly, through the political processes at work in Europe, a new form of political organization is developing, where sovereignty would not be concentrated in a state, since there would be no fixed source of sovereignty. Possibly, tomorrow, a political theorist will formalize it, as Montesquieu formalized the new political system developed by Britain in the seventeenth century.

In the same way, it has also been argued in the past that capital punishment is a good thing because, without capital punishment, homicides would increase. Capital punishment was abolished in many countries, however, without producing any increase in homicide rates. From that moment, it was perceived in many Western countries, not only as barbarian and as contradictory with basic values, but as useless, so that the public evaluation of it changed progressively, exactly as the Aristotelian notion of a conjectural turbulence being responsible for the movement of ships and arrows was progressively eroded.

Thus, the rational (or, as it can be alternatively labeled: the cognitivist) theory of moral and generally axiological feelings, which I am sketching here, is not only *not* incompatible with the fact that moral convictions change over time, but it can explain this change more easily than other types of theories. The fact that science is historical, that a statement that was treated yesterday as false is treated today as true was never held as an argument against the possibility of reaching truth in scientific matters; in the same way, in moral matters, the fact that some institutions were held as bad yesterday and are now considered as good is not an argument against the fact that moral evaluations are grounded on strong reasons in the minds of people. Moreover, it is hard to see how normative irreversibilities, as scientific irreversibilities, could be explained in a satisfactory fashion, if not rationally. The Newtonian principle of inertia is considered as irreversibly valid because it is objectively better than the principles it replaced. In the same fashion, as noted by Tocqueville, we will never again hear somebody explaining that he or she enjoyed being the spectator at a capital execution. Capital punishment can be reintroduced depending on political circumstances; but we will never be able to experience and express the feelings of Madame de Sévigné.

By so saying, I do not contend that there are no historical contingencies. On the contrary, for, if there were no contingencies, there would be no innovations, either scientific or moral. Tomorrow, totalitarian regimes can reappear. But unless human memory is destroyed, the idea that democracy is better than despotic regimes will remain present in human minds. "Il n'y a pas plus de recul d'idées que de recul de fleuves," wrote Victor Hugo ["as rivers, ideas never go backwards"].

The argument that change in moral values confirms relativism rests finally on a fallacy. The research of truth, positive or normative, *is* historical. But truth, either moral or positive, *is not* historical. The fact that science has a history is not an argument against the possibility of scientific truth. The fact that morals have a history is not an argument in favor of moral relativism.

The False Evidence of a Gap between Ought *and* Is

If our moral convictions rest upon strong reasons, why then is the similarity in this respect between the positive and the normative ill-perceived?

The main reason is that it contradicts many influential traditions, which I have already mentioned.

On the whole, the idea that moral and generally axiological statements cannot be objectively grounded was treated as evident by a host
of influential thinkers who differ from one another in all other respects. Strangely enough, empiricism converges in its interpretation of
moral feelings with the irrational *sociological* theories inspired by
Marx and Nietzsche or derived from a misreading of Durkheim, and
also with the irrational *psychological* theories inspired by Freud. All
these theories contend that moral convictions cannot be grounded rationally. To them, the reasons the subjects see as grounding their
beliefs should not be considered as their genuine causes, but as mere
"rationalizations," in other words, as false reasons, as the effect of
"false consciousness." Existentialists could be added to the list, since
they consider that moral beliefs cannot be grounded and propose to
treat the reasons given by subjects as illusory. Moral decisions would
be "absurd" in Sartre's vocabulary. In other words, they would be
ungrounded and ungroundable.

Thus, empiricism, Marxism, Freudianism, neo-Durkheimianism, existentialism, postmodernism and other—*isms*, different as they are from
one another in most respects, agree on one point, namely that moral
and generally normative convictions cannot be rationally grounded.

Consequential Reasons

But the idea that normative beliefs cannot be grounded has also
been reinforced by another factor worth being stressed, namely the
relative weakness of the rational theories of moral and normative feelings developed notably by the social sciences. This will be my *second*
main theoretical point.

These theories are rational in the sense that, to them, the reasons on
which the normative beliefs of a social actor are grounded in his mind
are their causes. But, with the exception of Max Weber and a few
other writers, most rational theories of axiological beliefs developed
by the social sciences propose to explain the moral evaluation of an
action or of a state of affairs by their consequences. Some of these
theories are powerful, but, because of this consequentialist restriction,
none of them can be considered as a general theory of normative
feelings. Consequently, they cannot efficiently counterbalance the powerful influence of the culturalist and generally of the irrational theories
of normative beliefs.

We can consider *functionalism* a classical example. In its most acceptable versions, it says that an institution is perceived as good if it has happy consequences on a social system which people appreciate. The example of Piaget's marbles game is again relevant here. Cheating is considered bad because it destroys a game children are interested in. In the same fashion, restricting the admission of new candidates to a "club" in the broad sense—namely, to a Church, to a sect, to a prestigious teaching institution, to an academy, etc.—is generally considered good because free admission would be detrimental to the aims followed by the club.

These functional explanations can of course be easily accepted. But functionalism cannot be considered a general theory which could explain *all* value statements. Thus, it can explain why admission to "clubs" is generally restricted, but not such a simple point as to why we consider that people should be free to *leave* a club. We are morally shocked when sects, for instance, retain members against their will. The source of our moral indignation obviously cannot be explained functionally.

Consider, as another classical example, the *contractualist* tradition, revitalized in recent years by John Rawls. Rousseau has written that we should accept being "forced to be free." By this famous statement, he meant that, in the absence of legal and social constraints, we would be tempted to act as free riders, to our own disadvantage as well as to the detriment of all. Without traffic lights, an unpleasant constraint would disappear, but traffic would freeze. So, we are better off with traffic lights and this is the reason why we accept them. In the same fashion, we are better off with all kinds of political constraints, and for this reason accept them. In this case also, the bad consequences of what he calls "natural freedom" is the reason why, according to Rousseau, exchanging our *natural* freedom with all its advantages for *civil* freedom is a good thing.

Another very influential contemporary theory, the so-called "*rational choice theory*" belongs also to this set of consequentialist theories: "rational choice theorists" have tried namely to show that social norms should always be explained by the anticipation of their consequences.[3] Many current beliefs in private or public life can effectively be accounted for by this "Rational Choice Model." Hence its influence. But many others cannot.

Axiological Reasons

The axiom common to many rational theories of values developed by the social sciences, notably to functionalism, contractualism, and the "rational choice theory," according to which "X is good" or X is considered by people as "good" if the consequences of X are good and bad if they are bad, is a powerful one. These theories are sufficient to explain many axiological beliefs. But they cannot, however, be held to provide a *general* theory of our axiological feelings. This results from the fact that the reasons underlying the axiological belief that "X is good" or that "X is bad" do not always deal exclusively with the consequences of X.

Examples are easily found, in other words, of normative and particularly moral feelings which cannot be explained by consequential reasons.

But it does not follow from the fact that they cannot be explained by consequential reasons that they cannot be explained rationally, for they can be explained by axiological-non-consequential reasons. By deference and reference to Max Weber, these non-consequential reasons can be called *axiological-in-the-Weberian-sense*. Recognizing the existence of axiological-non-consequential reasons extends the power of the rational theory of moral feelings and symmetrically considerably weakens the irrational position. This is my *third* main point.

I am ready to recognize that the distinction between instrumental and axiological rationality is not entirely clear in Weber's writings. But it is greatly clarified, it seems to me, as soon as it is related to the distinction between consequential and non-consequential reasons. For, if the reasons of social actors were only of the consequential type, the category of instrumental rationality would be sufficient. Traffic lights are good because, without them, the situation of all would be worse. Therefore, consequential and instrumental rationality are one and the same thing. Thus, by creating the notion of *axiological rationality* (*Wertrationalität*), Weber states clearly that some of our normative beliefs are inspired by reasons (otherwise he would not have chosen the word *Rationalität*), without these reasons being of the consequential type (otherwise, he would not have opposed *Wertrationalität* to *Zweckrationalität*, nor claimed that they are distinct, though complementary).

Thus, although corruption has a negative effect on the well-being of taxpayers and consumers, this effect is in "normal" circumstances, namely as long as it does not reach the level it has reached, say, in contemporary Russia, so negligible and hardly visible that it is ignored by most people. People tend to be highly sensitive to corruption, however. Thus, a few years ago, the Spanish and French governments were dismissed by voters, mainly because they gave the impression of not having struggled against corruption with sufficient energy, and were even themselves sometimes involved in corruption. As they are certainly not produced by the consideration of the consequences of corruption on the well-being of citizens, the negative feelings against corruption are produced in the minds of people by reasons, but by reasons of the axiological, rather than the consequential type.

The example I have just mentioned is taken from ordinary life. Other examples can be taken from political life, such as the already cited example of the action of Western powers against *apartheid* in South Africa. Introducing democracy in South Africa was *ex ante* risky: the process was exposed to potentially severe dangers. Hence, from a consequential viewpoint, it was difficult to decide whether the action should be taken. But axiological reasons prevailed here over consequential reasons and over axiological principles of a lower order. This explains why the political pressures against *apartheid* were generally approved by public opinion everywhere. In the same way, even though the lowering of child mortality, thanks to the progress of medicine, is partly responsible for poverty in many poor countries, no one would obviously consider it a bad thing.

3.5. Communitarianism Revisited

As this rational theory of values is directly opposed to the theory of values supported by communitarians, I will finally return to my earlier discussion on communitarianism.

In his brilliant book on the subject, *One for All*, to which I have already alluded, Russell Hardin (1995) raises crucial questions. In spite of the romantic positive evaluation of communities developed by communitarians, he stresses convincingly that the particularistic values defended by communities, which communitarians see as the only genuine values, so to say, have a dark face that should not be forgotten.

The sense of community is actually, he says, basically a sense for one's group interests. Thus, in the sixteenth century, the aristocrats, who saw themselves as threatened by the ascending bourgeois classes, invented an institution aimed at maintaining their social identity and superiority: the duel. Fighting in a duel was a sign that they had a sense of honor. Hence, according to aristocrats, only aristocrats could have a sense of honor. From the viewpoint of the interests of the aristocrats, this institution was consequently fully functional. It contributed to maintaining the social identity and superiority of the group. For this reason, it spread all over Europe and lasted three centuries, until the first World War.

This example stresses an important point, a point ill-perceived by communitarians, namely that identification with a community means exclusion of non-members. When Voltaire offered to fight a duel with the Chevalier de Rohan, who had insulted him, the answer of the aristocrat was to send his servants who struck Voltaire, in order to make clear to him that, though world famous, he was not an aristocrat.

The influence of community values also explains (without, obviously, justifying) the massacres in the old Yugoslavia. As I mentioned before, to communitarians, these massacres are to be explained by the fact that, from the moment when the artificial unity between culturally heterogeneous ethnic groups maintained by the communist regime was dissolved, the members of ethnic communities were offered the opportunity of revealing their vital preference for living in a community where they could develop fully their cultural identity. As Hardin rightly contends, however, this theory is incompatible with the fact that mixed communities had lived peacefully during the communist era, and that intermarriages between members of the various communities were not rare. Many episodes in the history of post-communist Yugoslavia can be explained more convincingly, he contends rightly, by group interests than by the cultural needs postulated by communitarian theories. Numerous Serbs have, for instance, spontaneously approved Milosevic's aggressive stance against Croatia about Krajina, because this Croatian province included a strong Serb minority. As, in the old Yugoslavia, the army and the police were in majority Serb, trying to get Krajina to Serbia was for many Serbs an attractive and, moreover, a politically realistic enterprise. The enterprise was rational in terms of the interests of the community and consequently of the members of the community. It led, however, to fights and massacres incompatible with universal values.

From the history of the duel, post-communist Yugoslavia, and other similar examples, Hardin draws several important conclusions: that interests rather than "cultural needs" explain the social and historical influence of community values; and also that community values have often very undesirable effects, notably because they generate negative attitudes and eventually actions against non-members. Finally, communities tend to support group values incompatible with universal values.

At this point, Hardin raises a theoretically and practically crucial question. The myth of Antigone illustrates the competition between particularistic community values on the one hand and universal values on the other. One remembers the story of Antigone's two brothers, Eteocles and Polynices; one fought on the side of Thebes, the other against Thebes. Hence, Creon, the master of Thebes, decided that the Eteocles would be buried with national honors, while Polynices would remain unburied. As Antigone decided to bury her brother against Creon's will, Creon decided that she would be herself buried alive. This happened to the applause of the Theban people.

The myth is of lasting value because it illustrates the conflict between the universal values represented by Antigone and the particularistic community values represented by Creon. But, as a sociologist, Hardin is essentially interested in the reaction of the people. The people of Thebes were in majority on the side of Creon, exactly as the Serbs were in majority on the side of Milosevic, or the aristocrats on the side of the duelists. This shows, according to Hardin, that community values are strong because they serve the interests of people: their ultimate function is to protect the interests of the group and, beyond the group itself, of the members of the group. By contrast, the universal values would be weak, as the loneliness of Antigone illustrates. Hardin sees in the myth of Antigone an illustration of the unequal competition between community values and universal values. To him, the massacres in Yugoslavia also have to be explained in the same fashion, by the weakness of universal vs. community values. The failure of Chancellor Francis Bacon in England or of Cardinal Richelieu in France in their political struggles against the duel should also be explained by the weakness of universal against particularistic community values.

On the whole, Hardin draws from his analyses very pessimistic conclusions: to him, this weakness of universal values would be structural, so to say. The strength of communitarian values would come from the fact that they serve the interests of the group and its members, while the universal values would have no direct relation to interests. Hence, the competition between the two types of values would be unequal. Universal values would have a strength, to him, exclusively in the case of dyadic relations, where instrumental and axiological rationalities appear as convergent: I keep the promise I have made to B, because I have an interest in doing so: preserving my future exchanges with B. But in the general case, instrumental and axiological rationality would be divergent.

This analysis, although profound, is, in my opinion, unfinished. While Hardin is himself a follower of the so-called Rational Choice Theory, he recognizes—at least implicitly—that universal values also exist, and that they are not grounded in individual interests. In Weber's vocabulary, he recognizes that social actors are moved not only by instrumental rationality but also by axiological rationality. But, as a follower of Rational Choice Theory, he assumes that, in the last instance, individual interests are the main factor accounting for behavior, beliefs, attitudes, and actions: to him, actors are basically moved by their individual and group interests. Hence, he concludes that axiological rationality would be structurally weak, while instrumental rationality would be structurally strong.

Hardin, however, refutes himself unwillingly. Namely, he has no doubt that he is himself on the side of Antigone, not Creon, and that he has negative feelings against the institution of the duel that he analyzes beautifully, and against the massacres in Yugoslavia. He also sees clearly that most people would have the same feelings. No spectator of Antigone has ever been on the side of Creon. No spectator of the *Merchant of Venice* has ever been on the side of the judge Portia. And, if universal values are often hurt in the short term, they can also win in the long term. The institution of the duel has disappeared, as well as the hierarchical social organization it reflected.

At this point, we are confronted with a question symmetrical to Hardin's question. To the question, "where does the strength of particularistic values come from?" he answers : individual interests mediated by group interests. But he has no answer to the question: "where does the strength of universal values come from ?"

It comes actually from two sources: this will be my *fourth* theoretical main point. The strength of universal values comes firstly from "axiological rationality": we are all convinced that Portia and Creon were wrong. We are all convinced that they were wrong on the basis of strong reasons, of strong axiological reasons. Secondly, one should be aware of the fact that while in some situations the interests of social actors are relevant parameters, in many other situations they are not. When the sixteenth-century aristocrats had to have an opinion on the duel, their class interests and, through their class interests, their individual interests were a crucial parameter: they were normally concerned with the question of how to maintain their social superiority in a situation where they were threatened; and, consequently, they approved generally an institution which served their interests. By contrast, the interests of, say, the nineteenth-century bourgeois did not play any significant role in their evaluation of the duel: they were not concerned by the institution, and they evaluated it on the basis of universal axiological reasons. So, after a while, once the aristocracy had lost any significant social role, the duel appeared as meaningless to a majority of people and became, moreover, ridiculous, because it was more and more frequently practiced by *parvenus*, who wanted to demonstrate, by fighting in duels, a purely imaginary social superiority. Moreover, in the last decades of its life, the duel entailed neither big risks nor big courage. In the more than twenty duels in which Clemenceau was involved, only one of the fighters was slightly hurt.

In other words, the social actors are not only actors pushed on all subjects by their interests. They are also spectators. But spectators are also actors–as spectators—on the social and political stage. This is one of the basic weaknesses of Rational Choice Theory. It does not take into account the fact that, in many situations, social actors have on such and such subject an opinion that is not dictated by their interests, for the very simple reason that they are not directly concerned by the subject, that the subject does not cross their interests. In other words, Rational Choice Theorists forget—or ignore—the existence of public opinion. Now, public opinion does exist and has beyond a doubt a strong influence on political, social, and historical processes. And it appears as being guided by axiological rationality (though it is obviously not clearsighted in all circumstances). For public opinion is nothing else than the aggregation of opinions of actors who, on many issues, are not directly concerned in their interests by the issues in question and who, consequently, do not form their evaluations in accordance with their own class and individual interests, but rather by axiological reasons. That I am not concerned in my personal or in my group interests by an issue does not mean that I have no axiological interests about it. Evidently, most people are not directly concerned by capital punishment; they have, however, strong convictions on the subject.

Finally, to come back to the question I raised at the beginning: that the "cultural" rights of groups and subgroups should be recognized is one thing; whether this should imply endorsing axiological relativism is another. Supporting the rights of cultures and subcultures does not imply that we forge a picture of the world where it would be composed of a mere juxtaposition of cultures and that we forget the dimension of universality of social action and of values, which has been well recognized by the greatest classical sociologists, and, before them, by the greatest philosophers.

Pareto wrote that we feel attracted by some theories because they are useful, rather than because they are true. It seems to me we have here an illustration of this important idea. Value relativism is widely endorsed, notably by influential currents in the social sciences, essentially because it is useful (in the sense that it legitimates the claim of cultures and subcultures to see their rights recognized), rather than because it would be true. This is, it seems to me, one of the basic misunderstandings in contemporary social sciences.

Notes

1. Public Conference, "Colloquium of the Austrian, German and Swiss Societies of Sociology," September18–19, 1998, Freiburg im Breisgau. Published as "Multiculturalism and Value Relativism," in C. Honegger, S. Hradil, F. Traxler, eds., *Grenzenlose Gesellschaft*, Vol. I, Leske Budrich: Opladen, 1999: 97–118.
2. As shown for instance by Damon (1988).
3. We can ignore in the context of this discussion that it adds a further restriction besides the consequentialist one, namely that actors pay exclusive attention to those consequences of an action or state of affairs that are related to their own interests.

4

A Seminal and Difficult Notion: "Axiological Rationality" [1]

The concept of "axiological rationality" (my translation of *Wertrationalität*) is possibly one of the most difficult of all the concepts Weber put on the market. Sometimes the expression is understood as describing situations where a social actor acts in conformity with the values he has internalized. Sometimes it is entirely rejected as meaningless, as a contradiction between the two terms "value" and "rationality." I have conducted no systematic review of the interpretations of the concept. But I would contend that these two attitudes toward the concept are probably the most frequent, namely either the pedestrian interpretation making axiological rationality a synonym of "value conformity" or the skeptical interpretation according to which the expression would not have a clear nor solid meaning.

My own interpretation is that, although Weber has never been entirely clear or analytical on the notion, it is perhaps, once it is properly understood and developed, one of the most fruitful he has ever proposed.

Before I proceed, I would like to make my design as clear as possible. My primary objective is less to reconstruct what Weber "has really meant" when he has conceived and decided to introduce this notion than to stress its "present relevance." The former task would be interesting as such; it would imply collecting the passages where Weber uses or discusses the notion and submitting them to a hermeneutic analysis in the sense of Schleiermacher. But my interest is rather to develop what I perceive as a crucial and extremely fruitful intuition on the part of Weber, to make it perhaps more analytical, and finally to

show that it sketches a powerful theory of collective axiological beliefs.   However, when the notion is replaced in the context of Weber's
general methodological principles, one gains the feeling that the theory
of axiological beliefs I propose here is a plausible interpretation of
what Weber had in mind.

4.1. Weber Often Ill-Understood

Weber as Nietzschean?

What I called the "pedestrian" interpretation of the notion of
axiological rationality may be more profound than it may seem at first
sight. This first interpretation makes axiological rationality synonymous with "value conformity." In other words, endorsing such and
such values would in this interpretation not be rational in itself; what
would be rational would be the congruence between the values one
endorses and one's actions. In other words, this pedestrian interpretation hides possibly a strong thesis: that accepting and endorsing values
is not rational; only being congruent with values could be qualified as
rational.

This interpretation illustrates a position often represented in economics. Behavior is rational to economists to the extent that it is
congruent with preferences. As to preferences themselves, they have
to be considered as mere data. They can be rational only in the sense
that they should not be contradictory with one another. But economists, with some exceptions, believe that preferences as such cannot
be qualified as rational.

Pareto had a similar position. Actions are rational (he would rather
have written "logical") to the extent that they aim at some goal with
the help of means objectively adequate to the goal.

Thus, this first pedestrian interpretation implies that Weber would
have accepted the idea, considered by Pareto and many economists as
trivial, that rationality is a concept which cannot be applied to goals,
preferences, or values, but only to the capacity of the means used by a
subject to reach his goals, to satisfy his preferences, or to realize his
values. An action would be rational to the extent that it would mobilize means adapted to the goals, preferences, or values.

The famous Weberian thesis of the "polytheism of values" suggests
that, to Weber, values are a matter of personal choice in modern

societies. Modern societies would be such that they do not impose prescribed values to social subjects, but propose to them to choose among many sets of values. The positive evaluation of individualism in modern societies would make this choice possible and legitimate. As to the fact that a given individual chooses rather one set of values than another, we can interpret it for instance in a Nietzschean fashion (the values endorsed by an individual are the product of instincts deeply rooted in his personality) or in a Sartrian fashion ("choosing" one's values is a free act that cannot be inspired by any forces or considerations if it is to be effectively free; in Sartre's words, value choices are "absurd").   Undoubtedly, Weber sometimes takes his inspiration from Nietzsche (Hennis, 1987). His insistence on the point that science would be value-free is well known. But it would be hazardous to reverse the statement and to contend that to him value would have been science-free, still more, that he would have interpreted value choices in a Nietzschean fashion, or in a Sartrian one. [2]

Is Weber trivial (that would be the case if value rationality would simply mean value conformity)? Is Weber a pragmatist in the sense of Pareto or of the economists (that would be the case if he would have implicitly meant that the notion of rationality is applicable exclusively to the relation means-ends)? Is Weber rather Nietzschean (that would be the case if he would have interpreted values as coming from deep hidden irrational forces)?

Weber as Kantian?

Other writers, as Lukes, have rejected these interpretations (Lukes, 1967: notably 259–60).

The British sociologist criticizes severely the use made by Weber of the notion of "rationality": "The use of the word 'rational' and its cognates has caused untold confusion and obscurity, especially in the writings of social theorists," he writes. This remark is explicitly directed against Weber, as a footnote appended to this passage makes clear: "I think Max Weber is largely responsible for this. His use of these terms is irremediably opaque and shifting." From the context, it can be detected that this "opacity" is mainly due to the distinction between "instrumental" and "axiological" rationality. "Instrumental rationality" is alright: it corresponds more or less to what Lukes himself proposes to call "rationality" shortly. But this means that, beside instrumental rationality, no other type of rationality could be defined. What then can be done with the notion of "axiological rationality?" Is it not a contradiction in terms? To Lukes, the notion of "axiological rationality" most likely has exclusively one possible meaning: it would indicate that the choice of values can be rational. In other words, he probably reads the expression "axiological rationality" as meaning that not only the choice of means but the choice of ends could be rational.

In other words, Lukes probably takes seriously Weber's typology of action as it appears notably in the first pages of *Economy and Society*. In addition to the familiar category of "instrumental rationality," Weber introduces in this famous pages another type of rationality, "axiological rationality." And so, to Lukes, it is evident that rationality in this expression cannot merely mean "conformity." To the British sociologist, the notion of rationality can mean only one thing: the adequation of means to ends, preferences, values. This is what Weber calls "instrumental rationality." Thus, to Lukes, the idea that there would be another type of rationality, characterizing not the adequation of means to ends but the choice of ends, seems meaningless.

In contrast with the interpretations I referred to above, Lukes takes seriously the word "rationality" in the expression "value rationality." He refuses to assimilate value rationality to value conformity. I think he is right. Why would Weber have written rationality when conformity would have been clearer? Why did he ostensibly create two kinds of rationality? Hence, as rationality can mean only instrumental rationality to Lukes, he fails to understand what "value rationality" could mean and rejects the expression as useless.

Lukes's criticism has the advantage of dramatizing the discussion. It is true that it is very hard to accept that Weber would have meant conformity and said rationality. It is on the other hand very clear that value rationality has nothing to do with instrumental rationality, nothing to do in other words with the relation between means and ends.

What does it mean then?

The most immediate interpretation would be that Weber would be Kantian, in other words, that "value rationality" should be interpreted as an echo to the Kantian notion of "practical reason." Kant was, of course, beside Nietzsche, one of the influential thinkers that molded Weber's thinking. Possibly, Lukes has such an interpretation in mind. As a social scientist, however, he cannot accept the Kantian idea of a universal practical reason. Nor can he probably accept the idea that Weber's Kantianism could be literal. Consequently, he fails to see what the notion of axiological rationality really means. This can be easily sensed in his tone: a strange, un-understandable, on the whole, a confused notion, he suggests.

How Can a Coherent Positive Content be Attributed to "Axiological Rationality?"

My own contention is that, if Weber has taken part of his inspiration from Nietzsche and from Kant, his notion of axiological rationality cannot be reduced to any of the interpretations which I have just gathered. To me, the notion is clear, fruitful, analytical, original, and can be reduced neither to Kant nor to Nietzsche. It is, moreover, crucial to the social sciences.

But before I try to make the meaning of the notion clearer and to make explicit and develop the program it contains, it is necessary to go back to some key points in Weber's sociology and methodology.

4.2. The Methodological Principles of Weber's Sociology

Methodological Individualism against "Kollektivbegriffe"

In a famous letter to R. Liefmann,[3] Weber makes clear that what we now call "methodological individualism" (MI) should be adopted, not only by economists, but by all social scientists. The letter is addressed to an economist, to an economist moreover belonging to the marginalist school. So, when Weber writes in this letter "…auch Soziologie kann nur—strikt "individualistisch" in der Methode…betrieben werden," the "auch" is unambiguous: it means that, as marginalist economics, sociology can and should use an individualistic methodology. The expression "methodological individualism" is written almost literally ("individualistisch in der Methode"). What does Weber mean by so saying? That the ultimate stage of any sociological explanation of a social phenomenon can and should consist in finding out why the actors behaved the way they did to the effect of producing the phenomenon in question. "Methodological individualism" as we know it does not say more. It does not say more under Weber's pen either.

The letter goes as far as to propose what can be read as a "demarcation," in Popper's sense, between good scientific sociology and bad sociology. The bad one is a sociology where "Kollektivbegriffe herumspuken." Thanks to the MI postulate, these collective concepts currently in use as far as the explanation of social phenomena is concerned can be avoided. It is difficult to identify what Weber had in mind specifically and even whether he had anything specific in mind by introducing this distinction, but the meaning of the expression is clear. He wanted to exclude from sociology the pseudo explanations evoking obscure social factors (for example, "national mentality") and making them the causes of sociological phenomena. He even goes so far as to claim that he became a sociologist to eradicate such pseudo-explanations.

Meaningful to the Actor

Thus, to Weber, explaining a social phenomenon is making it the outcome of individual actions, attitudes, or beliefs. This is the very definition of MI. But Weber's sociology rests on another principle: the "understanding principle": *explaining* the actions, beliefs, attitudes of an actor means "understanding" them; understanding them means *reconstructing their meaning to the actor*. I would add moreover that reconstructing their meaning to the actor means in most cases reconstructing the reasons he has to endorse them.

It is essential to recall and comment upon these basic principles of Weber's methodology, for they are frequently misunderstood. The notion of "understanding" (in Weber's sense) is notably very often presented and discussed in a caricatural fashion, as Abel's article illustrates (Abel, 1964).

It should also be stressed that the individuals sociologists deal with in their analyses are, according to Weber, ideal-typical individuals rather than actual concrete individuals. Here again, Weber suggests that sociologists follow a principle familiar to economists. Economists, too, explain the macro-phenomena they are interested in by making them the outcomes of understandable actions of ideal-typical individuals (for example, the "consumer," the "producer," etc.).

An other essential remark: "understanding" is not a mysterious activity. It is on the contrary an operation familiar in any scientific discipline: the sociologist introduces conjectures as to the reasons accounting for some action, and checks that these conjectures are compatible with observed data. If I see somebody cutting wood, I introduce the conjecture that he will put the wood in his chimney to get warmer. If he cuts wood on a sunny summer day, I will have to reject the conjecture and find some other more acceptable one. Of course, any "understanding" operation involves an empathic moment. In the famous example I refer to here, I introduce the statement "he wants to get warmer" because I know from my own experience that being cold is unpleasant and that he probably feels like me on this point. For the rest, the conjectures about the reasons have to be checked against data exactly as any conjecture in any scientific discipline.

Another essential point of Weber's methodology is contained in his famous typology of actions contained in the first pages of *Economy and Society*, to which I alluded earlier. Actions can be explained by reasons belonging to the register of instrumental rationality, by reasons belonging to the register of axiological rationality, by the submission of the actor to traditions, or by affective reasons. *Examples*:

> *First type*: I wear a coat because the weather is cold and because a coat is an easy way of struggling against cold.
> *Second type*: I do not steal because I believe one should not steal.
> *Third type*: I shake his hand because he is French and because Frenchmen shake hands when they meet.
> *Fourth type*: She protected him because she liked him.

Understanding an action to Weber means: locating the action in the proper category in this typology, and, within this category, reconstructing the causes of the action.

Another important principle of Weber's methodology is what Popper was to call later the "zero hypothesis" (Popper, 1967): try to interpret an action as rational, as grounded on reasons; if this appears impossible, try the explanation by tradition or by affective factors.

The most plausible assumption about the woodcutter is that he cuts wood because he wants to get warm; if not, because he wants to show his neighbor how to cut wood; if not, because he belongs to a sect of woodcutters in which cutting wood is a duty; if not, he may cut wood because in his country everybody cuts wood everyday at that time of the day (traditional action); if not, he may cut wood because he feels a compulsion to cut wood (affective action), etc. This variation on a familiar Weber example aims at illustrating the natural character of the "zero hypothesis": sociologists are concerned chiefly, as economists, with all these prosaic individual actions which produce, once aggregated, the collective phenomena they are interested in. They are essentially interested in these situations where many people behave in the same way, so that these individual actions produce a collective effect. Now, in the circumstances where these prosaic actions are the same from one individual to the next, this results generally from the fact that they are inspired, not by individual idiosyncrasies, but by simple more or less obvious reasons. Hence the advice given by Weber and Popper to social scientists: try to find the simple reasons behind the individual actions before sketching more complicated conjectures.

4.3. Why These Principles?

Why these principles? I leave aside their realism. I mean that it is true that social phenomena are very often the aggregate outcome of actions inspired by simple reasons. Thus, the French landlords of the eighteenth century leave their land and buy a royal office *because* it gives them influence, prestige, and power (Tocqueville, 1986 [1856]: 1036sq.). The farmers whom they put on their land have not the capacity for innovation. On the whole, what Tocqueville calls the "administrative centralization" of France has the effect that buying a royal office is more rewarding in France than in England. This circumstance generates a strong landlord absenteeism and hence a stagnation of agriculture. This famous analysis is a good illustration of Weber's principles: methodological individualism, understanding the *meaning* of the decisions taken by the ideal-typical landlords and farmers, in other words reconstructing the reasons of the decisions they took.

I considered this example because it makes clear a crucial point, namely that explanations that are able to make a social phenomenon the outcome of understandable individual actions is "final" in the sense that it contains no black boxes. Here, the macro-phenomenon represented by the stagnation of French agriculture relatively to the British one is explained as the effect of understandable actions on the part of the ideal-typical French landlords. Once such an explanation is produced, it generates no further question. It does not contain any black box.

By contrast, when a Lévy-Bruhl explains magical beliefs by referring to a "Kollektivbegriff" as "primitive mentality," he creates a big black box. The sociologist who learns that some ritual can only be explained by the fact that the members of a far tribe are governed by a "primitive mentality" would perhaps ask the biologist to explain to him why the brain of the so-called primitive is wired in a different fashion from ours. At any rate, explanations using concepts as "primitive mentality," "national spirit," "socialization," etc., are not "final." I am not saying they should be rejected, merely that they suggest immediately further questions: what are the mechanisms behind the words "socialization," "primitive mentality," etc.

One of the main appeals of the set of methodological principles advocated by Weber is that it produces "final" explanations without black boxes, as well as being realistic.

Applications: Two Examples from Weber

Mithraïsm. Weber's analyses, although powerful, are often sketchy. Why did the Mithra cult penetrate so easily into the Roman Empire? (Weber, 1922). Why was it particularly appealing to the Roman civil servants? Answer: because they had strong reasons to find it appealing. The traditional Roman religion was a religion of peasants: it did not speak to civil servants. Why would they consider the landmarks between the fields as gods? By contrast, Mithra religion gives the stature of a god to a unique figure, half-real, half-unreal; the Mithra believers are promoted from one rank to the next higher by being submitted to uniformed, well—defined, impersonal procedures. They have reasons to feel drawn to this religion: it appears to them as familiar, since its general features can easily be seen as a transposition of the rules and rituals governing the Roman civil service. Roman civil servants are promoted also after having been submitted to standardized examinations. At the top of the hierarchy sits the Emperor, who is both a human figure and the symbolic representation of an entity, the Roman Empire. Thus, the civil servants have reasons to prefer Mithraïsm to the traditional Roman religion. These reasons are understandable. The theory explains why the Roman civil servants were a powerful vector in the diffusion of Mithra cult. Of course, the reasons are not of the utilitarian or instrumental type; still they are reasons; these reasons are the genuine causes of the individual conversions of the civil servants and, by aggregation, the causes of the macrophenomenon "diffusion of Mithraïsm in the Roman Empire."

Magical Beliefs. In a few lines of *Economy and Society*, Weber sketches a powerful theory of magic: "Wie das Quirlen den Funken aus dem Holz, so lockt die 'magische' Mimik des Kundigen den Regen aus dem Himmel. Und der Funken, den der Feurquirl erzeugt, ist genau ebenso ein 'magisches' Produkt wie der durch die Manipulationen des Regenmachers erzeugte Regen" (Weber, 1922, II, Kap. IV, §1: 227).[4] In a few words: to the magician and his public the moves the former makes to produce fire and to generate rain are equally magical; "the action of the fire-maker is not less magical than the action of the rainmaker," he writes. This means: we, Westerners, make a difference between the fire-maker and the rainmaker and we consider this difference as obvious. The former believes in a causal relation which is true, the latter in a causal relation which is false. To us, the latter belief is magical, the former is not. But why do we make the difference? Because we have strong reasons to do so. As we have been taught the theory of the transformation of energy, we know that kinetic energy can be transformed into thermic energy, so that the fire-maker behaves in congruence with a valid causal belief. By contrast, we do not see any grounded causal belief underlying the behavior of the rainmaker. But what about the primitives themselves, asks Weber? They have no means of knowing the theory of the transformation of energy, nor of having an intuitive access to a theory which mankind has taken centuries to discover it. So the primitives have no reason to make a distinction between fire-making and rainmaking, while we have strong reasons to consider the distinction as obvious. To them, the two are equally magical.

These two examples are sufficient to show that Weber applies effectively his methodological principles in his empirical analyses. Moreover and more importantly, they show that these methodological principles are the source of the "final" character of his analyses. Compare the theory of magic sketched by Weber to Lévy-Bruhl's. The latter rests upon a big black box ("primitive mentality") no corporation has been able to open. The former contains no black box at all.

4.4. Moral Feelings

If we keep in mind the basic principles of Weber's methodology, we see easily that, to him, explaining collective beliefs means: reconstructing the meaning to the social actors of these beliefs.

Understanding that collective beliefs, as individual beliefs, can be positive or normative, we can believe that something is true or that something is right, legitimate, good, wrong, illegitimate, bad, etc. Why could not the general principles used in the case of collective descriptive beliefs be applied to the case of prescriptive, normative, axiological beliefs? I submit, in other words, that, given the general methodology of Weber, the category of "axiological rationality" expresses the principle that normative and more generally axiological beliefs should be understood as meaningful to social actors, and, moreover, exactly as descriptive beliefs, as meaningful to the actors because they are grounded in their minds on strong reasons. Actions can be meaningful to social actors because they are grounded on instrumental reasons ("instrumental rationality"). But they can also be meaningful to social actors because they are grounded on axiological reasons ("axiological rationality"). This interpretation has possibly two arguments in its favor. First, it excludes the conjecture that, for some obscure reason, Weber would have confused rationality and conformity. Second, it is tightly congruent with Weber's general methodology.

Values Rest on Strong Reasons

Accepting the idea that normative, moral, and generally axiological feelings and beliefs can be grounded on strong reasons does not lead evidently to the endorsement of the Kantian theory of morals. The notion of "axiological rationality" is, in other words, "cognitivist" (as Kant's theory of morals) in the sense that, to Weber as to Kant, moral beliefs are caused by reasons. But the similarity between the two authors stops at this point. The same distinction would be true of many theories of moral feelings and generally of axiological beliefs produced by contemporary social sciences: they are also cognitivist without being Kantian in any way. Moreover, they can be considered as particular versions of the general theory sketched by the notion of "axiological rationality." I will consider some examples of these theories.

Functionalism. I will insist on a first theory of moral feelings and generally axiological beliefs that is "cognitivist" in the sense of moral philosophers (it explains moral feelings by the reasons actors have to believe in them). This theory is clearly not Kantian though. And it appears immediately as an illustration of Weber's notion of "axiological rationality."

A very simple example shows that we can explain familiar moral reactions by the strong reasons which inspire them. Piaget, the Swiss psychologist and sociologist, made himself famous notably by his memorable pages on the marbles game (Piaget, 1985). When one of the children playing marbles cheats, he will attract immediately a negative reaction from the others. Why? Not because the children would have internalized cultural norms according to which playing marbles and following the rules of the marbles game would be good, for, without having been told that cheating at the marbles game is bad, any child reacts negatively against cheating. So, the rejection of cheating is not inspired by socialization or tradition. Why this reaction? Because the children find the game interesting, and for this reason play it. Now, cheating destroys the game: it makes it uninteresting. Thus, the children have strong reasons to reject cheating and, as many observations show, they are very early aware of these reasons. The basic assumption of *functionalism* (in the most interesting versions of this theory) is, as this example makes clear, that an attitude, an action, a decision, an institution, etc., are perceived as good, legitimate, acceptable by individuals when they have the effect of making certain that the interaction system individuals are interested in functions properly, efficiently and smoothly. In the same way, an attitude, an action, etc., will be considered negatively when they have detrimental effects on the interaction systems individuals are interested in. This assumption is illustrated by the case of the marbles game. It can be illustrated by many more complex examples.

First of all, it can be noted that many observations have confirmed Piaget's views. Even very young children can explain that cheating is bad because it generates detrimental effects on a social interaction system they like (the marbles game). In other words, they believe that something is good or bad because they feel they have strong reasons for thinking so, and not because they would have been socialized to the idea. This illustrates, according to my basic contention here, Weber's category of "axiological rationality": they think that cheating is bad because they have strong reasons for thinking so.

Though it is a particular illustration of Weber's "axiological rationality" theory, the functionalist theory is powerful. Simple as its principles are, it explains a host of moral feelings. To wit: why do we consider it legitimate that many organizations select their members? Because, without this institutional disposition, members could eventually be attracted into the organization that would be detrimental to the very objectives of the organization. For this reason, selecting their members is considered a legitimate right of many organizations. Nobody has ever struggled against the idea that a football team or an academy should be deprived of its right of selecting its members. As cheating, in the case of the marbles game, being deprived of this right for a football team would be detrimental to the objectives of the team and threatening to its very existence.

The functionalist theory provides also a convincing explanation of the collective feelings related to social inequalities. Against a current but false view, people accept easily social inequalities provided they can see their functional basis. Thus, people accept easily the idea that those with heavier responsibilities, those exposed to particular risks in their occupational life, those who have gained their competence thanks to a long and difficult training, those who have to deal with more difficult tasks, those who are less easily replaced in their function, etc., are more highly rewarded.

It can be easily observed in this respect that social life produces very normally and very spontaneously such inequalities of rewards with a functional basis. These inequalities not only are not discussed, they are on the contrary positively perceived. Thus, the football player whose talent has made possible the victory of his team will be particularly admired. The composer who expresses with sounds categories of emotions which had not been expressed before and who by so doing makes the language of music more powerful will be admired and celebrated, perhaps not immediately, but in the long run. Take the obvious example of Beethoven: before him, one would have considered as crazy the idea that highly complex feelings, as those of freedom, of hope, of optimism, could be expressed in a musical score. By this achievement, notably, he gained a unique position in the collective memory, as does the scientist who has produced an important discovery or who has produced a fruitful change in our representation of the world. In the same way, the political man who has brought his country into a peaceful and opulent situation will be admired, even if he is severely criticized as any political man normally is as long as he remains active on the political battlefield. Obviously, negative examples could obviously as easily be mentioned.

I evoke these familiar and diverse examples to give an exact impression of the wide scope of the collective moral feelings and generally axiological beliefs that can be effectively explained by the functionalist theory I have considered in this section and more generally by the "cognitivist" theories that make moral and axiological beliefs the effect of strong reasons.

Rational Choice Theory. A highly influential theory today, the so-called *"Rational Choice Theory"* (RCT), is another example, not entirely unrelated to functionalism, of a theory which is also "cognitivist" in the sense that it explains normative beliefs by the reasons actors have to endorse them (Coleman, 1990; Oberschall, 1994; Opp, 1983). As functionalism, it is also inspired by the utilitarian rather than the Kantian tradition, and it can, moreover, as functionalism again, be considered as a particular illustration of a more general "axiological rationality" theory that I attempt to sketch here, following Weber's lead.

Many current decisions in private or public life can effectively be accounted for by this "Rational Choice Model."

Take for example the judge who studies a case or the teacher who examines a candidate. They will have, after some time, the impression that they have spent the *appropriate* time on the task. They will have the feeling that spending less time would have been *unfair* and more time *inadequate*. Why? Because they know that in spending less time they would have run the risk of being unfair to the candidate, or in the case of spending too much time, since they have a limited amount of time, they would have been unfair to the other candidates or cases. By the nature of the situation, the problem the teacher or the judge have to face is namely to minimize the sum of two costs. The longer the time spent on the decision, the more likely the decision to be fair. The longer the time spent on a given case, the less time left to the others and the greater the risk of unfairness to the others. As the information tends to be redundant over time, the curve relating the two types of costs will be convex. The first type of cost is a monotonic decreasing convex function of time. The risk of being unfair decreases with the time spent, but more slowly over time. The other curve is a monotonic convex increasing function of time. The risk of being unfair to others increases more and more quickly with time. The two functions can be represented in a graphical way. If a case is more difficult, or a candidate more difficult to evaluate, the parameters of the curves will move and the minimization points, the points where the curves cross one another, will also move. If the number of cases to be treated is lower, the congestion curve will obviously have another form.

I use this example because it shows that prosaic value statements such as, "I have spent the right time on the case," can be analyzed in a satisfactory fashion with the Rational Choice Model. Moreover, the example shows that the reasons underlying ordinary everyday value statements can be so strong that they can easily be represented in a mathematical fashion. [5]

Why Weber Introduces Two Kinds of Rationality

At this point, an important distinction should be introduced: functionalism, as the "Rational Choice Theory" of norms, as well as most theories of norms proposed by modern sociologists are "consequentialist." In other words, for these theories, an action, a decision, an institution, etc., is positively or negatively valued considering its potential positive or negative effect on social systems (in the case of functionalism) or on individuals (in the case of the RCT).

Weber's notion of "axiological rationality," more precisely the theory which can be developed on the basis of this notion, not only contains these theories as elements, but it transcends them in the sense that it does not say that the reasons underlying the normative beliefs are necessarily of the consequential type. This point is very important in any discussion of Weber's two "rationalities." If the ultimate ground of normative beliefs is to be found on the side of the potential consequences or effects on systems or individuals of actions, decisions, attitudes, institutions, etc., then "axiological rationality," being consequentialist, would not be clearly distinct from "instrumental rationality." "X is good" would be synonymous with "X generates good outcomes," or with "X is a good means to reach the objectives followed by such and such individual or system." In other words, Weber's distinction implies that, to him, "axiological rationality" cannot (or at least cannot *always*) be reduced to "instrumental rationality."

That the reasons underlying axiological beliefs are not always consequential or instrumental is a crucial point in itself, as far as the analysis of axiological beliefs is concerned. It is also essential, if one wants to understand why Weber introduced an autonomous category of "axiological rationality."

The most classical example in discussions about morals, the example of the negative value attached to the act of stealing, shows namely that many moral feelings are not the product of instrumental rationality. The idea that moral judgments would be basically irrational was probably in modern times expressed in the most provocative fashion by Mandeville. Stealing provokes a negative feeling. But this feeling cannot be rationally justified, suggests Mandeville. Of course, stealing has negative consequences as far as the victim is concerned, but the consequences are good to the thief. Of course, society mobilizes all kinds of threats and penalties against thieves. But if the thief can be deterred from stealing, he cannot be convinced that stealing is bad. Mandeville's argument was a blessing to Karl Marx, who evokes it and makes it more systematic (Marx, 1968: 399–401). The social consequences of stealing are ambiguous, he contends, some being socially bad, some good. It is bad to the rich, but provides jobs to lawyers and locksmiths. We could easily go further than Marx. Thieves are a blessing to insurance companies. And not only to them. Look at what happens today in poor urban areas: thanks to thieves, poor people can get at lower prices many goods, such as electronic goods, they could not afford otherwise. They are not even necessarily aware that the low price they pay for these goods results from the fact that the goods have been stolen. In many cases, they have simply the impression of being offered a bargain. This dual market has the happy consequence of inverting Caplovitz's famous theorem (Caplovitz, 1967). As the poor, because of their scarce resources, are limited to low quality products, said Caplovitz, it turns out that "the poor pay more" for their refrigerators or washing machines. Right. But, thanks to thieves, "the poor pay less" for their video—and tape-recorders, or hi-fi sets. Possibly, this unintended redistribution from the rich to the poor is more efficient than the redistribution generated by fiscal policies. In that case, thieves would achieve what political men are unable to accomplish. Moreover, since it makes the demand broader, stealing has a positive effect on supply. Thus, stealing is possibly good, not only from a social, but as well from a macroeconomic viewpoint, since it has plausibly the positive effect of reducing unemployment. Mandeville's and Marx's sarcasm and paradoxes are finally more profound than they seem. They demonstrate by a *reductio ad absurdum* that it is impossible to show that stealing is a bad thing when starting from a consequential viewpoint.

Nobody has proposed to legalize stealing, however. From which source then comes our conviction that stealing is bad? Not from its consequences. From which origin then? To show that stealing is bad, to explain in other words the normal feeling which expresses itself through the value statement, "stealing is bad," one has to reconstruct the non-consequential reasons behind it. They are not difficult to find. Social order is based on an adequation between retribution and contribution. With the exception of particular circumstances, when, for instance, citizens are physically or mentally unable to contribute, a retribution must correspond to a contribution. Now, stealing is a typical violation of these basic principles of social organization, since the thief attributes to himself unilaterally a retribution without offering any contribution as a counterpart. Hence, any theft violates the basic principles of the social link and as such cannot be accepted.

This case, obvious as it is, shows that reasons, though of the non-consequential type, can easily be discovered behind the negative feelings normally aroused by the act of stealing. This example has important consequences: it shows that the basic argument on which the irrational theories of morals are grounded, namely the argument that no reasons can be found behind the negative feelings produced by stealing and other deviant forms of behavior need not be accepted. No consequential argument can prove that stealing is bad. No instrumental reasons can convince that thieves should be prosecuted. But axiological reasons can. This example suffices to suggest that the Weberian notion of axiological rationality, once properly developed, solves very important theoretical problems and many sociological puzzles. It explains why a theft, even of very little importance from a utilitarian viewpoint, produces such a strong reaction on the part of the victim. Sociological analyses often fail to understand this crucial point: "Why such a strong reaction to a minor theft, while the thief is a poor man, a marginal individual toward whom society is so unfair?" is a question often heard. Yes, but unfairness is not a valid answer to unfairness and what counts in a theft is the fact that it violates the basic principles of any social exchange and thus breaks the social link. This example has also the advantage of showing that a utilitarian analysis in the style of the Rational Choice Model is irrelevant here. The indignation of the observer of a theft will grow, other things equal, if the thief has robbed a weak human being, an old woman for instance. But it will hardly grow with the amount stolen. The so-called minor delinquency is an important social problem today, not because the amount of the minor violations of the law has increased, but because the small rate of prosecution gives the public the feeling that political authorities do not care enough about enforcing the basic principles of the social link. All these puzzles cannot be explained without the category of axiological rationality.

Thus, the category of "axiological rationality" invites the development of a theory which would make the functionalist theory, the Rational Choice Theory, but also the so-called "exchange theory" (Heath, 1971; Homans, 1958) or the contractualist theory (the two important latter theories will be only mentioned here without further developments), particular cases of this theory.

4.5. *"Gesinnungsethik"* and *"Verantwortungsethik"*

The example of stealing and the other examples I have evoked makes clear that at least some of our moral feelings are not grounded on consequential reasons. It illustrates the category of "axiological rationality." Also, it helps in understanding another classical Weberian distinction.

These examples show namely that one should not present the choice between *Verantwortungsethik* and *Gesinnungsethik*, the "ethics of responsibility" and the "ethics of conviction," as constituting always an open choice, for in some cases, axiological rationality dominates consequential rationality. Thus, the progress in medicine has reduced infant mortality and this circumstance is generally and rightly acknowledged as being responsible for underdevelopment and hence for all the evils generated by underdevelopment. But who would accept that reducing infant mortality was not a desirable progress? In that case, axiological rationality dominates consequential rationality, and the ethics of conviction dominates the ethics of responsibility. [6]

The "cognitivist" analysis of these sentiments which can be derived from Weber's notion of "axiological rationality," has the advantage of explaining easily why, when I believe that "X is good, legitimate, fair, etc.," I am at the same time normally convinced that the generalized Other (Mead, 1934) should endorse the same statement: my sentiment being grounded on reasons which I see as trans-subjectively valid, the other people should have the same sentiment.

4.6. Back to Kant?

So far, I have presented an interpretation of Weber's notion of "axiological rationality." Moreover, I have sketched a general theory of moral feelings which could be inspired by this famous category. In this final section of the chapter, I would like to sketch an answer to some views likely to be opposed to this theory.

The marbles players have strong reasons not to accept cheating. Generalizing from this example, I would contend that, when we believe that X is good or bad, we *always* have strong reasons—though we can be more or less conscious of these reasons—for believing that X is good or bad. This assumption implies, in other words, that moral convictions are not different in essence from positive convictions. I believe that the square root of 2 is irrational in the mathematical sense, that it cannot be expressed as the ratio of two integers, p and q, because I have strong reasons for believing so. If we take seriously the notion of axiological rationality as I interpret it, we should also accept the idea that the source of moral convictions lies in strong reasons. To use a somewhat provocative formulation, I would say that moral truths are established in the same way as positive truths.

Strange as the idea may appear at first glance, it is not difficult to illustrate. I will start from a trivial example. Why is democracy considered a good thing? Because the statement that it is a good thing is grounded on solid reasons.

I need only refer here briefly to classical theories to make this point more concrete. A good government serves rather the interests of the citizens than its own interests. For this reason, the members of the government should be exposed to the risks of reelection. Electing the government does not insure that the best candidates will be elected, but limits the risk that they disregard the interests of the people. Democracy does not and cannot prevent corruption. But it makes it less likely than with other types of regimes. A legally elected government can overthrow democracy. But there is no absolute protection against this risk. An independent press and an independent judiciary system are indispensable elements of a democracy, since, by their critical function, they can avoid corruption or political mismanagement. Of course, judges and media can become corrupted. But other judges and media people will plausibly have an interest in denunciating the corruption of their colleagues.

If we examine these arguments, we see easily that they derive from principles, for instance that any government should serve the interests of the people rather than its own. Starting from this principle, the argument then shows that elections, an independent press or judiciary system are appropriate means to reach the goal of making more likely than less that the government serves the interests of the people rather than its own.

My objective is not to defend democracy, nor to be original in matters of political philosophy, but only to suggest that there is no substantial difference between the way positive and normative statements are grounded. We believe that the square root of 2 is irrational because we have strong reasons for believing so. We believe that democracy is a good thing because we have strong reasons for believing so, the reasons which have been developed by writers such as Montesquieu, John Stuart Mill, Tocqueville[7] and others. We would never dream of explaining our belief in physical statements by making them the effect of some obscure instinct or of socialization. Why should we evoke such mysterious mechanisms as far as normative statements are concerned?

The objection will possibly be made at this point that political philosophers develop their theories from principles, and that these principles cannot be demonstrated. Otherwise, they would not be principles. However, the objection can be raised against *any* theory, positive as well as normative. Any physical theory for instance rests also on principles. And the principles cannot be demonstrated except by other principles and thus *ad infinitum*. This paradox, christened as "Münchhausen's trilemma," because it evokes this legendary German figure who tried to get out of a pool by drawing his own hairs, has never stopped science. As K. Popper has shown (1976), the fact that we need frameworks to think on any subject and principles to develop any theory does not prevent us from criticizing the frameworks and principles. We endorse principles in normative as in positive matters because they are fruitful. If they are not, we reject them. Trivial as it may appear, this Popperian observation that we need principles before we can derive consequences from them and that we need to see the consequences before we can judge the principles implies that knowledge, against a received idea, is *circular*. This was stressed by some sharp-minded thinkers, such as Georg Simmel (1892). In the normative as in the positive case, we have to accept Münchhausen's trilemma and also the fact that, because knowledge is circular, the trilemma is not contradictory with the possibility of reaching truth and objectivity.

This example of democracy suffices to show that a value statement, "X is good," can be as objective as any positive statement. If the feeling that "democracy is a good thing" were not objectively grounded, one would not observe a consensus on the subject. One would not understand that against the principles—basic in international relations—which require respect of the sovereignty of foreign states, pressures on foreign governments to the effect of installing or developing democracy is generally well understood and approved by the public opinion. How could these collective feelings be otherwise explained? Theory and empirical sociology converge here. (Of course, I am not saying that consensus is a proof of truth, but only that when consensus appears, it has to be explained by making it the product of reasons likely to be perceived as objectively strong).

An objection can be made here: namely that democracy was certainly not always considered so. Even before the First World War, the universal voting right was criticized. A. Pareto, for instance, saw in this right another of these symptoms of human craziness he liked to collect and prophesied that it would generate social chaos. Does not this show that our belief that democracy is good is a product rather of socialization than of reason and that it has little to do with our beliefs in scientific statements? The fact that moral truths are historical, however, is far from being a deadly objection against the theory of axiological beliefs which I develop here on the basis of Weber's "value rationality."

Consider scientific beliefs. Aristotelian physicists believed that any physical move is produced by some force or set of forces.[8] This sheet of paper moves because I apply force to it. If I would not apply force, it would not move. This point seems so trivial that insisting on it can easily appear bizarre. What I want to say by evoking it is that Aristotelian physicists had strong reasons for believing that any move is the effect of some force. But they drew from this statement conclusions that appeared acceptable to them and are unacceptable to us, for instance that when a ship keeps on sliding after the wind has suddenly fallen, some force should be responsible for this move. They tried consequently to figure out what this force could be and introduced the assumption that the move of the ship produced a turmoil. This turmoil was for its part supposed to produce force pushing the boat, which was finally held responsible for the fact that it kept moving. But after a while, Buridan came and said: "if the argument were right, the hypothetical turmoil would have the effect that the straw on a straw heap should fly in opposite directions depending on whether the heap is located at the front or at the back of the deck."[9] As the direction where the straw flies does not actually depend on the location of the straw heap on the deck of a ship, Aristotelian physicists came—slowly—to the conclusion that the principle according to which there would be no move without force producing it was false. Finally, physicists came to a new principle, which we now consider as evident, namely, that a body that moves needs a force to be stopped, exactly as a body not moving needs a force to be brought into move. This is the so-called "principle of inertia." The feeling of obviousness that it produces today in our mind is well the product of history.

The same kind of story could be related on normative as well as positive statements.

As reported by George Trevelyan (1993), Voltaire, before he came to England, could not conceive that a society could function orderly when writers were allowed to publish what they wanted. And, to return to my earlier example, as long as actual democratic regimes or at least political regimes embodying some of the features of what we call democracy did not exist actually, they were not conceived; no one could imagine them, nor *a fortiori* give them a positive value. Then, at the occasion notably of civil struggles in England in Cromwell's time (I follow again Trevelyan here), the principle of the separation of the executive and legislative powers appeared and its effects started being evaluated and positively appreciated. Much later, theories of democracy were developed by analysts such as Montesquieu, John Stuart Mill, and others who presented the principle of the separation of powers as crucial. At this point, it started being perceived as evident, in the same fashion as the principle of inertia appeared as evident after it was understood that it solved many physical puzzles.

But the story does not end at this point and further objections were raised toward other principles of democracy that today we consider obvious. As I mentioned before, at the time of the First World War, the argument that universal voting right would produce chaotic political effects was being developed. But this right was introduced in many places and produced no chaotic effects. And so, an argument which was strong before became weakened under the attack of experience.

Freedom of the press, which would produce all kinds of undesirable effects, was also an argument frequently heard before it become eroded. Freedom of the press does produce undesirable effects, but restricting it produces still many more undesirable effects. No one would doubt that now. Capital punishment is necessary; without capital punishment, crime will increase, it was argued. Capital punishment was abolished in many places without producing any increase in crime rates. From that moment, it was perceived, not only as barbarian, as contradictory with basic values, but as useless, so that the public evaluation of it changed progressively, exactly as the Aristotelian notion of turmoils being responsible for moving ships and arrows was progressively eroded.

Thus, the rational (alternatively: the "cognitivist") theory of moral feelings I propose here following Max Weber, not only is *not* contradicted by the fact that moral convictions change over time, but it can explain this change more easily than other types of theories. The fact that science is historical, that a statement that was treated yesterday as false is treated today as true was never held as an argument against the possibility of reaching truth in scientific matters; in the same way, in moral matters, the fact that some institutions were held as bad yesterday and are now considered as good is not an argument against the fact that moral evaluations are grounded on strong reasons in the mind of people. Moreover, normative irreversibilities, as scientific irreversibilities, can hardly be explained if not by a rational history. The principle of inertia is objectively better than the principles it replaced. Because it is objectively better, it created historical irreversibility. In the same fashion, as noted by Tocqueville, we will never see again someone proclaiming that he enjoyed being the spectator of a capital execution.

The argument that change in moral values confirms relativism rests finally on a fallacy. Truth, moral or positive, *is not* historical. But the research of truth, positive or normative, *is* historical. The fact that science has a history is not an argument against the possibility of scientific truth. The fact that morals have a history is not an argument in favor of moral relativism. Truth cannot be reached at once. History does not legitimate historicism, contextual variability does not justify sociologism or culturalism.

Of course, I do not contend by so saying that there are no historical contingencies. On the contrary, the role of contingencies should be

stressed. If there were no contingencies, there would be no innovations, neither scientific nor moral. On this point, we must definitely
stop following Hegel's intuitions. No one can foretell that tomorrow
totalitarian regimes will not reappear and eventually spread over the
planet. But unless men's memory is destroyed, the idea that democracy is better than despotic regimes will remain present in human
minds.

I do not contend either that an axiological truth lies hidden ready to
be discovered on all subjects. This view is false as far as positive
knowledge is concerned. On many questions we do not know the
truth. We did not know until recent years whether bees have a language or not in spite of the fact that von Frisch got the Nobel prize in
1953 for having "proved" it. On many moral questions, we are in the
same situation. Life continually brings to the surface new positive and
normative questions, many of which remain provisionally unsolved,
while others are possibly unsolvable.

We are now in a position to answer the question raised by the title
of this chapter: the dynamic side of the moral theory which can be
derived from Weber is sufficient to show that the notion of "axiological
rationality" takes us far from Kant.

I conclude with a single sentence: Weber's hints are presently extremely relevant because they propose to overcome the shortcomings
of both the Kantian and the utilitarian traditions.[10]

Notes

1. Conference, "Economics and Ethics in the Historical School of Economics.
   Achievements and Present Relevance," Forschungsinstitut für Philosophie
   Hannover, March 27–31, 1996, published as "The Present Relevance of Max
   Weber's *Wertrationalität* (Value Rationality)" in P. Koslowski, ed., *Methodology
   of the Social Sciences, Ethics, and Economics in the Newer Historical School*,
   Berlin: Springer, 1997: 3–29.
2. Mommsen (1959) or Fleischmann (1964) go too far when they seem to draw from
   Nietzsche's influence on Weber and from the idea that science should be value-
   free, the idea that to him, values would be irrational.
3. "Wenn ich nun jetzt einmal Soziologe geworden bin…, dann wesentlich deshalb,
   um dem immer noch spukenden Betrieb, der mit Kollektivbegriffen arbeitet, ein
   Ende zu machen. Mit anderen Worten: auch Soziologie kann nur durch Ausgehen
   vom Handeln des oder der, weniger oder vieler Einzelnen, strikt 'individualistisch'
   in der Methode also—betrieben werden." Letter to R. Liefmann, March 9, 1920,
   quoted by Mommsen (1965: 44).
4. See Boudon (1993).
5. I lean here on my book (Boudon, 1995b).

6. Bell (1997) shows that the negative accent Weber puts on *Gesinnungsethik* has to be related with G. Lukacs, who was present at the private discussions Weber organized in his home and who frightened him by his fanaticism, as he frightened Thoman Mann, since he appears as the Jesuit Naphta in *Der Zaubeberg* (Lukacs was, it seems, proud of this portrait). The conceptual distinction transcends obviously these circumstances, however.

7. I have left aside here the consequentialist arguments in favor of democracy (as it makes economic development easier). They have been developed again by Olson (1993).

8. I follow here Duhem (1954), tome 1: 371–372: "Aucun corps inanimé ne peut être en mouvement s'il n'est soumis à l'action d'un moteur qui soit distinct de lui et extérieur à lui; il faut que ce moteur, pendant toute la durée du mouvement, lui soit constamment appliqué, soit sans cesse en contact avec lui."

9. J. Buridan, *Questions sur la physique*, develops the so-called "theory of impetus," according to Duhem a first formulation of the principle of inertia as we know it. Question 12 of Book VIII in particular criticizes the principles of Aristotelian physics using this example of the straw heap.

10. The ideas I have presented are developed in a more extensive fashion, notably in (Boudon, 1997a).

5

Generalizing the "Rational Choice Model" into a Cognitivist Model[1]

To the memory of my old friend Jim Coleman

The "Rational Choice Model" is of utmost importance for two reasons. First, because in the cases where it can legitimately be applied, it leads to final explanations, while explanations using concepts such as the "internalization of norms," "socialization," etc., lead to further questions as to which mechanisms are hidden behind them. Second, it explains efficiently a host of social phenomena, as recognized already by classical sociologists as Tocqueville or presociologists as Rousseau (see Boudon 1981).

But it suffers also a major weakness: it is namely of little use as far as the explanation of beliefs is concerned. Now, beliefs are not only a major object of sociological analysis in themselves, they are also in many cases an essential ingredient of actions: I did so because I believe that "X is good, fair, legitimate, etc." Weber (1922) described this type of action by his category of axiological rationality (*Wertrationalität*). This notion is often interpreted in a simple, and also, I think, wrong and uninteresting fashion, as describing actions inspired by values. If this had been the sense Weber had in mind, he would have plausibly spoken of "value-conformity" rather than "value-rationality." Although I do not wish to enter into a discussion here as to what Weber actually meant, I submit another interpretation: by "value-rationality," he meant that axiological beliefs are grounded in the minds of social actors on reasons which they see as valid and, consequently, as likely to be considered valid by others. Since Weber proposes to distinguish carefully between value—and instrumental rationality, it should also be stressed that, to him, these "axiological" reasons are not of the instrumental type.

Following Weber's lead, one should introduce additionally the notion of "cognitive rationality" to describe explanations of form: I did so because I believed that "X is true, likely, plausible, etc.." Thus, "cognitive rationality" would describe the situations where actors believe that "X is, true, likely, plausible, false, etc.," because, to them, these statements are grounded on reasons which they see as valid and hence likely to be considered as valid by others.

Now, the challenge sociological analysis often has to meet is to explain why an actor believes that "X is good, etc.," or that "X is true, etc.." As easily recognized, the Rational Choice Model has little to say on such questions for a simple reason, namely that my belief that "X is good" or that "X is true" is rarely the product of the cost-benefit rationality characteristic of the "Rational Choice Model."[2]

As the "Rational Choice Model" in its current version has little to say on beliefs or on actions grounded on beliefs ("I did Y because I believed Z was true," "I did Y because I believed Z was fair," etc.), the sociologist who has to explain a belief or an action inspired by some belief will turn easily to irrational explanations. Many traditions, the Freudian as well as the Marxian or the Durkheimian traditions, will put a host of irrational models at his disposal. Thus, to avoid the Charybdis of the irrational models and the Scylla of the narrow version of rationality the Rational Choice Model endorses, it seems advisable to borrow a third way.

I will call the model corresponding to this third way the "cognitivist" model, this adjective meaning that beliefs, either of the positive or of the normative type, are assumed in this model to be derived from reasons, although from reasons which cannot be reduced to mere considerations of costs and benefits. Thus, the "cognitivist" model is drawn from the "Rational Choice Model" by lifting the restriction that the reasons of social actors should always be of the cost-benefit type. Reciprocally, the latter model is derived from the former by introducing the restriction that the reasons of the actors should always be of the cost-benefit type. Again, the "cognitivist" model appears as more useful than the "Rational Choice Model" as soon as non-trivial beliefs appear as an essential ingredient of social action.

5.1. Explaining Collective Beliefs: The "Cognitivist" Model

For the sake of clarity, three types of beliefs should be distinguished.

- Type 1 includes the beliefs that can be validated, notably by an operation of confrontation with the real world and which are actually validated. For instance: "I believe that 2 and 2 are 4."
- Type 2 includes the beliefs that can be validated, notably by an operation of confrontation with the real world and which are *not* actually validated. For instance: "I believe that 2 and 2 are 5." Here, the belief will be explained in most cases by evoking some irrational cause (that is, a cause not having the status of a reason). Thus, the belief of the pupil that 2 and 2 are 5 will be explained by evoking his absentmindedness or eventually the deficiency of his cognitive capacities due to his very young age. Such explanations can be easily accepted. Although "absentmindedness" is a complex psychological phenomenon, its very existence is beyond doubt. Much more difficult to accept are, for instance, the explanations of the false causal beliefs underlying magical rituals which evoke, as in the classical case of Lévy-Bruhl (1923, 1928), a conjectural "primitive mentality" and make it responsible for the beliefs. To Lévy-Bruhl, magical beliefs as observed in what was called in his time "primitive societies" should be explained by the fact that the brain of the primitive would be, so to say, wired in another fashion than ours. Consequently, they would follow rules of inference different from the ones we use. Thus, they would not make the distinction that we make between relations of similarity and causal relations. This would explain, for instance, why, when they imitate the noise of rain, they believe this should facilitate the fall of rain. The reality of the causal explanatory factor evoked in such theories is obviously more controversial than in the case of "absentmindedness," say. As reported by Nisbett and Ross (1980), cognitive psychologists not infrequently introduce the assumption that ordinary thinking would be led by rules of inference which scientific thinking treats as invalid, and qualify it as "magical thinking." Two examples of cognitive experiments interpreted in a, so to say, "neo-Lévy-Bruhlian" fashion are presented in the following section of this chapter.
- Type 3 includes the beliefs that *cannot* be validated by an operation of confrontation with the real world. It can be illustrated by beliefs of the type: "I believe that it is good to. . . . " This type includes the normative beliefs and generally the evaluative or, in other words, axiological beliefs.

A superficial glance at the explanations provided by sociological literature shows that, as I mentioned earlier, the collective beliefs of

Types 2 and 3 are frequently explained by irrational causes. Thus, in the Marxian and in the Durkheimian traditions, they are explained as the effects of the internalization of collective beliefs through socialization processes. In the Paretian, Freudian, or Nietzschean traditions, they are explained as the effects of affective factors. In other traditions, they are explained in a naturalist fashion as the effects of cultural or biological evolutionary processes. In all these cases, the explanation evokes causes that have not the status of reasons.[3]

Undoubtedly, irrational factors, notably affective ones, can in many circumstances legitimately be evoked to the effect of explaining beliefs. But the strong appeal (on which I will add some additional comments later) of irrational factors as far as the beliefs of Types 2 and 3 are concerned allows for the fact that they are also used in circumstances where an explanation by reasons, along the line of the "cognitivist" model, appears as scientifically more acceptable. [4] I will illustrate the importance of this model with the help of examples borrowed from three fields, namely: cognitive psychology, the sociology of knowledge, and the sociology of norms. Selecting heterogeneous examples has the advantage of suggesting that the basic processes of conviction formation are the same, independent of the content and nature of beliefs: beliefs on public as well as private matters, normative ("I believe X is fair, legitimate, bad, etc.,") as well as assertive ("I believe X is true, plausible, unlikely, etc.,") beliefs, beliefs appearing in the field of scientific as well as ordinary knowledge are endorsed by the social actor once he sees them as "making sense" to him, in other words when he sees them, in a more or less confused way, as grounded on solid reasons.

The Weberian motto *"deutend verstehen"* (meaningful understanding) says nothing else. It says that explaining a belief, an action, an attitude amounts to finding out the meaning to the social actor of the given belief, action, or attitude, in other words to finding out the reasons as to why he endorses the belief or attitude, or undertakes the action. This motto includes, in other words, two postulates: individual beliefs should be analyzed as meaningful to the actor; collective beliefs result from the aggregation of individual beliefs meaningful to the actor.

This "cognitivist" model appears entitled to claim, on several points, its superiority over its irrational competitors.

1. It can explain a crucial subjective fact, namely that the social

subject has normally a feeling of conviction and not of internalization or of constraint. Why would the subject have a feeling of conviction that, say, "X is true" or "X is good" if this feeling is produced, as the Durkheimian tradition contends, by social constraints. Why would not the subject have a feeling of constraint, if his beliefs are actually produced by a constraint? Why has he actually a feeling which he normally identifies rather as a feeling of conviction? Why would he identify in an improper fashion the sources of his beliefs? This difficulty is often solved by evoking the assumption that consciousness would be "false." But, while it can be accepted that the assumption is valid in some specific circumstances, it is much more difficult to accept the idea that consciousness would be "false" by essence: I can for instance fail to recognize that I perceive what somebody tells me as true because I like him. In such a case, the assumption that my consciousness is "false" can be easily accepted. That consciousness should be systematically false is much more difficult to accept. This assumption is often, implicitly or explicitly, introduced, however, though in irrational theories of beliefs.

2. The irrational theories evoke often occult causes, the existence of which is not demonstrable. Probably because they were conscious of this difficulty, Weber (1988) and Popper (1967) invited social scientists to endorse a postulate, namely that it is legitimate to accept an irrational explanation of some piece of behavior only once the plausible rational explanations have been excluded as incompatible with the available observed data. If I see somebody cutting wood in his backyard, I will assume that he wants to burn the wood to make the room where he sits warmer. If this explanation appears as invalid (as it would be if the observation is made in summer), I will propose some other rational explanation, e.g. that he wants to show somebody how to cut wood. If he is actually alone in his backyard, I will possibly assume that he celebrates some cult of wood-cutters. If no such cult is observed in the social context, if he belongs to no sect of that kind, and if I have the impression that I have exhausted the gamut of plausible rational explanations, I will finally assume that he cuts wood because he is subject to a "compulsion" to do so. Weber and Popper saw well in other words that an irrational occult cause, as here "compulsion," can be granted a reality only when rational causes have been discarded: if A, B, C, D, E are to our knowledge the only possible causes of P and if the rational causes A, B, C, D must be discarded, I

can hold the irrational cause E as the cause of P, even though I cannot show its existence directly. Scheler (1954 [1916]) has rightly stressed the point that an action or a belief has always a meaning to the actor and that assuming that this meaning is *not* the cause of the action is a very strong and hence in many cases questionable assumption. A basic point of Freudianism and Marxism is, on the contrary, that the meaning to the actor of his actions or beliefs, in other words the reasons on which he thinks they are grounded, would in many cases be mere "rationalization" as Freudians would contend, or the product of "false consciousness," as Marxians would say: these reasons would not be the actual causes of the actions and beliefs. The lasting and diffuse influence of Freudianism and Marxism explains to some extent at least that social scientists introduce so easily the idea that the meaning to the actor of his beliefs or actions is false and consequently should not be treated as its cause.

3. When a social actor has the feeling that "X is good" or that "X is true," he also has the feeling that others should endorse these statements. Beliefs are not seen by social actors as preferences. I prefer white to red wine, but I accept easily that my neighbor has the opposite preference. By contrast, if I believe that "X is good" or that "X is true," I will normally expect that my neighbor holds the same belief. This normally "trans-subjective" dimension of beliefs is easily accounted for in the framework of the cognitivist model: if beliefs are endorsed once they are perceived by the social actor as grounded on solid reasons, he should expect that these reasons also convince his neighbor. This "trans-subjective" dimension of beliefs is much less easily accounted for by irrational theories. It is, however, an essential character of beliefs.

4. The "cognitive" model does not ignore socialization. A pupil believes that "2 and 2 are 4" certainly because he was taught this, but the belief "holds" in his mind because it is grounded on solid reasons. Socialization is a channel which should not be confused with its content, and which can be effective only for some contents. As Durkheim himself stresses, even a cat cannot be conditioned to believe that a ball of string is a mouse. Socialization is in other words never the only cause of beliefs: this corollary is immediately derived from the principles of the cognitivist model.

As I noted above, the "cognitivist" model is accepted as far as Type 1 beliefs are concerned. It is easily recognized that I believe that "2 plus 2 are 4" *because* there are strong reasons for believing that the statement is valid. It is easily accepted that this belief is "trans-subjective," in other words that I would normally expect that the generalized Other also believes that "2 plus 2 are 4." It is easily accepted that socialization is not the only cause of the belief. But the claim of the "cognitivist" model that the same type of analysis can also be conducted in the case of beliefs of Types 2 and 3 is exposed to more resistance.

I will now show with the help of some examples that the "cognitivist" model can be applied successfully to the case of beliefs of Types 2 and 3. I will illustrate the application of this model to Type 2 beliefs by examples drawn from cognitive psychology. I will explain further why I chose this field rather than another. Then, I will illustrate Type 3 beliefs by examples drawn from the sociology of knowledge and the sociology of norms.

5.2. Type 2 Beliefs: Examples from Cognitive Psychology

The experiments from cognitive psychology are interesting to the social sciences for several reasons. In many of them, a majority of subjects give a false answer to the problem to which they are exposed. Moreover, they give the same false answer. These experiments may thus be regarded as machineries generating false collective beliefs (that is, beliefs of Type 2). These false collective beliefs cannot be explained by affective factors (the questions are affectively neutral), nor by socialization effects (the subjects have never been confronted with the problem before), nor by contagion or influence effects (the respondents give their answer independently from one another). How should they be explained? In an irrational fashion, by introducing the conjecture that "ordinary thinking" would, like Lévy-Bruhl's "primitive mentality," be directed by inference rules incompatible with the rules recognized as valid ?[5] By the conjecture that "ordinary thinking" is affected by "biases" or by "frames," the origin of such has to be sought on the side of either cultural or biological evolution. Or is not the "cognitivist" model a more acceptable theoretical framework? In other words, do not the respondents believe in the false answer because they have strong reasons to do so? I will try to show that this latter path leads to a more satisfactory analysis.

Beliefs on the Validity of Aids-Test

A first example has the advantage of showing the importance of the "cognitivist" model, and also, of illustrating the notion of "trans-subjective" reasons with full clarity. As we deal here with beliefs of Type 2, these beliefs are by definition invalid. The "cognitivist" model assumes that they are endorsed by each subject because they appear to him as grounded on solid reasons. Moreover, these reasons are perceived as solid, not by some individual because of idiosyncratic factors that would characterize them, but rather, if not by all, at least by many. Consequently, these reasons are not objective, but they are not subjective either: they have some strength that explains why they convince many respondents. In the vocabulary I propose they are "trans-subjective": they will likely be perceived as strong, not by this individual in particular, but by many.

A group of physicians is asked the following question: "if a test to detect a disease, whose prevalence is 1/1000, has a false positive rate of 5 percent, what is the chance that a person found to have a positive result actually has the disease, assuming you know nothing about the person's symptoms."[6] The distribution of the answers is interesting for two reasons. Firstly, it is highly structured in the sense that the mode is very high and falls on a very specific value: a majority of physicians holds that the subject referred to in the question has a .95 probability of being actually ill; the average of the answers is .56. Secondly, the most popular answer is very far for the true one: only 18 percent of the physicians give an accurate answer. The correct answer is namely that the subject has a little less than .02 probability of being actually ill. So the experiment has generated a false collective belief (Type 2).

It is readily noted that, given the conditions of the experiment, the collective belief can be explained neither by affective, nor by socialization or contagion factors. The authors from whom I borrow these astonishing data propose to explain it, in a Lévy-Bruhlian fashion, by the existence of "biases" or "frames," which would lead human intuition on false paths as far as intuition about statistical or probabilistic problems is concerned. How should the existence of these biases be explained? The authors introduce here a phylogenetic conjecture: our intuition about statistical questions would have been structured in the early eras of the history of mankind as an effect of hunting experience and transmitted from generation to generation. This structuration would have had the effect of making us unfamiliar with Bayesian inference procedures. This conjecture is obviously interesting, but subject to several objections. First, it is strong, far-fetched, and hard to prove or disprove. Though theoretically falsifiable, it is not practically. [7] Moreover, how is it possible to explain that procedures leading to erroneous predictions are transmitted without correction from one generation to the next? Generally, evolution theory teaches that ill-adapted characters tend to be eliminated. Here it is curiously interpreted as suggesting that they are kept up over time. Why would our intuition about arithmetical or geometrical matters be generally unbiased, while our intuition about statistical matters would be biased? Moreover, the theory does not explain satisfactorily why the distribution is sensitive to variations in the formulation of the question. Finally, this phylogenetic theory explains that the collective belief is false, not the more specific findings produced by the experiment, notably that the distribution is characterized by a high mode corresponding to the specific value .95.

The "cognitivist" model gives a more satisfactory explanation of the puzzle raised by this experiment. The respondents are confronted with a question they have not met before. They do not likely mobilize a preformed answer that would be present in their minds as the effect of nature or nurture. Nor do they select in an arbitrary fashion a random answer. They try instead to develop an argument as solid as possible to derive a valid answer to the question. Many of them fall on the same argument. Although it is false, it is induced by the question. It has, in other words, a "trans-subjective" validity. This trans-subjective validity explains that it is picked up by a majority of the respondents.

Here is the implicit argument of the subjects giving the modal answer, as I reconstruct it. The physicians know exactly what the notion of "false positive" means. However, they are not told how the word "rate" in the expression "false positive rate" should be read. To which denominator should the number of false positive be referred? To the number of the "true positive" or to the number of the "true negative"? The first solution is simpler. Moreover, the notion of test is a "success word" in Ryle's vocabulary (1966): in the same way as a false theorem is not a theorem at all, a test which would not have a minimal validity would not be a test at all. Given the purpose of any test, a person positive to the test should have a probability as close as possible to the value 1 of being actually ill if the test is worth its name.

The argument is in other words: (1) As a test is valid by nature, the probability I am asked about should be close to 1; (2) I am not told to which denominator the number of false positive should be related; (3) It is simpler to refer the false positive to the true positive than to the true negative; (4) Referring the false positive to the true positive generates a high value of probability. This argument leads to the following computation:

T (number of persons positive for 100,000 people) = M (number of people ill) +5% M = 100 + 5%(100)= 105.

Hence it is readily drawn:

$$Pr(M/T) = 100/105 = .95.$$

In fact, the correct argument is:

$$T = M + 5\% \text{ (not M)} = 100 + 5\% \text{ (99,900)= 5,095}$$

Hence,

$$Pr (M/T) = 100/5,095 = .02.$$

The "cognitivist" theory I submit suggests in other words that the false answer is chosen because it is supported by reasons likely to be evoked and perceived as good. The question includes an objective ambiguity. The ambiguity can be solved in two ways. One way (the wrong one) is attractive, because it is simpler and much more congruent with the very notion of the test than the right one. Although the reasons mobilized by the respondents are false, they have an intrinsic strength that explains why they are retained and generate a false collective belief. To introduce a sociological parenthesis: the experiment explains why ineffective policies, notably in the field of public health, can be accepted by public opinion without much resistance. Suppose a test, the validity of which would be as poor as in the example, were to be made compulsory by political decision makers and financed by taxpayers. Because of the cognitive reasons hypothesized in my analysis, such a political decision would not likely meet with opposition from public opinion, as long at least as the question of the validity of the test would not be publicly raised.

The "cognitivist" explanation of the findings of the above experiment introduces exclusively "light" psychological assumptions which are easily credible. They are not *ad hoc*, in the sense that the same kinds of assumptions could be used in other situations. Moreover, the theory explains easily why the value .95 corresponds to the modal answer. Given the criteria generally used to appreciate the validity of a theory, the "cognitivist" theory explains more of the observed data and explains them with lighter and more acceptable assumptions than the irrational phylogenetic theory of the naturalistic type originally proposed by the authors of the study. The "cognitivist" explanation could also inspire experimental designs which would make direct testing of it possible. An easily devisable design could check, for instance, whether the modal value is changed with a change in the parameters introduced in the question or with a change in the wording of the question where the ambiguity of the notion of "rate" would be eliminated, etc. In other words, the "cognitive" theory has not only a greater explanatory power, it has also a greater heuristic value.

Beliefs on the Relation between Symptom and Disease

Many experiments from cognitive psychology where a collective false belief is generated are interpreted by their authors in an irrational fashion ("biases," "frames" from cultural or biological origin leading "ordinary" intuitive inference to false paths). Most of them can be reinterpreted along the principles of the "cognitivist" model.

To the effect of showing the generality of this claim, I will present briefly an additional example, taken from the numerous ones I have presented elsewhere (1994). These two examples have the advantage of being excellent illustrations of the notion of "trans-subjective" reasons, and also of confirming the superiority of the "cognitivist" model on irrational theories.

In an illuminating study, Shweder (1977) presents several experiments where respondents are offered statistical data.[8] A strong majority draws from that data conclusions that the canonical rules of statistical inference do not allow. Shweder concludes that ordinary inference follows principles of its own, and proposes to qualify these rules as "magical thinking," well in the Lévy-Bruhlian tradition. He postulates, in other words, that ordinary thinking, for reasons he does not make explicit, would follow rules normally considered invalid in scientific thinking. Shweder's findings are fascinating. They propose to sociologists as well as psychologists an interesting challenge. His irrational interpretation, however, is controversial.[9]

In one of the experiments, a group of nurses is presented with a set of 100 cards, each representing a hypothetical patient. Two items of fictitious information are written on each of the cards: whether the

Table 5.1
A Negative Correlation Perceived as Positive

Disease Symptom	Ill	Not ill	Total
Symptom: yes	37	33	70
Symptom: no	17	13	30
Total	54	46	100

patient displays a given symptom, and whether or not he is affected by a given disease. The nurses are then asked whether the symptom is a symptom of the disease, in other words whether the disease is the cause of the symptom. Table 5.1 gives the overall information, as such not given to the nurses, which can be derived from the information contained on the individual cards presented to them.

The nurses use, it seems, only one piece of information to determine their answer: the proportion of cases where the patient has contracted the given illness *and* displays the symptom. These cases are "relatively frequent" since they are thirty-seven among a total of 100. Obviously, this information is insufficient to conclude from it the causal relationship, "Illness is the cause of the symptom." Verifying this relationship would require a comparison of the proportions of those having the disease among those respectively characterized by the symptom and those not characterized by the symptom. Such a comparison would include four pieces of information. As can be seen in table 5.1, the proportion of those having the disease is actually slightly lower (and not higher as the nurses' modal answer would suppose) among those displaying the symptom than among those not displaying it: $37/70 = .53$; $17/30 = .57$.

Why then is the modal answer of the nurses wrong? Why is a slightly negative correlation perceived as positive? Why does the experiment generate a false collective belief? For the general reasons I have indicated, I will not spend time discussing the assumption according to which the ordinary rules of inference would have a "magical" character. The modal conviction of the nurses can be more easily explained by analyzing it as resulting from their effort to master a complex problem-solving situation as meaningful to them, in a word, as deriving from reasons likely to be perceived as strong by many of them. Of course, by contrast with the previous example, the reasons cannot be claimed to be valid. There is no ambiguity here in the question, and the causal belief of the nurses is objectively incompatible with the data. However, the reasons on which their conclusion rests may be said to be "trans-subjective" in the sense that they can likely occur in many minds. Because of this trans-subjective character, the answer is modal and the belief *collective* (and as such of interest to sociologists).

Here is the way these reasons can be reconstructed. Here again, I have no empirical proof of the validity of this reconstruction. But, as in the previous case, with this reconstruction in mind, a design of experiment could easily be devised to check whether it holds or not.

It is true that in principle a causal statement derived from a binary contingency table mobilizes four independent pieces of information. But practically, one piece can often be sufficient, notably in the case where we have some implicit knowledge on the order of magnitude of others, as when we know for instance they are very asymmetrical. By the very nature of things, this latter feature is characteristic of the distribution of diseases and symptoms: it results from the fact that pathological are less frequent than normal phenomena.

Here, the nurses have possibly considered in a meta-conscious fashion that the frequency of the disease should be weak, as the frequency of most of the diseases with which they are confronted. In the same fashion, they would normally consider the frequency of any particular symptom as weak by essence. True: these frequencies are not actually weak in table 5.1. But this feature makes the table unrealistic. The data appear in other words as implausible, given their supposed meaning. Now, if the marginals would have been more realistic, if symptom and disease would have had a more realistic lower frequency, the fact that thirty-seven people out of 100 have both the symptom and the disease would be a serious indicator of the existence of a causal relationship between the two variables. Thus, let us suppose that a disease strikes 20 percent of the patients in a hospital and that a symptom is observable on 20 percent of the same population. As soon as the percentage of those presenting both the symptom and the disease would be greater than 4, a presumption would hold that the symptom is a symptom *of* the disease (table 5.2). In other words, when 37 percent of the patients in a hospital have some disease and present some symptom, the plausibility of the symptom being a symptom of the disease is actually high.

Table 5.2
A Causal Presumption Can Be Derived from One Piece of Information

Disease Symptom	Ill	Not ill	Total
Symptom: yes	4	16	20
Symptom: no	16	64	80
Total	20	80	100

A current objection against such an analysis can be easily discarded. The nurses do not develop consciously the argument I have just developed. But nothing prevents the assumption that they see in a meta-conscious intuitive fashion that, when the marginals are asymmetrical, the combination of two characters should also be rare. In other words, it can be assumed that statistical intuition is reliable and that it leads here to a false answer because it is applied to an artificial situation very different from the ones the nurses meet in the real world. At any rate, we do not need to draw from the experiment the strong conclusion that natural inference follows specific rules considered illegitimate in scientific inference. This irrational theory is not only strong, it is flawed: either these specific "magical" rules, which would guide natural inference do actually exist and they can be described with the same accuracy as the rules of legitimate inference, or they cannot be listed because they are confused. But in this case, how can they be used by the nurses and explain their beliefs? How can they generate highly structured distributions and *collective* beliefs?

Also, it can be observed that the answers of the nurses show that they have some correct intuitive notions about the complexity of causal inference from statistical data. Among the cards presented to them, some represent fictitious patients that have the symptom but not the disease. This does not disturb their belief though that the symptom is a symptom of the disease, possibly because they know that a cause can be present without the effect appearing.

In the two examples and in all the other examples that could be considered, the beliefs of the respondents can be more satisfactorily analyzed by supposing they meet the problem-solving situation they are exposed to by building plausible conjectures, by mobilizing in an intuitive fashion—sometimes with virtuosity—implicit information ("a test is a test under the condition it has a high validity; a given disease is rare; a given symptom is rare, etc.), by synthesizing this likely information and these plausible conjectures and deriving from them a conclusion meaningful to them, because they are grounded on reasons good to them. Again, this line of analysis has the advantage of introducing weak, easily acceptable assumptions, of explaining the data in a more detailed and specific fashion, and of explaining easily the collective character of some answers. Moreover, this reconstruction of the reasons behind the beliefs can in principle be tested by appropriate designs of experiment. Thus, I propose the interpretation of the answers of the nurses suggests that it would be helpful to reproduce the experiment, using various marginal distributions. Also, it would be interesting, not only to register the answers of the nurses, but also to use what Lazarsfeld has called the "art of asking why" to try to disentangle the reasons as to how they reached their conclusions.

Although drawn from psychology, these examples are important to the sociologist since they analyze collective beliefs (generated *in vitro*). I will turn now to examples *in vivo*.

5.3. Type 3 Beliefs: Examples from the Sociology of Knowledge

The examples drawn from cognitive psychology that I have just examined deal with beliefs of Type 2. The sociology of knowledge provides for its part a host of examples of beliefs of Type 3 (that is, of those beliefs which cannot easily be confronted by an external "truth"). I will consider two classical examples showing also that in this case the "cognitive" model is particularly powerful.

The first example is drawn from Marx, the second from Tocqueville. It is interesting to note that these two writers, who are so opposed to one another on so many points, seem to endorse implicitly a Weberian "cognitivist" methodology in their analyses in the sociology of knowledge, thus indirectly testifying to its powerfulness. Also it is interesting to note that Marx's methodology appears very different in practice from what it is in theory. The notion of "alienation" which appears in Marx's early theoretical texts is not used in the later works. On the contrary, Marx seems to assume that collective beliefs, even when they are detrimental to the interests of the individuals, are endorsed because they are grounded on good reasons in their minds. But the notion of "alienation," as well as Mehring's notion of "false consciousness," is widely used by the neo-Marxist tradition, and described by this word or by an equivalent word.

An Example from Marx

In *Capital*, Marx wonders why the workers so easily accept exploitation.[10] One need not endorse his theory of the surplus value nor any other point of the Marxian doctrine to appreciate the ingeniousness of his answer. No false consciousness, but strong reasons ground the acceptation, he suggests. A subsidiary advantage of his sketchy theory here is that it proposes a cognitivist interpretation of the classical "reference group theory."

The implicit argument that Marx puts into the head of his ideal-typical worker can be reconstructed in the following manner:

1. Is my salary fair?
2. My salary is fair if it reflects the value of my work.
3. I know obviously my salary, but I cannot determine directly the value of my work.
4. Are indirect evaluations possible?
5. A system of rewards is fair if it retributes in the same fashion two workers whose contribution to production is similar.
6. So, comparing my salary to a worker whose work is the same as mine is an indirect way of testing whether my salary is fair.
7. However, there is a possibility that the two of us are exploited. So, the equality of our salary is not the appropriate test for the fairness of my salary.
8. A more reliable test would be to compare my salary to the salary of a similar worker in another firm, and preferably in a non-capitalist firm (since exploitation can be a feature common to all capitalist firms). The best indirect test would be to compare my salary to the salary of workers doing the same work as me in small independent firms. Suppose I work in an industrial bakery: the baker at the corner of the street will be my "natural" reference person. Moreover, I can evaluate his standard of living and his income.
9. If his earnings are not definitely greater than mine, I will conclude with good reason that my salary is fair.

The analysis suggests first that the worker endorses a theory of justice (proportionality between contribution and retribution). Why this theory rather than another? Because the worker contributes to the production with the purpose of deriving a retribution from it. The salary should consequently reflect the contribution. Then he looks for the best means available to him to check whether the correspondence between retribution and contribution is secured or not. Obviously, the worker will not take into account the fact that the costs of production are lower in an industrial bakery. But the notion of the economy of scale is not more intuitive than the law of the transformation of energy. Why would he be aware of this law that requires some familiarity with economic theory which he is not likely to know? Thus, the worker will accept "exploitation," not because his consciousness is "false" or obscured by the perverse *habitus* produced by alienation, but because he has good reasons for accepting it. He is not passive. On the contrary, he wonders whether his salary is fair. He is not irrational. On the contrary, he tries to explore the best tests available to him to check whether his salary is fair or not.

This example is interesting for another reason: it shows namely that collective axiological beliefs ("our salary is fair") should, as representational beliefs, be analyzed as meaningful to the actors, in other words, as grounded to them on trans-subjectively good reasons.

An Example from Tocqueville

Tocqueville always analyzes collective beliefs with the help of a methodology grounded on two principles. He treats them as the aggregate effect of individual beliefs, more precisely of beliefs which can be likely attributed to ideal-typical individuals. Then he postulates that reconstructing the meaning of these beliefs to the individual, that is, retrieving the reasons he has to endorse them, is the appropriate way of explaining them. To this end, he shows that the beliefs derive from a network of reasons, some of them being context-indexed others eventually not.

In the *Old Regime and the Revolution*, Tocqueville wonders why French intellectuals at the end of the eighteenth century are so enthusiastic about the notion of Reason with a capital R, and why this idea of Reason spreads so easily and so quickly, while no similar phenomenon can be observed in England at the same time.

The main line of his explanation is that the intellectuals of the end of the eighteenth century, the so-called "Enlighteners," have all kinds of reasons to believe in Reason. France at that time is in such a state that Tradition, that is, all the institutions which draw their force from their antiquity, appears to many as the source of the present evils. To take one example, the gentry is entitled to get from non-noble people signs of respect and deference. But no one sees the grounds for this superiority. Rich noblemen buy royal offices corresponding in many cases to ill-defined duties. They spend their time at the Court in Versailles. As to the poor noblemen, those whom the peasants are likely to meet, they cling insistently to their privileges, since they are the only source of their status. They are so unpleasant that, when they were designated *"hobereaux"* (a name for a small ugly carnivore bird), the metaphor spread immediately: it described vividly the behavior of these poor noblemen. As Tocqueville notes, the word *"hobereau"* is untranslatable into English. In England, the members of the gentry fulfill by contrast visible local and national political and social functions. Hence, by contrast to what happens in France at the same time, its official superiority is seen as legitimate and well accepted. The same analysis is conducted by Tocqueville on other institutions. In all cases, he shows that they appear with good reasons to the people as a-functional, as ungrounded. From this feeling, they draw the conclusion that the social and political institutions grounded on traditions are bad, that Tradition with a capital T is bad, and that good institutions should be grounded on the contrary term, namely Reason, that is, on blueprints similar to the blueprints used by engineers or architects:

> Au dessus de la société réelle dont la constitution était encore traditionnelle, confuse et irrégulière, où les lois demeuraient diverses et contradictoires, les rangs tranchés, les conditions fixes et les charges inégales, il se bâtissait ainsi peu à peu une société imaginaire, dans laquelle tout paraissait simple et coordonné, uniforme, équitable et conforme à la raison. . . . On se désintéressa de ce qui était, pour songer à ce qui pouvait être, et l'on vécut enfin par l'esprit dans cette cité idéale qu'avaient construite les écrivains (Tocqueville, 1986 [1856: 1040).

Obviously, Tocqueville himself considers the faith of the Enlighteners in social planning full of dangers and disillusions. But he does not interpret this faith as irrational. On the contrary, he sees it as the conclusion of a practical syllogism grounded on good reasons: a good society should be grounded on rational planning rather than on traditions, since traditions appear as bad and a-functional. The words and arguments, the utopias built up by the Enlighteners, were adopted quickly because they gave an expression to the diffuse feelings of many people. Significantly, Tocqueville not only does not use the assumption that the popularity of the ideas of the Enlighteners would be due to a contagion effect, he even explicitly discards the assumption when he discusses one point of their doctrine, namely their anti-clerical stance:

La rencontre de plusieurs grands écrivains disposés à nier les vérités de la religion chrétienne ne paraît pas suffisante pour rendre raison d'un événement si extraordinaire; car pourquoi tous ces écrivains, tous, ont-ils portés leur esprit de ce côté plutôt que d'un autre? (Tocqueville, 1986 [1856]: 1042).

The hostility toward the Church is due to the fact that this institution is seen, not only as the product, but as the gate-keeper of Tradition, and hence as one of the main obstacles against the necessary political renovation of the country. The anticlericalist stance of the Enlighteners derives again from a practical syllogism, the premises of which are perceived as analytical or empirical obvious statements. Anticlericalism becomes a collective belief because each ideal-typical citizen in particular has good reasons to give it a positive meaning. The collective belief results from the aggregation of individual beliefs grounded on strong reasons. This explains why it spread so quickly, says Tocqueville. If its diffusion would have resulted essentially from a contagion effect, it would have spread much more slowly.

Tocqueville's analysis uses up to this point the "cognitivist" model (people have strong reasons to believe what they believe, to do what they do). But it contains also an additional part worth being mentioned in the context of this discussion, where Tocqueville suggests that some other people moved toward anticlericalism rather on the basis of utilitarian reasons in the style of the "Rational Choice Model" than on the cognitive reasons evoked up to this point. Anticlericalism was also endorsed by many people, he says, because they found it useful to follow what they perceived to be the dominant mood. In other words: the cost-benefit balance of conformism appeared to them as more favorable than the balance of anti-conformism. In most cases, they kept their Christian faith, since religious conversions rest rarely on opportunistic decisions, but they understood that it was better for them not to raise their voice against the anti-clerical propaganda. On the whole, some had "cognitive" reasons to be anti-clerical, others "utilitarian" reasons not to oppose the anticlerical actions and declarations:

Ceux qui niaient le christianisme élevant la voix et ceux qui croyaient encore faisant silence, il arriva ce qui s'est vu si souvent depuis parmi nous, non seulement en fait de religion, mais en tout autre matière. Les hommes qui conservaient l'ancienne foi craignirent d'être les seuls à lui rester fidèles, et, redoutant plus l'isolement que l'erreur, ils se joignirent à la foule sans penser comme elle. Ce qui n'était encore que le sentiment d'une partie de la nation parut ainsi l'opinion de tous, et sembla dès lors irrésistible aux yeux-mêmes de ceux qui lui donnaient cette fausse apparence (Tocqueville, 1986 [1856]: 1045).

Thus, anticlericalism is analyzed by Tocqueville as an aggregation effect, well in the style of methodological individualism: it makes sense for many, either for cognitive or cost-benefit reasons. Those who are anticlerical for cognitive reasons create a context which pushes the others, if not to endorse their anticlericalism, at least not to oppose it. The combination of the two effects, the cognitive effect that led many people to believe that traditions were bad and that religion, because of its narrow relationship to tradition was also bad, and the cost-benefit effect which pushed those who had no hostility toward religion and even remained faithful to their religious beliefs to refrain from opposing the non-believers, generated finally in the minds of those who were rather indifferent to the question the strong impression that religion belonged to the past. Though Tocqueville's analysis is individualistic, he sketches a dynamic complicated model.

The same methodology inspires all Tocqueville's analyses in the field of the sociology of knowledge. They do not simply assert in a naturalistic fashion the existence of frames; they make understandable why the actors endorse such and such frames (Goffman, 1974). This methodology is responsible for the solidity of his theories. It inspires for instance his analysis of the American religious exceptionalism. Why have Americans kept up a religiosity which has disappeared in European countries? Because they have not the same reasons as the Germans or the French to be hostile to religion. The sectarian character of American religious institutions has prevented them from entering into a competition with political power. They have as a result kept up a number of social functions notably in the field of education, health, and welfare which have been lost in European countries as a consequence of their competition with the state. To Americans, religion is present in institutions that have an existential meaning to them in their everyday life. Moreover, the plurality of the sects has had the consequence that the dogma is not unified. The common denominator of the numerous American protestant sects is, as a result, moral rather than dogmatic. This made the competition of science with American Protestantism much less acute than, say, with French Catholicism or German Lutheranism. Hence, religion was less eroded as an effect of the progress of science in the U.S. than in France or Germany. On the whole, Americans have not the same reasons as Frenchmen or Germans to reject the traditional religious doctrines. Important corollaries can be derived from this theory. I mention just one: that religion is more moral than doctrinal in the USA, explains plausibly why moral conformity is greater in the USA than, say, in France. A survey[11] has shown for instance that Frenchmen tolerate more easily than Americans that positions are filled on the basis of personal relationships rather than on impersonal rules. Current observations show also that the former are more tolerant about corruption and privileges. They seem in other words to have a more tolerant attitude toward the violation of basic moral values. My guess (which would have to be confirmed by adequate research) would be that moral values are stronger in the U.S. because they are more loosely connected to religious dogmas than in France. By contrast, moral values would suffer in France from their connection with religious dogmas, which some people endorse, while many others do not. Again, this is just a guess. I mention it for methodological reasons: it suggests that even macroscopic diffuse cultural differences such as the ones I am evoking here can be explained as the aggregate result of reasons.

5.4 Type 3 Beliefs: Examples from the Sociology of Norms and Values

The example from Marx has shown that normative evaluative beliefs could, as "positive" beliefs, be analyzed as the effect of reasons. This point is so important that I would like to reinforce it by two additional examples that illustrate the fruitfulness of the "cognitivist" model in the important field of norms and values.

C. W. Mills

In the pages of his famous *White Collars*, C. W. Mills (1951) describes women clerks working in a firm organized along Taylor's principles. They all do the same tasks. They are settled in a great room, all have the same desk, the same work environment, etc. Violent conflicts frequently occur on "minor" issues: being seated closer to a source of heat or light, etc. The outside observer would normally consider such conflicts as irrational, eventually as "childish," because he would use implicitly and intuitively the "Rational Choice Model": why such a violent reaction to such a minor issue? As the behavior of the women would appear to him strange in terms of the "Rational Choice Model," he would turn to an "irrational" interpretation: childish behavior. A cognitivist interpretation, however, is much more convincing: the conflicts appear frequently; they are independent of the idiosyncratic characteristics of the persons; the actors within the firm understand the conflicts; they do not consider them "childish"; they do not find them un-understandable; they do not find the reaction out of proportion with its cause, etc. Any irrational explanation fails to account for this set of facts in its entirety.

In fact, the conditions in which the clerks are placed is such that any departure from a strict equality between contribution and retribution can be immediately and easily perceived. Moreover, it is normally treated as intolerable. Because the white collars are all equal, are all devoted to similar tasks, any minor advantage is perceived as an illegitimate privilege. From a utilitarian viewpoint, it matters little to sit a little closer to the window. But, as soon as this advantage to the benefit of X results from a decision of the supervisor, it is perceived by Y, not as a disadvantage to himself, but as an injustice: I am here to get some retribution from my contribution; I am in a situation of social contract with the firm; any unjustified advantage in favor of X, however minor, is a violation of this basic contract and consequently morally intolerable, even if materially of weak relevance. Again, any irrational analysis fails to account for the apparent disproportion between cause and effect, but a "rational choice" analysis is not better off here. An irrational analysis does not account for the fact that the conflict occurs independently of the personal idiosyncrasies. The rational choice analysis fails to account for the disproportion between the importance of the issue and the strength of the reaction.

It should be noted incidentally that, as this example suggests, exchange theory may be seen as a special case of the cognitivist theory proposed here. It makes the point, namely, that many actions and evaluations can be grounded, as in the just evoked example, on considerations of equilibrium in exchange processes. But in other cases, as many other examples in this chapter suggest, other types of reasons will ground actions and evaluations.

The sentiments of justice or injustice, legitimacy or illegitimacy, are rightly called, since they include an affective dimension: nothing is more painful than injustice. But they are at the same time grounded on reasons. Moreover, the strength of the sentiments is proportional to the strength of the reasons: I suffer more from injustice if I am convinced of the strength of my rights. Finally, the "cognitivist" analysis of these sentiments has the advantage of explaining easily why, when I believe that "X is good, legitimate, fair, etc.," I am at the same time normally convinced that the generalized Other should endorse the same statement: my sentiment being grounded on reasons which I see as trans-subjectively valid, other people should have the same sentiment. In its "cognitivist" version, methodological individualism appears as definitely and clearly immunized against the objection of atomism.

French Doctors

I will discuss briefly a final example. A few years ago, two French doctors were condemned in a trial dealing with the transfusion of blood contaminated by the AIDS virus. A petition was signed by numerous doctors and scientists throughout the world, including thirty Nobel Prize winners, making the point that the trial had been unfair and entreating the French president to use his prerogative of presidential pardon, which could effectively be applied in this case, to the effect of extracting the doctors from jail. A strong majority disapproved the proposal. Already before, influential members of the government made clear they would not recommend the pardon. This is an example of these current collective beliefs which the social sciences should be able to explain. The example is taken because the collective belief in this instance appears unusually strong. Can the "Rational Choice Model" explain this social fact satisfactorily? Can the sociological classical "internalization of norms" model explain it? Evidently not, while the "cognitivist model" can: the petition rests on the argument that no one should be condemned until those equally guilty are condemned. If this rule was applied, no one would ever be condemned. As this consequence is unacceptable, so are the principles on which it is grounded. The collective rejection on the petition was grounded neither on the advantage to be derived from this rejection (which advantage?), nor on an aversion against the condemned doctors, but on the reason that it was contradictory to the very existence of a system of justice.

I evoked briefly this last example because it suggests that the "cognitivist model" easily explains the collective moral feelings that are continuously expressed by people in routine political and social life.

5.5. The Need for a Non-Utilitarian Notion of Rationality

In all the examples I have presented, the "cognitivist model" explains, better than its competitors, collective assertive ("X is true, plausible, etc.,") and normative ("X is fair, legitimate, etc") beliefs. "Better" in the sense that the theories derived from this model explain more specifically the observed data with the help of assumptions more acceptable in themselves. They satisfy more easily, in other words, the two types of criteria normally used to appreciate the validity of any scientific theory (Boudon 1997c). These scientific qualities explain that we are still impressed by the theories which I have evoked above of Tocqueville for instance and that we consider them as true. Moreover, the "cognitivist" theories explain much more easily than their competitors a number of "psychological" data, notably the fact that, when we are convinced that "X is good, legitimate, etc.," that "X is true, likely, etc.," we normally feel that the Other should think as we do. Though psychological, these facts cannot be ignored by a good sociological theory. It should also be noted that the "cognitivist" theories are not exposed to the same objections as the irrational theories which evoke heavy conjectural causes to explain beliefs.

As I have mentioned, the "cognitivist" model can be considered a general model of which the "Rational Choice Model" is a particular case. The "Rational Choice Model" can be defined namely as the set of explanations of form: "he did so because he had strong reasons for doing so, these reasons being of the cost-benefit comparison type." The cognitivist model generalizes the "Rational Choice Model" by dropping the final restriction. It can be defined as the set of explanations of form: "he did so because he had strong reasons for doing so; these reasons can be in some circumstances of the cost-benefit comparison type, but in other circumstances of other types." These "other types" include the reasons evoked by Weber when he coined his expression "axiological rationality," but also the cognitive reasons I evoked when talking about "cognitive rationality." The expression "cognitive rationality" includes, say, the reasons of the subjects in the first two examples, but also, generally, the type of reasons which lead scientists to believe in the truth of their scientific theories.

As the example from Tocqueville shows, we definitely need a model, including a definition of rationality, broader than the one used in the "Rational Choice Model" if we want to explain social action. The basic shortcoming of the "Rational Choice Model" resides in the fact that, except in trivial cases, social action rests on beliefs and that the "Rational Choice Model" in its current version has little to say about the question of how to explain collective beliefs.

Finally, I will introduce some remarks to the aim of answering possible objections. Inspired as I am here by Weber's distinction between instrumental and axiological rationality, I assume obviously that rationality can be non-instrumental and hence non-consequential. To those who want rationality to be instrumental and consequential, I will object, citing that Mandeville, Marx, Pareto have demonstrated each with his own words that there is no convincing consequential argument for or against many things which we evaluate positively or negatively. Weber's notion of axiological rationality as distinct from instrumental rationality takes this theorem into account and postulates the further essential point that there is a kind of rationality which is not of the instrumental type and which explains some of our actions or beliefs. To use a very simple example, my indignation at the fact that an old lady I do not know, who is not aware of my reaction and who never will be aware of my very existence, has had her handbag stolen is not grounded on the reason that I would suffer from this fact. Still, my indignation is strong and it is grounded on strong reasons. Possibly, Weber (1922) had simple examples as this one in mind when he created the notion of axiological rationality.[12]

In the examples of the first part of this chapter I introduced the idea that reasons can be wrong and still appear as strong to the actor, so strong that he has the impression that other people should have the same view as he does. This idea is less paradoxical than it appears as soon as we think of the fact that strong-wrong reasons are typical of scientific beliefs. Pareto (1935) has said that the history of science is a churchyard of many ideas that in their time were held as true for very strong reasons. Thus, the Aristotelian physicists had strong reasons for believing that when a ship continues sliding after the wind has fallen, it is because the ship produced whirlwinds that pushed it from behind. They devised this explanation because they thought that any move of a physical object was due to a force. As they observed that the ship went on moving after the wind had fallen, they tried to identify the force responsible for this move. It took time before it was discovered that the apparently innocent principle "no move without a force causing it" was inadequate in spite of its apparent obviousness, and that it had to be made more precise: "no move *of a body at rest* without a force causing it, no rest *of a body in motion without a force stopping it.*" The new formulation implies that no force is responsible for keeping the ship moving. In the same way, many scientists had strong reasons to believe in phlogiston or ether.

The reasons of the Aristotelian physicists were both strong and wrong, given the cognitive context in which they were located. The earlier example of the nurses is exactly of the same nature: given the cognitive context, they had strong (though wrong) reasons for believing in the existence of a causal relationship between symptom and disease.

This discussion leads me to an additional remark, which would require long development, namely that the criteria which make a set of reasons good are hard to define absolutely and should rather be defined relatively. Thus, one set of reasons may be better than another because the latter includes a statement incompatible with some data, or because it leads to "highly conjectural" notions (as in the case of the Aristotelian turmoils). But a "highly conjectural" statement can be good as long as I have not found a set of reasons definitely better that could eliminate it. Again, the history of science can be evoked here to suggest that we should not expect a too rigid definition of these criteria. For a while, those who believed in phlogiston and those who did not had strong reasons for believing what they believed. The statement "those who do not believe in phlogiston are right" was made possible only after the discussion was extended to the point where one of the systems of reasons in competition became so immune against doubts and objections that it dominated the other and where it could be concluded that phlogiston was a mere fiction that could be forgotten.

On the whole, scientific discussions are a good illustration of rationality as I understand it here. In this chapter I have attempted to suggest that the type of rationality which we observe in scientific discussions is not different in nature (even though it can obviously be different in degree) from the one we find at work in ordinary life, when people mobilize their cognitive resources to find the—in their view—the best possible answer to the host of questions, either positive or normative, that confront them in everyday life.

Notes

1. Published as "The Cognitivist Model: A Generalized 'Rational Choice Model,'" *Rationality and Society*, 1996, 8, 2: 123–150.
2. This article summarizes for one part ideas I have developed elsewhere (Boudon 1993). But it goes what I believe to be an important step further in the sense that it considers normative beliefs beside positive beliefs. This extension was the main purpose of another recent work. Also, I have greatly benefited from the critics addressed to the two books, so that several points are presented in a more satisfactory fashion in the present paper.
3. For a sociobiological evolutionary explanation of moral beliefs, see Ruse (1993).
4. I use the word "cognitivist" because I failed to find a better one. I am aware it can cause confusion, since it qualifies occasionally the models developing a naturalistic view of the "frames" of thinking. "Rationalist" would be possible, but it would expose one to still more confusion.
5. Lévy-Bruhl has developed a model for the explanation of beliefs which can be held as the prototype of many modern models, though he is unfairly held as obsolete.
6. *The Economist*, 4 July 1992: 81–82.
7. Popper's falsification theory is mute on this case where a theory is theoretically but not practically falsifiable.
8. The discussion I present here of this study is different from my discussion in Boudon (1989).
9. Shweder, as Tversky, assumes that "ordinary" thinking follows specific rules, "frames," etc. The "cognitivist" model I present assumes, on the contrary, the continuity of ordinary and scientific knowledge. The two try to disentangle the complexity of the situations they meet with the help of the most solid conjectures they can form, given notably their cognitive resources.
10. I lean here on a suggestion in Elster (1985: ch. 8).
11. *The Economist*, 25 August 1995: 49.
12. For a more precise discussion of axiological rationality, see Boudon (1995b).

6

The Cognitivist Model Applied to the Analysis of the Feelings of Justice[1]

6.1. Philosophy and Sociology on Axiological Feelings

Feelings of justice and more generally axiological feelings are perhaps the most important social phenomena and the least mastered scientifically. One reason for this unsatisfactory situation is that theories of justice are, for the most part, philosophical. Their aim, in other words, is mainly normative: it is to determine what is good or bad, right or wrong, or what should be done, rather than to explain why people see some state of affairs as good or bad, right or wrong, or as congruent with what should or should not be done. A philosophical axiological theory is obviously expected to be congruent with people's axiological feelings, but how far it should be congruent remains unclear. Kant (1797) considered that lying can never be treated as being good, against B. Constant's view, that lying can, in some circumstances, be normally perceived by people as a good thing. Such a fact would disqualify a descriptive theory or at least be considered incompatible with it, while it is unclear whether it disqualifies a prescriptive one.

Empirical sociological research on justice and generally axiological feelings, on the other hand, seems often eager rather to collect data on people's axiological feelings than to explain them.[2] Thus, Frohlich and Oppenheimer (1992) conducted an original experiment with the objective of checking whether people endorse some leading theories of justice, such as Rawls's (1971; 1993) or Harsanyi's (1977). They found that people are, for the most part, neither Rawlsian nor

Harsanyian: an interesting finding. But they made little effort to explain this fact, nor to construct an alternative theory aimed at reproducing people's justice feelings. This is surprising, since they hold Rawls's or Harsanyi's theories explicitly as explanatory theories, that is, as theories aimed at reproducing people's actual justice feelings.

But the unsatisfactory state of the social scientific art about axiological feelings is due mainly to the fact that the available theories of justice and, more generally, of axiological feelings are themselves unsatisfactory. To take major examples: Kant's theory is contradicted by the already mentioned fact that people would normally consider it good for a prisoner to lie for instance when a Gestapo officer asks him to deliver the names of his compatriots. The utilitarian theory is contradicted by the fact, well seen notably by Durkheim (1979 [1912]), that people can be genuinely altruistic. Rawls's theory is contradicted by the mentioned experiment. Habermas's "communicative" theory (1981) is contradicted by the fact that pure and perfect communication can generate false as well as true theories, as the history of science shows; why would then "communicative rationality" be immunized against errors as far as normative questions are concerned? To evoke a final example, the relativistic theory for which all axiological feelings are local ("vérité en deça des Pyrénées, erreur au-delà," wrote Pascal (1977 [1670]), is contradicted by the existence of axiological universals: stealing is held everywhere as bad in principle and tolerated only in specific circumstances. Corruption is treated as bad in principle by all cultures.

6.2. A Cognitivist Theory of Axiological Feelings

My claim in this chapter is that axiological feelings and justice feelings, in particular, can be more satisfactorily explained if we start from an intuition we see as contained in Weber's notion of "axiological rationality" (Weber, 1922).

Many interpretations of this notion have been given. In general, it is held as controversial. Thus, Lukes (1967: notably 259–60) contends that it is meaningless, while Sukale (1995), one of the best contemporary commentators of Weber, sees the concept as misleading ("irreführend").[3] To him, as to Lukes, rationality and instrumental rationality are synonymous. Hence, they reject the very notion of a type of rationality which would not be instrumental. But Weber uses the distinction repeatedly. Thus, Lukes's or Sukale's rejection of "axiological rationality" as a genuine form of rationality is possibly rather a projection of the dominant contemporary definition of rationality than a convincing interpretation of Weber's notion. This skeptical interpretation of Weber's "axiological rationality" is presumably reinforced by the fact that Weber is often described as supporting a "decisionist" theory of values, namely a theory according to which ultimate values cannot be grounded. But if values were endorsed without ground by social actors, how could their behavior be *understandable*? How could Weber advertise a "comprehensive" sociology? The ultimate values cannot be grounded for the reason that, if they could, they should be grounded on other values and thus would not be ultimate. But this trivial statement does not lead to the conclusion that people would endorse values without ground.

My own proposal is to take the notion of axiological rationality seriously, rather than to introduce the debatable conjecture that Weber would have committed a *lapsus calami*, so to say.

If so, what does the notion mean? One can start from the remark that rationality is currently used as a major concept by two disciplines, namely economics and philosophy of science. To economists, rationality means instrumental rationality, in other words: adequation between means and ends. To historians and philosophers of science, being rational has an entirely different meaning: I am rational if, to the best of my knowledge, I endorse a stronger rather than a weaker theory. Thus, it became irrational to believe that the earth is flat once the proofs had accumulated showing that it is round. Let us call this form of rationality "cognitive."

Radnitzky (1987) has proposed to build a bridge between these two basic meanings of the notion of "rationality": it became irrational to believe that the earth is flat from the moment when it became more difficult, in other words more *costly*, to defend this theory than to accept its competitor. But the costs of defending an obsolete theory T are higher than the costs of defending an alternative theory T' if the latter explains more easily observed phenomena than T. Without knowing and understanding the arguments used by T and T' to explain, say, why the sails of a ship disappear at the horizon after the ship itself, I cannot evaluate the *costs* of endorsing respectively T and T'. Thus, the reduction proposed by Radnitzky of cognitive to instrumental rationality appears as artificial. What matters is that T' explains more convincingly a number of phenomena P, P', P'', etc., than T. Little is gained by translating "T' explains more convincingly . . . " into "T' explains in a less costly fashion." In other words, "cognitive rationality" (the type of rationality that historians and philosophers of science refer to) cannot, except artificially, be reduced to "instrumental rationality."

A more natural bridge relates "cognitive" and "instrumental" rationality, though it retains the distinction between the two types of rationality. When an actor follows a goal G, he can be convinced that M is an adequate mean because a solid theory T shows that G can be reached via M. The actor believes T because he is "cognitively" rational; and, as he uses M in order to reach G, he is, moreover, "instrumentally" rational.

My contention in this essay is that Weber had this distinction in mind when he coined the expression "axiological rationality." In other words, I interpret this notion as indicating that what I call here "cognitive rationality" can be applied, not only to descriptive, but to prescriptive questions; not only to representational, but to axiological questions.

But I will leave aside the question of whether my interpretation of Weber is correct: this point has been discussed elsewhere (Boudon, 1997a; Boudon 1997c). My aim is rather to develop a theory of axiological feelings in general and justice feelings in particular starting from this interpretation. I propose to call this theory "cognitivist." It rests on three postulates. First, that theories can be built on axiological as well as descriptive questions; that, moreover, prescriptive theories can, as descriptive ones, be stronger or weaker. Second, that people tend to choose the theory they see as stronger. Third, that they tend to endorse a value statement and to experience the feeling that "X is good, bad, legitimate, fair, etc.," when it appears to them—more or less vaguely though—as grounded on strong reasons. My claim is that this theory is useful to explain axiological feelings generally and justice feelings in particular, as they are observed by sociological and psychological empirical research.

It is often contended that axiological theories are basically different from descriptive ones, because *ought* cannot be drawn from *is*. This is true. Still, prescriptive arguments can be evaluated: some prescriptive arguments are clearly weaker or stronger than others. Thus, to take a trivial example, under general conditions, people prefer driving a car faster rather than slower in city traffic, and for this reason consider traffic lights as a "good" (though unpleasant) thing. The value statement "traffic lights are a *good* thing" is the conclusion of a strong argument grounded on the empirical undebatable statement that traffic is more fluid with traffic lights than without. Though simple, this example is typical of many normative arguments. It shows that a normative argument can be as convincing as a descriptive one. Whether A is a cause of B is a non-normative question. Now I will accept the statement "A is a cause of B" if it is a consequence of a strong argument. If, moreover, I prefer B to non B, A is demonstrated to be a "good" thing for me. If all prefer B, A is demonstrated to be a good thing for all. Thus, the gap between *ought* and *is* exists undoubtedly. But when axiological statements can be interpreted consequentially, that is, when "A is good" means "A leads to consequences considered as good by people," their validity can be demonstrated as solidly as the validity of descriptive statements. As "A leads to consequences considered as good by people" can be translated into "A is an appropriate means to reach a state of affairs considered as good by people," the argument can be called instrumental as well as consequential.

However, as well seen by Weber, axiological statements cannot always be considered as the conclusion of consequential arguments. By creating his notion of "axiological rationality," Weber wanted possibly to insist on the point that people may have in some circumstances strong reasons for believing that "A is good, bad, legitimate, illegitimate, fair, unfair, etc.," without these reasons belonging to the instrumental-consequential category. My contention is that by so doing he introduced a powerful idea, crucial to my understanding of axiological feelings and of justice feelings in particular.

To summarize, I would define a feeling or a statement as "axiologically rational" if people would consider it as grounded on strong arguments which *can be* but are not necessarily of the consequential-instrumental type. I propose, in other words, to define axiological rationality as a form of cognitive rationality characterized by the fact that it deals with arguments where at least one statement is axiological, since *ought* cannot be derived from *is*, or, more precisely, since an *ought*-statement cannot be exclusively derived from *is*-statements.

While Weber was probably the first author to suggest conceptualizing the notion of "axiological rationality" as we understand it, he is not the first to use it.

This reference to Weber should not be misunderstood. By associating "axiological rationality" and "cognitive rationality" and making the latter a species of the former, I introduce a strong thesis, not only as far as the interpretation of Weber is concerned, but still more as regards the theory of moral feelings. It proposes actually to reorient, to a large extent, sociological theorizing about justice feelings. I will concentrate on the defense and illustration of the thesis and will treat only marginally important questions, such as the question as to whether individual justice feelings set limits to macro justice (see for instance, Brickman et al., 1981), which is considered only briefly in my section on Rawls, leaving entirely aside other interesting questions which do not at all belong to the scope of this chapter. Thus, my cognitive theory states that subjects have the feeling that "X is fair" if the statement is perceived by them as derived from a system of arguments they consider as strong. I will not consider here in general terms how subjects reach the conclusion, though I give some hints on this point in my discussion of Bazerman. [4]

6.3. Smith's Example

An example drawn from Adam Smith (1976 [1776])—but other examples could be found—can illustrate concretely Weber's notion of "axiological rationality," as I interpret it.

In his *Wealth of Nations*, Smith (1976 [1776]) wonders why his fellowmen have the collective feeling that miners should definitely be paid more than soldiers. Why this collective agreement on the value statement "miners should be paid more than soldiers"?

His answer consists in showing that this feeling is grounded on strong reasons, which can be reconstructed in the following fashion:

- A salary is the retribution of a contribution.
- To equal contributions should correspond equal retributions.
- Several components enter into the value of a contribution: the investment required to produce the type of competence required to produce the contribution, the risks involved in the realization of the contribution, etc.
  - The investment is comparable in the case of the miner and of the soldier. It takes namely about as much time and effort to train a soldier as a miner. The two jobs are characterized by similar risks. The two cases include above all the risk of death.
- Nonetheless, there are important differences between the two types of jobs. The soldier serves a function that is central in any society. He

contributes to preserving the identity and the very existence of the nation. The miner fulfills by contrast an economic activity, among others. His function is no more crucial to society than, say, the function fulfilled by textile workers.

- This difference, and others, results in the consequence that the death of the two men has a different social meaning. The miner's death will be identified as an accident, the death of the soldier on the battlefield as a sacrifice.
- Because of this difference in the social meaning of their respective activities, the soldier should be entitled to symbolic rewards, in terms of moral prestige, symbolic distinctions, funeral honors in case of death on the battlefield, etc.
- For symmetric reasons, the miner is not entitled to the same symbolic rewards.
- As the contribution of the two categories, notably in terms of risk and investment, is the same, the equilibrium between contribution and retribution can only be restored by making the salaries of the miners higher.
- This system of reasons is responsible for our *feeling* that the miner *should* be paid a higher amount than the soldier.

6.4. Lessons from Smith's Example

The approach used by Smith could be easily illustrated by examples taken from modern writers. A contemporary theorist of ethics, M. Walzer (1983), proposes several analyses of our moral sentiments similar to Smith's. Why do we consider conscription a legitimate recruitment method in the case of soldiers but not of miners, he asks? The answer is again that the function of the former, but not of the latter, is vital. If conscription could be applied to miners, it could be applied to any and eventually to all kinds of activities, so that it would lead to a political regime incompatible with the principles of democracy. In the same fashion, it is easily accepted that soldiers are used as garbage collectors to meet situations of emergency. But it would be considered illegitimate to use them to fulfill such tasks in normal situations. In these examples, as in Smith's example, the collective moral feelings are grounded on solid reasons. These reasons can be called "trans-subjective" since they would likely be considered as strong by most people.

Hence, Smith's analysis proposes implicitly a general theory of axiological feelings and of feelings of fairness in particular. His analysis suggests to the consideration that axiological feelings are grounded on reasons and that these reasons are not necessarily instrumental.

Smith offers here, not an "instrumentally rational," namely, but rather a "cognitively rational" explanation of the collective feeling he examines: "X (that miners are paid more than soldiers) is fair." The feeling that "X is fair" is collective and strong because it is grounded on strong reasons in individual minds. Thus, the collective feeling that "X is fair," though a *feeling*, is not a feeling in the personal idiosyncratic sense of the word. It illustrates rather a type of feeling that a social actor cannot experience without having at the same time the conviction that everybody would and should feel like him.

The connection between the feeling "X is fair" and the feeling that all should judge so becomes clear as soon as one supposes, as Smith does here, implicitly, that we experience this feeling as a consequence of strong reasons. In other words, he assumes that feelings of the type "X is fair, legitimate, etc., "are the effects of reasons, exactly as feelings of the type "Y is true." Prescriptive statements as descriptive ones are produced by reasons. Consequently, I expect naturally the "generalized Other" in Mead's sense to judge (Mead, 1934), as I do myself, that "X is fair" exactly as I expect him to judge that "Y is true" if I do so.

The individual statements used in Smith's argument, as I reconstruct it, belong to several types. But all have in common that they can be easily accepted.

Some of these statements are empirical. For instance: it takes as long to train a soldier as a miner; both occupations are exposed to deadly risks. These statements are undebatable. Some of the statements derive from "sociological theory": reinforcing the security of a nation is a central social function; mining is rather a particular economic function. Classical sociological functional theory, as developed after Smith, says that retribution should be higher, the more central the function; exchange theory says that people expect retributions to reflect contributions. These statements can hardly be rejected. Some statements are rather sociological observations: death is not perceived as having the same meaning when it is the effect of an accident rather than that of self-sacrifice; symbolic rewards can be used to reward the latter but not to compensate the former, etc. Such statements can also be easily accepted.

On the whole, it can be easily noted that all the individual statements used in Smith's argument are acceptable. For this reason, the conclusion "X is fair" is normally perceived by people as strong. In other words, Smith suggests a "cognitivist" theory in my sense of the collective axiological feeling "X is fair."

Moreover, it should be noted that the *consequences* of paying the miners more than the soldiers are not evoked in Smith's analysis with the exception of the fact that doing so is likely to generate public approval. Thus, the reasons grounding the statement "X is fair" are not consequential, except indirectly. In other words, the rationality inspiring the belief in the statement "X is fair" is not instrumental but axiological: it is rational to pay miners more, not because of the eventual consequences resulting from paying them more, but because paying them more is congruent with strong principles, such as the principle of equality between contribution and retribution.

That Smith's analysis is axiological rather than instrumental-consequential is worth being stressed, since it is extracted from a book generally considered not only as grounded on the utilitarian paradigm but as grounding this paradigm, in which rationality is defined as instrumental-consequential.

Obviously, Smith does not assume and need not assume that the reasons explaining the feeling "X is fair" are explicitly and clearly present in the head of all, but he assumes visibly that they are present in an intuitive fashion.

6.5. Application of the Model to Two Examples

The "cognitivist model" can build a bridge between theory and empirical studies on axiological and, particularly, justice feelings more easily than other models. Two examples will show that, with the help of this model, the interpretation of the findings from empirical studies can be made clearer, while the model suggests at the same time more efficient observation—and research procedures.

The Frohlich-Oppenheimer Study

The first example was already alluded to (Frohlich, Oppenheimer, 1992): the Frohlich-Oppenheimer study aimed at determining whether Rawls's and Harsanyi's theories of justice are able to reproduce the actual feelings of people as to whether some distribution of goods is fair or not. A sample was asked to choose a fictitious income distribution among a set of distributions. We need not describe the ingenious experimental procedure used by the authors of the study. It suffices to say that the set of distributions was built in such a fashion that the choice of a given distribution among those that were proposed allowed them to infer which one of four principles the subjects had in mind when they made their selection. The four principles were as follows:

- The principle drawn from Harsanyi's utilitarian theory (Harsanyi, 1955), namely: select the distribution with maximum mean.
- The "difference principle" drawn from Rawls's theory of justice: select the distribution maximizing the floor income.
- The principle: maximize the mean and define a minimum floor. By contrast with the "difference principle" derived from Rawls's theory, the principle requires, not that the value of the floor is maximum, but that it should not fall under a given value.
- The principle: make the mean as high as possible, provided the variance does not exceed a given value.

The two first principles are grounded on well-known theories. The third is not properly drawn from a formally developed theory of justice, but it reflects the distribution policy generally enforced by political authorities in most democratic countries. The fourth is drawn from sociological functionalist theories. Well before Rawls, sociological theorists had raised the question as to under which conditions inequalities are held acceptable or not by people. The answer of functionalist theorists is that inequalities tend to be accepted as long as they are perceived by people as having a function. They should, in other words, be limited to the amount necessary to fulfill this function. Thus, if we suppose that above a certain difference between the best and the worst paid, the worst paid would be demotivated, a degree of inequality above this threshold would be too high; it would be dysfunctional with regard to the system. In the same way, if, below a certain difference, the best paid would be demotivated, this other threshold should not be overstepped. The Frohlich-Oppenheimer study introduces the assumption that respondents having in mind a theory of justice more or less inspired from these functionalist ideas, should pay attention to the standard deviation of the distributions they are proposed.

Rawls's assumption on the "veil of ignorance" was simulated in the experiment by the fact that the subjects were told they would be located in random fashion, once their choice is made, into one of the income classes and that they would get a reward, the amount of which being proportional to the income of the class. Thus, their choice would affect their reward. But their judgment as to which distribution is fairest could be held as unprejudiced in the sense that it could not be inspired by their interests, since they did not know whether they would belong to the highest, to the lowest, or to one of the intermediary classes of the proposed distributions.

The study has been conducted on a sample of Americans and on a sample of Poles. It is illuminating for this discussion. It shows, namely, that people reject the Rawlsian principles of justice. In other words, Rawls's theory cannot be held as a valid reconstruction of the axiological feelings of people about the distribution of primary goods. By far the most frequent choice of the respondents was to maximize the mean and to define a minimum income. Harsanyi's principle (maximization of the mean without any constraints on floor and deviation) comes next, but far behind; the maximization of the mean with a constraint on deviation is still more seldom retained. On eighty-one experimental groups, the principles were chosen precisely with the following frequencies:

- Constraint on the floor and maximization of the mean: 77, 8 percent.
- Maximization of the mean: 12, 3 percent.
- Maximization of the mean and constraint on the deviation: 8, 64 percent.
- Difference principle (Rawls): 1, 23 percent.

Another interesting finding from the experimental study should be noted: that the same structure of answers characterizes the American and the Pole samples. In the two cases, the first choice is by far much more frequent than the three others.

Cognitivist Interpretation of the Frohlich-Oppenheimer Study. When, as here, the distribution of answers is highly structured, one can suppose that strong causes are responsible for the distribution. Moreover, when the structure is similar from one cultural context to another, it can be assumed that these causes are trans-contextual. Finally, it can be supposed that the high structuration of answers and their trans-contextuality is produced by strong reasons.

The study proposes to the respondents a very abstract decision-making situation. They have to answer the question of whether one distribution is fairer than the others. They have no information as to how the income inequalities have been generated, and they know nothing about the occupations of the population. The discussions which were conducted with the respondents have shown that they accept the idea that income inequalities should reflect functional inequalities: I am entitled to get a higher income if the tasks I am supposed to fulfill given my occupational role are functionally more important. But given the context of the experiment, they could not answer the question of whether or not the income distributions reflected functional inequalities: they missed the relevant information which would have been necessary to make the question meaningful. They probably started from questions they could answer: is it a legitimate goal for a government to try to make the mean of an income distribution as high as possible? They answered obviously yes to this question. Is it a good thing for a government to try to make the standard deviation lower? With the functional theory in mind, it is easily checked that trying to make the deviation lower can be dysfunctional and have the effect of making the mean lower. It is not implausible to accept the assumption that the respondents endorse some rough version of the functional theory. But, as they do not know whether the inequalities reflected by the distributions are functional or not, the most prudent assumption open to them is that they are and, consequently, to draw the conclusion that an effort to reduce the standard deviation can be dangerous. On the whole, given the cognitive conditions of the experiment, an attractive answer is to reject any constraint as far as the standard deviation of the distribution is concerned. On the other hand, it is a good thing to introduce a constraint on the floor, since it is normally expected of government that it try to install some protection against the hazards of life to which citizens are exposed. Hence, the fact that a constraint on the floor is widely accepted by the respondents. On the whole, the solution most widely chosen is: maximize the mean, attempt to provide a minimum income, and do not attempt to minimize standard deviation since it is produced by multiple unknown mechanisms and since it can be counterproductive to lower it.

In other words, the high structuration of the respondents' answers can be analyzed as the effect of strong reasons. It can be noted, incidentally, that the same strong reasons explain presumably that actual governments make, more or less generally though implicitly, the same choice as the respondents. They usually consider it good to take the decisions likely to increase the mean of the income distribution, in other words, to enhance growth. On the other hand, most governments consider that people should be provided insurance against the hazards of life: even the less "social" governments care about poverty and about making the proportion of the poor as low as possible. All are concerned, moreover—though, of course, to various degrees—that no one, ideally at least, be "excluded" from society. Finally, all recognize that inequalities are the product of complex micro-phenomena, that they are partly functional, that it is impossible to determine what the ideal standard deviation of income distribution should be, etc. They also consider that a lower standard deviation is not necessarily better. For these reasons, most governments are prudent in this respect. Their efforts to reduce the standard deviation of incomes are, in many cases, marginal when they are not merely symbolic.

Governments, as people, have most likely a more or less diffuse minimal philosophy about income distribution. This philosophy includes a set of arguments which they consider as strong. From these arguments, they draw conclusions as to whether it is good or not to try to make the standard deviation as low as possible, the mean as high as possible, etc.

Reciprocally, the strong rejection of Rawls's difference principle by governments as well as by the samples in the considered experiment is due to the fact that there are strong reasons to reject it: notably, it is impossible to determine effectively the threshold under which a reduction of the standard deviation of income distribution would have a negative effect on its mean.

It should be added that the system of reasons at work in the answers of the respondents would have plausibly been different if the experimental conditions had been different. Suppose, for instance, that the distributions proposed to the attention of the respondents would have been presented as reflecting, not fictitious, unidentified "societies," but the distributions of salaries in organizations, that the organizations would have been described as similar to one another, and that information would have been given to the respondents on the types of occupations and functions corresponding to the income classes. In that case, the respondents would probably have considered the standard deviation and tried to see whether it reflected functional inequalities. While it is impossible to determine what the good standard deviation would be as far as the general society is concerned, it would not be impossible in the case of an organization. At any rate, with the cognitivist model in mind, it would be possible to build a design of observation where the contextual fictitious conditions and the set of distributions would be systematically modified to the effect of check-ing assumptions on the systems of reasons leading the respondents to the choice of such and such principle.

The Example of Bazerman's Study

Let us consider as a second illustration of the interest of the "cog-nitivist" model for empirical research on axiological feelings Bazerman's illuminating study on collective negotiations (Bazerman, 1985). The methodology of Bazerman's study is rather complex, but derives from simple ideas. Its aim was to study a set of arbitrarial decisions in the context of a collective negotiation. The study involved sixty-nine arbitrators to whom twenty-five hypothetical disputes were submitted.

To illustrate, one of the cases submitted is as follows:

In a town with 102,000 people, workers with skills and backgrounds similar to the employees of a radio and broadcasting company were paid $8.31 per hour, while the national wage for this industry was $8.23 per hour. The financial outlook for this company is fair in light of the 11 percent inflation rate. The present average wage for this company's union is $8.44 per hour. Contract negotiations have reached an impasse. Both sides, however, have agreed to submit final offers to you, the arbitrator, and to be bound by your decision for the period of one year. Comparable pay increases from collective bargaining agree-ments in the industry are running about 8 percent this year. Management's final offer is $8.56 (a 1.4 percent increase), while the union's final offer is $ 9.55 (a 13.2 percent increase) (Bazerman, 1985: 564).

Bazerman introduced the assumption that the decisions of the arbi-trators should be inspired by a number of variables: actual salaries (X1), increase of salaries in the branch as decided on the basis of a collective negotiation (X2), economic health of the fictitious corpora-tion (X3), salaries in the environment (X4), salaries in the industrial branch (X5), proposals of the management (X6), proposals of the unions (X7). I leave aside the measurement problems raised by these variables, which are of no interest for my purpose. The data analysis has consisted essentially in a regression analysis of the arbitrarial decisions on these independent variables, with the objective of determining the relative weight of variables X1 through X7 on the decisions.

The main questions raised by Bazerman were to evaluate the convergence of the decisions and to determine the principles inspiring them. He retained three classical principles of justice: absolute equity (to each according to his contribution); the principle of equality, not in its Rawlsian ("difference principle") but in its traditional version (retributions equal for all); the principle of relative equity (increase of salaries equal for each according to his contribution).

Bazerman then introduced assumptions as to the meaning of the independent variables as indicators of the principle implicitly selected by the decisions. He interpreted three of the variables as indicators of the importance the arbitrators grant to the principle of absolute equity: the rate of inflation, the economic health of the firm, and the difference between local and national salaries for the same qualification. The health of the firm has for instance been retained because taking it into account in the decision means applying the principle: "to equal capacity, equal contribution." The weight of the differences between the unions' and the management's proposals and the average level of salaries in the branch are interpreted as reflecting the importance given to the equality principle by the arbitrators. The importance of the relative equity principle is measured through the weight given by the judges to the discrepancy between the salaries in the firm they are supposed to be concerned with and the salaries at the national level (Tversky et al., 1982). It is measured by the weight given to actual salaries, to the health of the firm, and to the average increase of salaries in the branch.

The hypothesized relations between the indicators and the principles of justice mobilized in the decisions could be discussed, but I am not concerned here with this aspect of Bazerman's study. My main concern is that one can gain a more interesting and probably more valid interpretation of the findings if one supposes, not simply that the judges mobilize principles they would have internalized under the effect of unknown causes, but that they reached their decisions by grounding them, more or less consciously, on systems of arguments including eventually the principles retained by Bazerman, among many other arguments.

Interpretation of Bazerman's Study. Particularly striking among the findings of this study is the fact that the answers appear as statistically highly structured: firstly, among the seven independent variables, three (X1, X2, and X3) account for 52 percent of the variance; secondly, the proposals of management and the unions account for a small part of the variance. My contention is that these findings (as well as further findings to be considered below) can be satisfactorily interpreted if it is assumed that the judges have had in mind a sequence of arguments such as the following:

- A decision has to be better than alternative possible decisions.
- The best decision is the outcome of the application of adequate principles to a situation of which the relevant parameters are taken into consideration.
- Since it is advisable to start from the assumption that, objectively, the best decision has to be found, the proposals of unions and management can be given secondary importance.
- The company I am concerned with is a system whose aim is to produce some goods or service. The workers are there to get a salary as the counterpart of their contribution to production.
- Hence workers expect normally that their salaries reflect their contributions. Salaries are fair, in other words, to the extent that they are determined in consideration of the equity principle (retribution should reflect contribution).
- The principle of equality, even in its Rawlsian version, is irrelevant in the considered situation.
- A good decision is a decision which can be applied and is likely to be applied because it is perceived as legitimate.
- The health of the company is a good indicator as to whether a decision to the effect of increasing salaries can effectively be applied.
- Imposing an excessive increase of salaries on a company in bad economic condition can generate negative effects (the firing of workers, and a decrease of salaries in the long run, eventually threatening to the very existence of the company).
- The criteria leading to the conclusion that salaries are fair or unfair must be perceived as legitimate.
- The salaries of the workers of a firm can be compared either to the salaries of workers with similar qualifications in the workplace or to the salaries of other workers in the branch.
- The first comparison is more "sociological": it supposes that the workers in a company tend to compare their own situation with the situation of workers they are likely to meet in their social environment. This comparison uses, in other words, a "psychological reference group theory" approach.
- The second comparison is more "formalist": it supposes that the workers in a firm tend to compare their own situation with the situation of

workers employed in the same type of job. Even though they are un-likely to meet them, they can be informed on the subject through unions and other media and use a "formalist reference group theory" approach.
- The two types of comparison are possible, likely, and legitimate. Both are equally valid conjectures.
- So the choice of comparison is open.
- In the cases proposed to the arbitrators, the retributions to equal qualifi-cations or types of jobs are presented as unequal.
- This inequality can be interpreted in different fashions. The inequality can be legitimate, as this would be the case for instance if it were due to the fact that in a company where the salaries are higher, the workers, other things being equal, would on the average have been employed a longer time by the firm. In this case, it should not be proposed to reduce the inequality.
- So it can be unfair to apply the principle of absolute equity rather than the relative equity principle.
- Absolute equity can be preferred to relative equity under two condi-tions: if information is available on the causes of inequality between the firms and if it turns out that it is illegitimate.
- If not, relative equity should be preferred to absolute equity.
- With imperfect information on the causes of inequality, applying the principle of absolute equity can be unfair and, moreover, can possibly generate undesirable effects.
- Absolute and relative equity are two versions of the same theory of justice. The choice between them should be guided by the available information on the causes of inequalities.

If it is assumed that this system of arguments can likely be put into the mind of the ideal-typical arbitrator, it becomes easier, not only to understand their decisions, but also to explain the most striking fea-tures of the statistical distribution of their decisions. One both better understands and explains why they seldom care about the proposals of management and the unions. Why, namely, should they be taken into account, if one can assume that there is an objectively best decision that any unprejudiced person should be able to identify? The hypoth-esized system of arguments explains also that relative equity appears empirically as the most frequently chosen principle. This principle is congruent both with the nature of the firm (it should reward the work-ers proportionally to their contributions) and with the imperfect and exclusively synchronic character of the information available to the arbitrators. Arbitrators have in summary strong reasons to choose this principle of justice in the situation with which they are confronted.

Each of the arguments in this hypothetical argumentative system appears effectively as easily acceptable.

The same system can also explain easily the other major finding of Bazerman's study, namely, that three major types of decisions have been made by the arbitrators, the three groups being of unequal size.

The first group, the more important, includes the arbitrators that can be supposed to have reasoned along the previous system of arguments. They do not take into account the proposals of management and unions. They choose a formal "group of reference" rather than a "psychological" one, since the two choices can be made. They are aware of the fact that a good decision should be applicable and care about the health of the company. They are conscious of the fact that they know little on the causes of interfirm inequalities. They choose consequently the relative equity principle with the branch as "reference group."

The second group, less important in number, differs from the first by the fact that it chooses the "psychological" rather than the "formal" reference group. It assumes, in other words, that the ideal-typical worker is more sensitive to the inequalities with the reference workers he is likely to meet than with the workers belonging to the same branch but whom he is unlikely to know personally and that, to him, exist so to speak in an abstract mode, as statistical beings. To which extent do the arbitrators of the two groups project their own experiences in their choice? It is clearly impossible to tell, given the available data. The fact that the first assumption is more frequent can possibly be explained by the fact that it is simpler, or perhaps because the arbitrators have had more juridical than sociological or psychological training. The first assumption can more easily appear to them as treating people in a universalistic fashion. As to the choice between absolute and relative equity, it is also open to a certain extent. But, given the available information, preferring the latter is more prudent. Applying the principle of absolute equity would possibly be more fair, but it can also be unfair and bad from a consequential viewpoint. The greater popularity of relative equity is at any rate more satisfactorily explained in the frame of the cognitivist model than with the notion of "anchored equity," which proposes a mere word to explain the preference for relative equity when it is observed.

The third group, the smallest, chooses a compromise between the proposals of management and those of the unions. They also possibly have in mind the system of arguments that I have just presented. But they may object that the views developed by the actors themselves should be taken into consideration since, though they can be self-interested, they are also almost certainly inspired by a familiarity with the field which outside observers cannot equal. Nothing prevents the men from management and unions having in mind the above arguments, even if their views are biased by the consideration of their own interests. Being confident to those "who know" is a possible strategy in a situation where one has the impression that much relevant information is missing. Besides being simple, this third type of solution has the advantage of being able to eliminate the biases introduced by the interests of the two parties by proposing a solution located halfway between the proposals of management and the unions. This solution entails several types of costs, however. It is mechanical and lazy. It contradicts the rules defining the role of the arbitrator. Moreover, in spite of the fact that it appears as prudent, it supposes much: that the proposals of the two parties are likely biased to the same extent for instance. Briefly, there are strong reasons to choose this third solution, but also strong reasons to prefer the two other main solutions.

The cognitivist interpretation I have just proposed explains Bazerman's main findings: the existence of three groups of decisions, the unequal size of the three groups, the data about the proportion of variance explained by the independent variables, and notably the strong difference in the weight of the independent variables. The group largest in number starts from the assumptions: that they can decide by themselves, that there is a best decision given the constraints, that the information is leaky, and that the most prudent hypotheses are welcome in such a situation. Thus, the cognitivist approach explains the main findings in a satisfactory fashion. Moreover, it refrains from using the very strong assumption according to which the arbitrators would simply express a brutal preference for one of three popular justice principles, namely, equity, absolute or relative, and equality. Even if such an assumption would appear acceptable, it would not explain the existence of the three groups, nor *a fortiori* their unequal size. In the cognitivist analysis, by contrast, the arbitrators are presented, not as selecting a principle under the effect of unknown causes, but as trying to find out the best solution, given notably the constraints in matters of information they have to face. The analysis suggests that they all have the same conception as to what justice means in this case, namely, making the retribution as close as possible to the contri-

Figure 6.1
The Three Types of Arguments behind the Decisions
of Bazerman's Three Groups

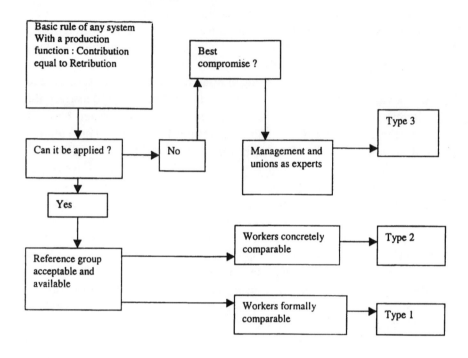

bution: a conception directly dictated by the very nature of the production system. But the cognitive ambiguity of the situation allows that several choices are possible at several crossroads (should, for instance, the reference group be "psychological" or "formal"? Should I decide by myself or follow the advice of the actors on the field?, etc.). As a consequence, several acceptable solutions are possible, even though the three most represented decisions appear as decreasingly convincing.

Many other examples, drawn from sociology or social psychology, would confirm another conclusion that can be drawn from this analysis: that it is impossible to reconstruct the feelings of justice experienced and expressed by people as resulting simply from the application of general principles (for other examples, see Boudon, 1995b). According to the cognitivist theory I propose here, these principles are only elements among others, though important ones, in the evaluation procedure more or less implicitly conducted by social actors. First of all, once they are confronted by a given situation, they will have to decide whether they should apply one principle or another.

This example entails also several general conclusions. It shows first that rationality can be, in Weber's terms, axiological rather than instrumental. The arbitrators care of course about their reputation and want to reach a decision likely to be perceived as good. But they do not try to guess the opinion of their audience. Rather they try to reach a good decision, namely, a decision which themselves and others would consider good because it is grounded on strong reasons. Secondly, the example shows that the conclusions are not reached on the basis of subjective idiosyncratic reasons. Otherwise, the statistical distribution of the decisions would appear as less strongly structured.

6.6. Checking the Importance of Contextual Effects

The previous examples have shown that people's feelings of justice could not be considered as deriving from an application of general principles, as the ones proposed by the "philosophical" theories of justice. This does not say, though, that we can avoid raising the question of the relation between the theories of justice and actual feelings of justice. Indeed, if we come to recognize that people, when they endorse a moral judgment, express not only subjective preferences but rather objective judgments, which can be potentially shared by others, it is hard to accept that the theories of justice cannot teach us anything on their feelings of justice.

Taking into account the contextual dimension of moral judgments allows us to clarify that question. More precisely, it can be claimed that the "philosophical" theories of justice have an explanatory value in a given situation as soon as the contextual assumptions they introduce implicitly can be considered as effectively satisfied in the situation. That is to say that we can observe that individuals endorse in reality feelings of justice congruent with the principles derived, for example, from some "intuitionist" or some "constructivist" theory if we interpret the hypothetical situation used by the author to ground his principles as characterizing the real context in which the individuals are actually located. Thus, in some situations, the assumptions introduced by some "intuitionist" theory will be satisfied, while the assumptions introduced by some "constructivist" theory, as Rawls's, will be rather realized in others. When the implicit assumptions of "philosophical" theories are actually met, the theories in question have an explanatory value. My guess, in other words, is that the validity of moral principles can only appear as grounded in real contexts with specific characteristics.

In order to make this idea more concrete, I will go back to the attempt made by Frohlich and Oppenheimer (F&O) to test the explanatory value of some theories of justice, thanks to an ingenious experimental simulation of the "veil of ignorance" and compare their findings with those of another experiment, quite similar in its orientation, but introducing explicitly a contextual variation. This latter experiment is due to Mitchell, Tetlock, Mellers, and Ordonez (MTM&O) (Mitchell et al., 1993).

Failing to have in mind the "cognitivist model," F&O did not manage to interpret their findings accurately, that is to say to reconstruct the system of reasons induced by the experimental context. Furthermore, they did not manage to exploit their findings to build a bridge between the general theories of justice and observed actual feelings of justice. Indeed, the greater popularity they observed of the "combined principle," previously described as "maximize the mean and define a minimum floor," does not mean that it should be considered as generally valid, that is, as able to predict people's feelings of justice in all contexts. As to the failure of Rawls's, Harsanyi's, and the functionalist theories among F&O's subjects, it does not say that these theories cannot have an explanatory value in other contexts.

According to Rawls's postulate –a postulate common to all "constructivist" theories—a hypothetical situation can be identified, such as the principles chosen in that situation can be considered relevant, whatever the context may be. F&O interpreted Rawls's philosophical postulate as a sociologically valid postulate, simulated the "veil of ignorance" situation, and checked whether people actually endorsed Rawls's "difference principle." As we know, it turned out that a very small minority appeared as Rawlsian.

But a crucial question is whether the experiment actually simulated the "veil of ignorance" situation. This situation can be defined as a context wherein people have to choose between lotteries: they can belong to each of the classes of an income distribution with unknown probabilities. If we postulate that, in such a context, people are likely to be careful about the risks involved, that is to say that they will choose the least risky distribution (or lottery), namely the distribution which maximizes the floor income, we can conclude that this real context is a good interpretation of the "veil of ignorance" and that it provides a local ground for Rawls's principle of justice. F&O's subjects preferred though the distribution which maximizes the mean and defines a minimum floor. In other words, the subjects appeared as seeking both a protection against risks and a maximization of potential gains. This discrepancy with Rawls's principle may be due to the fact that F&O's lottery does not adequately simulate the lottery of the life chances: aversion toward risk may be stronger in the latter than in F&O's lottery, since the stake is obviously of a greater order of magnitude. But the discrepancy can also be due to the fact that Rawls's "veil of ignorance" fails to take into account a consideration which might be essential to subjects in this hypothetical situation, namely the fear and reluctance to be arbitrarily treated. Indeed, under the "veil of ignorance," the individuals are considered as being rational exclusively in the instrumental sense of that word and are not supposed to have any moral intuitions. If we suppose though that individuals under the "veil of ignorance" fear arbitrariness, we derive Rawls's difference principle. Now, while people can hardly forget or put into brackets—even in a mental experiment—their actual aptitudes, achievements, and gifts, they may easily imagine living in a society where these qualities would not be taken into consideration and would have no effect on the social rewards they would receive.

The study by MTM&O has the interest of introducing an explicit variation of this crucial contextual dimension. In a few words, MTM&O's experiment consisted in asking people's opinion about the fairest economic reform in a society which was described as more or less meritocratic.

More precisely, the subjects were requested to choose between economic policies guided by the following alternative principles:

- The "difference principle" drawn from Rawls's theory of justice: maximize the floor income.

- The "combined principle": maximize the mean and define a minimum floor.
- The principle drawn from Harsanyi's utilitarian theory: maximize the mean.
- The principle of equality: minimize the standard deviation.

The alternative policies were presented as efficient: they were supposed to generate income distributions congruent with the principles. The subjects' choice was supposed to depend merely on the degree of morality and political acceptability of the alternative principles of justice. Moreover, the subjects were incited to avoid projecting themselves into one of the classes of the stratification system when evaluating the alternative economic actions. By difference with F&O's experiment, they were not motivated by an actual gain in money. On the whole, MTM&O sought to avoid having the subjects take into consideration their personal interests, either real or imaginary.

As in the case of F&O's experiment, the subjects were incited by the experimental situation to answer the following implicit questions:

- How have the income inequalities been generated? Do they reflect merit and/or achievement inequalities?
- Can income inequalities be considered as functional?
- Is it a legitimate goal for a government to try to make the mean of an income distribution as high as possible?
- To make the standard deviation lower?
- To define a minimum floor?
- To maximize the floor income?

Plausibly, the subjects have devoted special attention to the first question, since, by difference with F&O's experiment, they were given information as to the functional character of inequalities.

In the low and medium meritocratic conditions, the subjects know that income inequalities do not reflect their efforts, merits, and achievements. So income inequalities will likely appear to them as dysfunctional and, hence, as arbitrary. In such a context, we can assume that the individuals would not allow the government to maximize the mean without constraints, since this would possibly lead to an excessive enrichment of some individuals, to the detriment of others, who would also have contributed to the creation of wealth. Moreover, a constraint on the floor will possibly be considered sufficient if an income distribution can be considered as functional. But if it cannot, such a constraint will be unable to eradicate the feeling of unfairness raised by the distribution. In other words, when the inequalities appearing in a distribution are perceived as a-functional or dysfunctional, people will be incited to endorse Rawls's "difference principle," since it is the only one–among the proposed principles—which is able to compensate the feeling of arbitrariness aroused by the distribution. Indeed, as the "difference principle" maximizes the floor income, it should naturally generate a severe redistribution. Moreover, given that the distribution is supposed a-functional, the best way to restrict its arbitrariness is to impose a constraint on the ceiling. Finally, the Rawlsian principle is more attractive than the principle of equality, since it insures a higher mean. MTM&O's experiment supposed namely that the principle of equality is associated with a lower mean than the other distribution principles.

On the whole, in a context where inequalities are supposed a—or dysfunctional, the subjects tend to wish: a protection against risk, a constraint on the standard deviation to the effect of correcting the arbitrariness of the distribution, with the provision that this constraint should not lower the mean. In agreement with this reconstruction of the reasons of MTM&O's subjects, one of the two main findings of MTM&O is, effectively, that in low and medium meritocratic conditions, a majority of the opinions appeared as endorsing effectively the Rawlsian" difference principle."

The second main finding of MTM&O is that, in a high meritocratic hypothetical context, a majority chooses rather, as in the F&O's study, the "combined principle" (maximization of the mean, definition of a minimum floor). If an income distribution is perceived by individuals as reflecting adequately their merits and achievements, and if we suppose that most individuals have in mind some rough version of the functional theory, trying to make the standard deviation lower would appear to the subjects as unjustified and dysfunctional: it would have the effect of demotivating social actors. As to the principle of equality, it is hard to see how it could be preferred in such a context. But Rawls's principle will not likely be attractive either: when a distribution is perceived as functional, the subjects have no reasons–except in the case where they would be exclusively motivated by envy—to see a reduction of the standard deviation as justified. As in F&O's experiment, however, the subjects have strong reasons to wish a protection against the risks of life, provided it does not lead to distorting the functional character of the distribution and has no negative effect on the mean. On the whole, in a highly meritocratic context, the subjects have strong reasons to choose the "combined principle" (maximize the mean and define a floor income).

It can be noted incidentally that the principle of equality is almost never chosen in the experiments where individuals are proposed to choose a distribution principle for the society. Plausibly, because it is difficult to find strong reasons that could support this principle.

To sum up, Rawls's "difference principle" describes adequately the feelings of justice actually experienced by people notably in a context where the distribution of goods is perceived as arbitrary. When it is not perceived as arbitrary, but rather as functional, the same principle is rejected by a strong majority. Maybe people would appear as Rawlsian in other contexts, besides the context where the distribution of goods appear as arbitrary. Identifying these other contexts would be an interesting goal for further sociological research on justice feelings. But the main conclusion to be derived from the analysis of F&O's and MTM&O's studies is that no single theory of justice is able to reproduce the feelings of justice experienced by people.

This is due to the two complementary reasons that (1) all these theories are implicitly contextual (though they are generally presented as a-contextual) and that (2) the feelings of justice experienced by people are inspired in them by reasons taking the parameters of the context into consideration. With these reasons in mind, it becomes easier to understand why people appear, for instance, as Rawlsian in some circumstances and anti-Rawlsian in others. No single criterion nor theory of justice can predict in all contexts the feelings of justice as they actually are. The "general" theories of justice are actually special applications of the "cognitivist model," valid in special types of contexts.

6.7. Which Criteria of Fairness, Legitimacy, Etc.?

The previous examples suggest that collective feelings of the type, "X is fair, legitimate, good, unfair, illegitimate, bad, etc.," can be explained fruitfully as the product of strong reasons. This raises the question as to what makes a reason strong or weak. In other words: on the basis of which criterion can I judge that a reason is weak or strong? As paradoxical as this may appear, would contend that most theories of justice and more generally most axiological theories fail because they naively tend to associate simple criteria to the ideas of goodness, fairness, legitimacy, etc., and their contraries.

It is almost unnecessary to accumulate the examples. Against the Kantian criteria of universalization, it has been objected that lying and other deviant types of behavior can in some circumstances be moral. Against the utilitarian criterion, it has been objected that people can be very hostile to a state of affairs without any consequences or even with positive consequences to their well-being. Axiological theories as the Kantian and utilitarian theories owe their success to the fact that they start from the principle that a criterion of morality, fairness, justice, etc., could be easily defined (Taylor, 1997). But this reason of their success is also a major cause of weakness.

It is surprising that Kant tried to propose a general criterion of morality, for this appears contradictory with a just and profound remark he makes in his *Critique of Pure Reason*. Those who look for general criteria of truth, he writes (Kant, [1787] n. d., I, I, 2nd part [*Die transcendentale Logik*], III [*on der Einteilung der Allgemeinen Logik in Analytik und Dialektik*], p. 93), remind us of these two idiots one of whom attempts to milk a male goat, while the other one holds a pail under the belly of the animal. The joke stresses an important point. There are effectively no *general* but merely *particular* criteria of truth. Thus, there are criteria, defined by Tarski (1936), of the truth of observational statements: "snow is white" is a true statement, if and only if snow is white. But there are no general criteria which could be mechanically applied to evaluate the strength of a theory or generally of a system of arguments. Take a scientific theory considered as totally uncontroversial, as Huygens' theory of the pendulum. On which criteria do we hold it as true? Popper (1968) would have said that we hold it as true because, to date, we have failed to discover facts which would contradict it: all the pendula we can observe under a variety of circumstances behave in a way congruent with the predictions derived from Huygens' theory. The theory appears to date as unfalsified and in that sense as true. But we do not only accept Huygens' theory as true because it leads to predictions congruent with observations; we also accept it notably because it does not introduce concepts we would consider as unacceptable in a scientific theory. But on which criteria do we consider a concept as scientifically acceptable? The move of the pendulum is analyzed in Huygens' theory as resulting from the combination of "forces," one force drawing the pendulum toward the center of the earth, another drawing it toward the point in the ceiling where the thread holding the pendulum is fixed, etc. We accept Huygens' theory because we consider the concept of "force" and the mental construct described by the "parallelogram of forces" as legitimate. It suffices to think of the objections raised against such totally unempirical notions, from Descartes to Carnap (see Boudon 1997c), to check immediately that there are no criteria by which we could easily determine that such concepts are acceptable, legitimate or not. Since we have no reason to consider the case of Huygens' theory as exceptional rather than typical, it follows that we normally cannot define criteria by which a scientific theory can be held as valid or true. Descartes was convinced that the notion of "force" is unacceptable. We are convinced that it is acceptable. There is no easy criterion thanks to which we would judge it acceptable, though, namely criteria which we would have identified and that Descartes would have failed to identify. We accept it because it explains many things and has repeatedly been successfully used in the history of physics. So, when Kant states that there are no general criteria of truth, he is correct.

Why then would there be general criteria associated with such notions as "fair," "good," "legitimate," etc., and their contraries, while no general criteria can be associated with the attributes "true" and "false"? Of course there is a strong demand for such criteria. But, as the case of Popper's "falsification" criterion shows, the criteria that have been proposed to meet this demand are only partial.[5] They can in particular circumstances be necessary. They are never sufficient.

Does this lead to an "intuitive" theory of truth, fairness, legitimacy, or goodness? Evidently not. We hold the notion of "force" as acceptable in a scientific physical theory and the notion of "God" as unacceptable, not for intuitive reasons, but because a historical Darwinian process has selected the first one as adequate, given the aims pursued by scientists, and rejected the second one as inadequate.

My claim here is that the situation is basically the same, whether we have to explain the collective feeling that "X is true" or the collective feeling that "X is fair, legitimate, etc." Such statements are endorsed when they are grounded in the minds of people on reasons perceived by them as strong, or as stronger than the reasons leading to the opposite conclusions. To this, it must be added that the empirical statements included in the system of reasons should satisfy the Tarskian criterion, that is, be congruent with the relevant observations, but that in most cases the system of reasons will also include non-empirical statements the validity of which, in the general case, will not be reducible to the verdict of some well-defined criterion.

And so, "cognitive rationality" and "axiological rationality" point to the fact that the feelings that "X is true" in the first case, "X is fair, legitimate, etc.," in the second one, are grounded in the minds of social subjects on systems of reasons perceived by them as strong; they differ by the fact that the "systems of reasons" include at least one prescriptive statement in the latter case.

6.8. The Universal and Contextual Dimensions of Axiological Feelings and Justice Feelings in Particular

Besides having the shortcoming of assuming wrongly the existence of criteria of goodness, fairness, etc., the general theories of axiological feelings, such as the ones mentioned at the beginning of this chapter, are unable to account satisfactorily for the contextual and historical variations of men's axiological and particularly justice feelings.

The "cognitivist model" I have presented makes it possible to catch more adequately than other models the combination of the contextual-historical dimension and the universal dimension characteristic of moral feelings.

Thus, in some contexts, people appear as intolerant toward any deviation from the principle according to which retributions should reflect contributions, while in other contexts they appear rather lax in this respect, accepting without any protest strong deviations from the same principle. Why? Because strong reasons command the two contrasted attitudes in the two cases. Thus, the point made earlier about Rawls's "difference principle" can be held as general. Not only this principle, but others as well can be rejected or endorsed depending on the context.

On the whole, the "cognitivist model" makes possible an accurate explanation of the observed variation of feelings of justice from one context to another, because it takes into account the parameters of the contexts responsible for the variation (and assumes that these parameters are more or less consciously perceived by social actors). By so doing, the model solves the apparent "contradiction" between the sensitiveness to the context of the feelings of justice and the claim to coherence and objectivity more or less implicitly made by the social subjects who experience them.

This contextual variation of moral judgments is often presented as proof of the basic inconsistency and contingency which would govern the moral standpoints endorsed by individuals, [6] and consequently as justifying an investigation of the causes rather than of the reasons responsible for moral judgments, or alternatively as supporting a strategic interpretation of the feelings of justice (for example, Deutsch, 1975), an attempt which turned out to be unsatisfactory (Deutsch, 1986).

By contrast, the "cognitivist model" suggests that it is possible to reconcile the contextual character of the feelings of justice with their claim to "objectivity." We express a moral judgment as "this is fair, unfair, etc.," and by so doing expect that other people will agree as soon as we feel that the reasons on which our judgment is grounded– whether we can express these reasons clearly or are merely vaguely aware of their existence—take into account the characteristics of the context, far from being merely derived from abstract moral precepts or from our own subjective inclinations. Moreover, these reasons can be accepted as valid by any observer, provided he is informed of the characteristics of the context from which they emerged.

Of course, it is less easy to account for moral judgments or to ground our subjective axiological preferences in general. Also, it is possible–this is one of the sources of moral conflicts—that within certain limits an identical context is characterized in various fashions by various actors. The "cognitivist model" can also take this possibility into account, however, as we saw in the case of the several arbitrations proposed in the Bazerman's experiment.

On the whole, the model invites us to revise the received idea according to which the contextual variation of axiological judgments would be incompatible both with the existence of general principles and with the idea that such judgments could be "objectively" valid.

6.9. Contextual Variations of Tolerance to Inequalities

Finally, I will mention only sketchily a few examples to illustrate the generality of the idea according to which, depending on the context, a principle can be adopted or rejected. These examples will also stress the point that the theoretical and empirical fruitfulness of the "cognitivist model" derives from the fact that it reconciles rather than opposes singularity and universality, contextuality and universality, and by so doing possibly . . . sociology and philosophy.

To return to an example developed in chapter 5, in his *White Collars*, C. W. Mills (1951) describes women clerks working in a firm. They all do the same tasks. They are settled in a great room, have all the same desk, the same work environment, etc. Violent conflicts frequently occur among them on "minor" issues: being seated closer to a source of heat or light, etc. Why such a violent reaction to such minor issues with so minor *consequences*?

A cognitivist interpretation can easily explain them. In fact, the working conditions of the clerks are such that any departure from a strict equality between contribution and retribution can be immediately and easily perceived. Moreover, it is normally treated as intolerable. The white collars are all equal, they are all devoted to similar tasks. So that any minor advantage is perceived as an illegitimate privilege.

In other cases, people appear rather extremely lax in regard to the principle according to which retributions should reflect contributions. Thus, educational investments are very unequally and unfairly rewarded. The distributions of statuses and incomes corresponding respectively, say, to x and x+k years of education will generally overlap widely. This means that the probability of individual X with x years of education getting a higher status and a higher income than individual Y with x+k years of education is high. The lack of adequation between "contributions" (here: educational investment) and rewards (here: status and income) is massive. And yet, no one has ever proposed to correct this inequality. Moreover, this inequality is not generally perceived as unfair. Why? Clearly, because trying to correct it would be extremely costly if at all possible. It would suppose a general planification both of the educational and of the occupational systems which is properly inconceivable and certainly undesirable.

For the same reasons, the wide inequalities between generations are rarely perceived as unacceptable and unfair.

Many experiments on the feelings of justice have been conducted by psychologists. In most cases it would be easy to show that the cognitivist model can provide an acceptable explanation of the findings. Thus, in a well-known study, which was replicated in Switzerland and Germany, respondents were proposed the following case (Kahneman et al., 1986a; Frey, 1997):

A hardware store has been selling snow shovels for 30 Swiss francs (or 30 German marks). The morning after a heavy snow storm, the store raises the price to 40 Swiss Francs/German marks. How do you evaluate the price rise?

In Germany and Switzerland, as well as in the U.S., a strong majority perceived the behavior of the firm as unfair. Should we be content by stressing the fact that people do not always behave according to the utilitarian principles that are supposed to guide the *homo oeconomicus*? Or would it not be more interesting to understand the reasons for the strongly structured distribution of answers? It can plausibly be assumed that they result from the respondents' application of a theory likely to be perceived as strong, according to which windfall profits should be accepted remorselessly by a social actor, provided this has no negative effects on other people; otherwise, the subject would gain his profit at the expense of others without justification.

Finally, an important remark should be introduced, which I cannot develop here in a manner it deserves, that is, in the various examples mentioned the principle of the equality between retribution and contribution was frequently evoked. One should not believe, however, that it is the only possible axiological ingredient of justice feelings. Other arguments would, for instance, evoke the principle of the equal dignity of human beings or many other principles.

6.10. Beyond Kantian, Utilitarian, and Contractualist Theories

Some cognitive obstacles to the development of knowledge about axiological sentiments in general and justice sentiments in particular are easily identified. One of them is the attraction of simplicity. It explains the success of the Kantian or the utilitarian theory of moral and generally axiological feelings. These theories provide easy criteria thanks to which a statement of form, "X is good, fair, etc.," could be validated. But this easiness is the counterpart of a major weakness: these criteria appear as contradictory to the axiological feelings of people. Rawls's theory is exposed to the same diagnosis. It is simple. It provides in principle a criterion thanks to which fair inequalities could be distinguished from unfair inequalities as far as the distribution of primary goods is concerned. But this criterion does not predict correctly the feelings of people. In fact, as we have seen through the Frohlich-Oppenheimer study, people reject it.

Sociologists on their side have often a "relativistic" view of axiological feelings in general and of justice feelings in particular. This attitude derives from many causes and notably from the positivistic tradition in which sociology is anchored. This tradition is full of suspicion toward the idea of seeing reasons as genuine causes and particularly as the genuine causes of axiological feelings. Positivists traditionally prefer to introduce "material" causes, even very conjectural, rather than accept the idea that reasons can be the causes of feelings.

Another *a priori* frequently endorsed by sociologists is to consider that reasons are the causes of feelings only when they are objectively undebatable (traffic lights are good because removing them would be objectively detrimental to traffic). This *a priori* accounts for the effort made by some sociologists to develop an instrumental theory of norms and values. Rationality, however, cannot be reduced to instrumental rationality in spite of the intellectual comfort gained by reducing the former to the latter. As well seen, notably by Max Weber and before him by Adam Smith and others, axiological feelings cannot always be derived from instrumental, in other words, from consequential considerations. A promising path to eliminate these difficulties is to consider axiological feelings in general and justice feelings in particular as being generally the effects of systems of reasons perceived as strong by social actors. As already seen by Durkheim (1979 [1912]), prescriptive and descriptive beliefs should be explained in the same way: because they are perceived as grounded.

Notes

1. Published with Emmanuelle Betton as "Explaining the Feelings of Justice," *Ethical Theory and Moral Practice. An International Forum*, 1999, 2: 365–398.
2. Many exceptions can, of course, be evoked against this statement, as the work of the Swiss Sociologist J. Kellerhals, among other examples, shows. See for instance (Kellerhals et al., 1995).
3. M. Sukale writes (1995: 43): "Damit ist Webers Einteilung des rationalen Handelns in zweckrationales und wertrationales, als gäbe es zwei verschiedene Arten rationalen Handelns, aüsserst irreführend" ("Weber"s distinction between axiological and instrumental rationality, as though there would be two types of rational action, is extremely misleading.")
4. On this point, for instance, see (Tyler, Lind, 1992).

5. R. Boudon has discussed these points more thoroughly in (Boudon, 1994b) and (Boudon, 1997c).
6. For example, Hochschild (1981), where the fact that people endorse different norms of justice depending on the characteristics of the contexts they are located in is considered a sign of the inconsistency of their standpoints.

7

The Cognitivist Model Applied to the Analysis of Public Opinion[1]

"One may in fact doubt that war will ever become so terrifying as to discourage those who love it, particularly since they are not necessarily the people who wage it."
—*Julien Benda,* La trahison des clercs

7.1. A Free Interpretation of the Metaphor of the "Impartial Spectator"

Adam Smith is the author of two famous metaphors. One, the metaphor of the "invisible hand," has been widely assimilated, whereas the importance of the other, the "impartial spectator," has not received nearly as much recognition. It is not my intention to launch any further debate on what is known as *das Adam Smith Problem* since Knies (1883), but I do believe that these two metaphors sum up one and the same intuition and conceptual framework, even if this point was not clearly developed by Adam Smith himself.

The "invisible hand" reconciles specific interests with the general interest. It is not from the benevolence of the butcher that we expect our dinner. When he lowers his prices or buys better quality meat to attract customers the butcher does so in pursuit of his own egoistic interests, and also helps to generate an optimal structure of supply for the benefit of the consumer.

Another metaphor, that of the "impartial spectator," is generally not as well understood. Its fate is much the same as that of Max Weber's "axiological rationality." In my opinion it is a highly important notion,

181

but one that usually receives a only vapid interpretation. It seems to me that to Smith's way of thinking the impartial spectator is not a simple fiction, but rather it designates a complex process by which individual opinions and judgments, biased by the interests and passions of those involved, *may*, under some conditions, in the aggregate, produce an opinion or a judgment in keeping with the common interest.

In other words, the "impartial spectator" would be an "invisible hand" with the ability to transmute a biased opinion into one in keeping with the common interest, just as the "invisible hand" turns egoism into altruism.

I do not know whether my interpretation is accurate. In fact, I suspect that it literally goes even beyond what Smith's text says. There is no rule against trying to climb onto "the shoulders of giants," however, rather than pursuing the often frivolous goal of finding out "what they *really* meant to say." What is sure, at any rate, is that for political theory one essential question is as follows: either the saying *Vox populi, vox Dei*, fundamental to democracy, should be taken seriously, or we should follow Flaubert's example and make it a major piece in the *Dictionary of Received Ideas*. The former response, however–the positive one–assumes that the aggregate of biased opinions may produce and perhaps even tends to produce an opinion in keeping with the general interest or the common good. Barring this, there is no basis for democracy, and elections as well as opinion polls, those mock consultations, are meaningless. It is on the basis of the opposite response–the negative one–that analyses such as those produced by the Marxist tradition have developed. They contend that opinion is artificially "constructed" for the greater benefit of an oligarchy that wields the real power but is devoid of legitimacy, in an attempt to achieve artificial legitimacy.

Although the issue of the validity of the saying *Vox populi, vox Dei* is not directly raised by Smith, it underlies his main thesis in the *Theory of Moral Sentiments*, according to which each individual is composed of two "selves," so to speak, a "partial actor" and an "impartial spectator."

Just a word about Smith's literal theory. His *homo oeconomicus* is self-centered and self-seeking. His *homo politico-sociologicus*, as depicted in the *Theory of Moral Sentiments*, is capable of sympathy, a word designating both understanding, with a positive assessment of other people's psychological state, and empathy, in which that understanding foregoes any evaluation of people's feelings. This *homo politico-sociologicus* is subject to all sorts of passions, including asocial passions such as anger and resentment (incidentally, we notice that Nietzsche was not the first writer to reflect on resentment) which disturb his judgment. There is, within him, at the same time, an "impartial spectator" who is responsible, in particular, for the fact that he will normally have guilt feelings if, for instance, he gets angry for no good reason, and more generally speaking if he does not conform to what Smith calls "conventions," which he does not view as having anything to do with what we call conventionalism.

In the last analysis, the "impartial spectator" belongs to a large, important family of concepts, including Kant's "practical reason," Weber's "axiological rationality"[2] and Durkheim's sense of the "sacred"[3] With this figure, Smith heralds Scheler's analysis of pharisaism. The Pharisee himself attempts to pass off his own interest as the general interest because he is under the gaze of the impartial spectator. He himself is a partial actor but cannot disregard the views of the impartial spectator.

My intention, in the forthcoming remarks, is to delineate a general conceptual framework derived from Smith's work and nourished by recent research in the social sciences. This formulation may be summed up by the following three points.

- Significant research has drawn attention to the fact that individual judgments and opinions are affected by all sorts of biases. The idea of a "bias," although extremely widespread, is really not very felicitous. All it does, as in the work of Kahneman and Tversky, for instance, is put a label on a problem, the problem being the origin of those biases. Other contributions, both contemporary and somewhat older, not only evidence some biases, but provide a set of theoretical formulations which facilitate the comprehension of how opinions are formed, and above all, the fact that opinions may well be biased. These theoretical formulations represent a major contribution to contemporary work in the social sciences, in my opinion, but they have never been given the attention they deserve. Moreover, since they were developed independently of each other, there have rarely been attempts to make a connection between them, and even less often to view them as what they are: complementary pieces contributing to a theory of opinions. One of my intentions here is to attempt just that synthesis. These formulations are important, especially because they show that the reasons that account for opinions oscillate between the two poles of particularism and universalism, depending on the parameters defining the person and his or her social environment, as well as the questions asked. In other words, people tend to be closer to the "partial actor" or to the "impartial spectator" model depending on where they are located with respect to those parameters. The chances of my expressing myself as an impartial spectator are greater if I am questioned about an issue with which I am in no way directly concerned. Now, during a real or mock consultation, the probability of having the saying *Vox populi, vox Dei* apply depends on whether the majority of those questioned are in the "impartial spectator" position or not.

- Impartial spectators are not "conventionalist," in that they do not base their judgment entirely on the prevailing social usages. As Max Scheler, a severe critic of A. Smith, so rightly points out, Smith's theory is "judicatory" (*"urteilsartig"*), which is to say that it views the "impartial spectator" as capable of grounding his judgment in cogent arguments. I have shown elsewhere (Boudon, 1997a) that Smith's work is pervaded by this "judicatory" element of his theory. It is found in his *Wealth of Nations* as well as in the *Theory of Moral Sentiments*. For example, according to Smith, wage differentials between one category of workers and another are perceived as fair and actually are fair and legitimate as long as they may be justified by solid reasoning. Chapter 10 of book I of *An Inquiry into the Nature and Causes of Wealth of Nations* demonstrates that tavern-keepers, blacksmiths, craftsmen, miners, and soldiers must be ranked on a clear-cut ordinal scale of wages because of the very nature of those specific categories of jobs. In short, we may postulate that the "impartial spectator" is a sort of judge, making every effort to ground his conclusions in cogent arguments, which is to say, on arguments that may theoretically be endorsed by any Other whatsoever.
- The impartial spectator really is socially influential. Indeed, even an all-powerful group capable of imposing its interests must defend itself against the views of the impartial spectator.

This conceptual framework may be drawn from the writings of Adam Smith provided we consent to systematize them and return to the spirit of his thinking over and beyond the literal expression. I believe it yields a powerful theory of *collective sentiments and value judgments*. It has not drawn sufficient attention for the simple reason that the social sciences have tended to focus exclusively on two other models. The first stresses the sociocultural biases affecting the "partial actor's" perceptions and neglects that "impartial spectator" who also inhabits social subjects. The second, known as the Rational Choice Model, is not interested in the role of the "impartial spectator" either, since it is predicated on the idea that the behavior, attitudes, feelings and assessments of social actors are dictated by what they perceive to be their own interests.

7. 2. Effects of Social Affiliations: Special Interests, Group Interests, and Role Interests

It is a known fact for social scientists, since the eighteenth century at the least, that the judgments of social subjects pertaining to all sorts of subjects are affected by several types of biases. The first bias that comes to mind is of course generated by interests. It may be termed "concernedness bias," or "commitment bias." I find it difficult to approve what I perceive as going against my interests. Classical theoreticians of democracy, well before Marx and Nietzsche, had no objection to admitting that interests interfere with judgment formation, and this led them to ask whether public opinion may be viewed as guided by considerations of the common good or, at the least, as oriented towards the common good.

At first sight, Tocqueville seems to be highly skeptical in this respect: public opinion may err, and in fact does err normally. It is normally versatile and not very trustworthy in the *short term*, since in the heat of action, individual opinions lack distance and are dictated by interest. But, at the same time, again according to Tocqueville, in the long term opinions tend to incline towards those ideas that forward the public weal. For instance, our moral sensitivity has gradually led us to acknowledge that all human beings, irrespective of their attributes or merits, have their dignity. Furthermore, this trend is seen to be definitive. It is irreversible because it is based on an idea that has been accepted because of its conformity to the common good.

Thus, Tocqueville implicitly introduces the postulate that in the long term some ideas are selected by the "impartial spectator." It is that "impartial spectator" who decided that the idea–accepted by Aristotle, among others—that some individuals might alienate their will to the will of others was no longer acceptable. And it is because it was the "impartial spectator" who adopted that idea that it is definitive. To return to Tocqueville's metaphor, we may see the hand of "Providence" here. This actually does constitute an irreversible turn in our moral sensitivity. Although we live in a world pervaded by slavery, it is easy to see that it is neither advocated nor viewed as legitimate anywhere. It is hard to account for this irreversibility without the hypothesis of the "impartial spectator." The same is not true, we repeat, in the short term. The "impartial spectator" is in competition with partial, committed actors in the short term, and this explains why

Table 7.1
Opinions on the Thirty-five Hour Work Week

For each of the following category of individuals, tell me whether, in your opinion, the shorter work week is very positive, somewhat positive, somewhat negative or very negative:

	Sub-total positive	Sub-total negative	Neither positive nor negative	No opinion	Total
The unemployed	72	19	5	4	100
Salaried workers, public sector	66	20	6	8	100
Precarious workers	58	29	4	9	100
Salaried workers, private sector	58	29	4	9	100
Executives	56	28	7	9	100
Company heads	35	52	5	8	100

Source: BVA opinion poll, May 11, 1998.

a wide range of opinions about all sorts of subjects may be found in the political arena.

To illustrate Tocqueville's way of thinking, as well as the "commitment bias," I would like to take one present-day example, the example of the "law of the thirty-five-hour work week," voted in recent months by the French parliament. It is the principle that interests me here, rather than the details. Opinions on the subject differ with the person's social status, and they reflect individual and group interests. A majority of employees and blue collar workers are in favor of the law because it is in their interest to work less for the same salary. Job-seekers also tend to view the law as positive inasmuch as they believe it will spread work among more people, and therefore create new positions: it serves their interests as they perceive them. Company heads, on the other hand, tend to be opposed to the law of the thirty-five-hour work week. In short, the difference in opinions definitely reflects the difference in interests (see table 7.1).

Despite its apparent simplicity, this example raises a complex question. It would in fact be simplistic to place these opinions on the same plane. In the case of company heads, the assertion that they are against the law because it goes against their interests is insufficient. To be more accurate, many of them believe–rightly or wrongly–that it is contrary to the interests of their business, inasmuch as its immediate effect is to cause an increase in the company's production costs. It is not as individuals, then, that they tend to be opposed to the law, but as "people in charge," or as "role-holders." Of course, this financial burden may be more or less easily reduced, depending on the size of the company and a number of other factors. This explains why although there is more hostility to the law among heads of companies, on the whole, than among employees and workers, there are varying degrees of opposition (in this discussion I have set aside those businessmen whose position within the power oligarchy has led them to support the law in exchange for some advantages wheedled out of the government, as well as those, to a large extent, whose companies have been "relocated" abroad).

This example has the advantage, then, of showing that "interests" may be "particular" or a mixture of the "particular" and the "general." It is impossible for a company head not to feel concerned by the threat to the future of his firm, represented by heavier costs, and that future also concerns his workers. In short, the effects of interests on opinions do not necessarily go against the general interest, any more than they are necessarily in keeping with it. When an actor favors a given measure because it enables him to fulfill his social role, his judgment is based on his particular interest, but also on his "role interest," and therefore possibly on the general interest.

This case is interesting for another reason. It shows that a law, now generally agreed to be of dubious value for creating employment, is approved by most people because a majority of people are in a position that makes them think, normally, that the law will be good for their particular interests.

It is important to focus on these distinctions. In themselves, they point to the limits of models such as the Marxist one, according to which group interests balance each other out, as well as of those which, more subtly, portray the interplay of group interests as an admixture of the cooperation element and the conflict element. Neither of these types of models consider the eventuality that some interests may include both a particular dimension and a general dimension or, to put it otherwise, an egoistical and an altruistic dimension, in which altruism is not simply a more intelligent form of egoism.

7.3. Effects of Community Affiliations

Russell Hardin (1995) has drawn attention to another type of mechanism that may also cause people to lean towards self-centered values rather than universal values, as a result of which actors are not in a position to behave as impartial spectators, but, rather, may be seen to be "partial" actors.

When we perceive ourselves as belonging to a community, says Hardin, we tend to conform to its principles and ideas, not so much because of some obscure "conformist leaning" as because those principles and ideas are of functional value to us. Often we feel that we "belong" to a community and persist in these feelings, not only through pure, mechanical inertia but because the values of that particular community serve our interests.[4] Conversely, each individual's personal interest in these values reinforces the general consent to them. According to Hardin, Hirschman's cherished concept of "loyalty" is no more than a matter of interest. Perhaps the best way to explain the nature of this mechanism is to develop one of the examples given by Hardin.

Since Rousseau, there has been a tendency to idealize "communities." Hardin, on the other hand, sees them as having serious defects. First of all, where there is a community there is at the same time exclusion from it. One cannot feel like a member of a community without perceiving those who do not belong to it as outsiders. Hence the importance for a community of having identification signs. The slang used by youth groups in the French suburbs is the product of their need to have reliable, immediately comprehensible symbols by which to distinguish those who are "in" from those who are "out." Dueling, a development of sixteenth—century Italy that then spread throughout Europe, also served identification purposes. It enabled aristocrats to assert their superiority over commoners, at a time when they felt threatened by the social and economic dynamism of the latter. Both Chancellor Francis Bacon in England and Prime Minister Richelieu in France attempted to eliminate dueling, just as unsuccessfully as we would imagine anyone would be in trying to eliminate suburban slang today. Duels did disappear, in fact–after World War I– for reasons that were partly inherent in it. That is, when the *nouveaux riches* began dueling the practice gradually became meaningless and increasingly ridiculous. It is a fact that in their latter days duels were rarely lethal, since the distance between the duelers and the accuracy of the guns was such that the risk was limited.

Duels and suburban slang are two of the examples advanced by Hardin to illustrate those distinctive–and exclusionary–signs and more generally, the particularist values necessarily secreted by any "community." Each of the actors participates unwittingly in the creation of these signs, out of a feeling that the pseudo-institution to which they contribute fulfills a worthwhile function for the community—that of creating its identity and asserting its existence. This enhances the visibility of the community, and therefore its power, and is therefore useful to each of its members. Here we have what may be called a non-deliberate "coordinating effect." The advantage of the example of dueling is that is shows how these self-centered values may easily come into conflict with universal values.

Many opinions do indeed insinuate themselves in the minds of individuals because they perceive themselves as part of a "community" and realize that some particular "truth" serves the interest of that community and, by extension, serves their own interests. Such "communities" may be of several types. They may be based on where people live, but they may be social, political, religious, and so forth as well. They may be more or less clearly defined ("civil servants," "socialists," "the left," "right-wingers," etc.).

The example of civil servants may also be used to illustrate the Hardin effects. Civil servants are wont to believe that the government has the ability to regulate away virtually every social problem. This belief shores up and magnifies their own importance. We have here an instance of a "diffuse community" ("civil servants"), one that adopts ideas not so much because they are in line with the general interest or are the outcome of rational analysis, but because at the same time as they sustain and legitimate that very community, they serve its members. This example leads us to some interesting conjectures. One of the reasons, no doubt, why the differences between the programs of left—and right-wing politicians are so slight in France–to the point where the distinction between right and left is proclaimed obsolete by one and all–is that so many political leaders on both sides are civil servants (owing to the fact that a civil servant who loses an election and a seat in Parliament returns to a civil service job, as opposed to a doctor in private practice, or a company head, for instance, for whom a lost election may be catastrophic for his or her professional career). One would hardly expect French right-wing politicians to be very attracted to neo-liberalism, then. If we were to sum up the intellectual core of neo-liberalism, over and beyond its countless varieties, we might say that one of the basic rules of a political organization, as viewed by this conception, is that it demands respect of two principles: the principle of what is known as "subsidiarity," and that of minimal control, another term for which would be the "trust principle." The meaning of the latter is self-evident. The former implies that decisions pertaining to a social subsystem must theoretically be made at that level, except if there are some definite advantages in having it made at a "higher," or more "central" level. Obviously, government workers do not find a conception of this type, which tends to contain the administration even if it does not by any means endorse the doctrine of "minimal state," at all attractive. It means that only those functions that cannot be cared for by other agents located at less central levels are left to the administration, and therefore constitutes a threat to the civil servant's importance. It is most probably because so many French politicians are civil servants that the right hardly differs from the portion of the left that participates in government. This also probably explains why French politicians in general show signs of interest group loyalty and sometimes seem more anxious to defend the interests of their "community" than to serve the general interest. This attitude certainly accounts at least partially for its present discredit. The outcome is a class of politicians cut off from the rest of the nation, and conforming to "community-based" values.

More broadly speaking, interest group phenomena yield an interesting illustration of the mechanisms described by Hardin. Another example that immediately comes to mind is the way French teachers' unions defend their interest group. They protect their members, and the latter can hardly be asked to forego its beneficial effects. This explains why the different ministers of Education have been just about as successful in this field as Richelieu in his combat against dueling. Now there is no evidence that the values and principles underlying this particular special interest represent the best interests of the public as a whole. Some people are even somewhat belatedly discovering that it has had catastrophic effects on the French educational system.

Just a few words about one other anecdotal but telling illustration of the mechanisms described by Hardin. At one time "Act up," a French citizens' group, yielded a striking example of how "community-based" values and universal values may be in contradiction. In its attempt to support equal rights for homosexuals, this organization briefly considered denouncing a homosexual member of Parliament because he had demonstrated against the *"Pacte d'Association Civile de Solidarité"* (PACS) (a law instituting, among other things, a civil contract between homosexual partners) and therefore, according to "Act up," had lent his support to the social hypocrisy according to which homosexuality may be tolerated provided it remains socially invisible. Here we have an interesting case in which a "community," or at least the leaders of an organization claiming to defend the interests of a community, suggested that an individual be denounced and discredited, under the pretext of serving the interests of the "community." They would have sacrificed universal values on the altar of the particular interests of the community. Such, at any rate, was the case as of March 20, 1999. Actually, the threat was not carried out. Immediately thereafter, on March 22, "Act up" finally decided not to reveal the identity of the representative, no doubt out of fear of the gaze of the "impartial spectator."

Hardin was a prisoner of his Benthamian model, and overlooked the role of the "impartial spectator." This led him to conclude his analyses on a pessimistic note. According to him, since universal values, unlike "community values," do not serve the interests of individuals, one cannot see from whence they might derive any strength.

But let us return to our discussion of opinions. Out of interest, and not simply out of conformism, people tend to go along with the opinions of some concrete or nominal "community" to which they believe they belong. For instance, opinion polls indicate that socialist sympathizers were shocked by the way the highly controversial trial of the contaminated blood affair, which examined the penal responsibility of three socialist ministers, was conducted in early 1999. Like any ordinary citizen, they were probably disturbed by a number of facts: there was no contradictory debate, the private claimants were absent, the ministers were judged by a special court, etc. They were therefore touched by the fact that although the trial may not have violated the letter of the law, it certainly did violate the basic principles of law, justice, and morality. At the same time, socialist sympathizers seem to have been more indulgent than right-wing voters, according to the polls, because of "communitarian" considerations. At the same time, the severity of sympathizers of right-wing parties was also partly prompted by considerations linked to their own "community." It is easy to see how the findings of the BVA poll on the contaminated

Table 7.2
Confidence in the Special Court of Justice of the Republic

Are you confident that the court of justice of the republic, composed of elected officials and senior magistrates, will judge the three former ministers, L. Fabius, G. Dufoix and E. Hervé equitably? A: confident or relatively confident; B: not confident or relatively not confident.

	Total	Sympathizers						
		PC	PS	"Green"	UDF-DL	RPR	FN	None
A	38	45	53	37	34	37	12	30
B	57	55	44	63	63	62	88	58
No opinion	5	–	3	–	3	1	–	12

Source: BVA poll, February 18, 1999. (PC=Communist Party; PS=Socialist; UDF-DL=Center Parties; RPR=Gaullist Party; FN=Rightist Party)

Table 7.3
Opinions on the Criminal Responsibility of Ministers

In your opinion, is the fact that a minister may be brought to court for decisions made in the course of his or her duties (A) a relatively good thing, since political leaders are not above the law, (B) a relatively bad thing, since it may make being a minister an almost impossible job?

	Total	Sympathizers						
		PC	PS	"Green"	UDF-DL	RPR	FN	None
A	85	78	81	91	90	88	85	84
B	11	22	15	9	7	10	12	9
No opinion	4	–	4	–	3	2	3	7

Source: BVA poll, February 18, 1999. (PC=Communist Party; PS=Socialist; UDF-DL=Center Parties; RPR=Gaullist Party; FN=Rightist Party)

blood trial immediately become more comprehensible when our theoretical construct is applied to them. In a nutshell: we find the rejection of the credibility of the special court, in the name of universal values, as well as the differences produced by different community values (see table 7.2). It is indeed a known fact that at the time of the poll, the intention of the public prosecutor was to call for acquittal, and there was every reason to believe the ministers would get off very lightly, or even be absolved. Thanks to the "community effect," the prospect of that outcome made socialist sympathizers less vehement in their criticism of the court. An effect of the same type led sympathizers of the extreme right National Front (FN) to condemn the court particularly severely, in an exactly opposite reaction. The criminal responsibility of government members is widely acknowledged, but greater hesitation is found when the ministers incriminated belong to the same political "community" as the person questioned. The differences are slight, however, when the question does not specify that their responsibility will be determined by a special court. The community effect is less powerful than the evidence that political leaders are responsible to the criminal justice system (see table 7.3).

7.4. Effects of Position[5]

Company heads and salaried workers have different opinions on all sorts of subjects, not only because their interests differ, but because their respective social positions lead them to adopt contrasting *theories* about reality. Workers, for instance, tend to believe that the cause of unemployment is mechanization. They are right. When a new machine is introduced in a factory, the goal is to increase the worker's productivity. By replacing human labor by mechanical labor, the company lowers its production costs. The same is true when a new machine takes the place of an old one. The aim is always to make gains in productivity, the means being the destruction of human labor. Despite the efforts of economist and demographer Alfred Sauvy, who spent his life trying to convince people, and notably the French trade union leaders, that such collective credos as "machines create unemployment," "technological progress causes unemployment," "the laws of the market generate unemployment," and so on, are unacceptable, these credos prevailed and continue to prevail among those who are threatened with unemployment, as well as their representatives. It is easy to see why. Conversely, people whose social position naturally leads them to a broader perspective on the workings of the economy, as is the case for company heads and, naturally, economists, find it easier to realize that while, on the one hand, the new machine eliminates jobs, on the other hand it creates work, since it had to be developed, it requires maintenance, and new, improved versions must be worked out. But people who are worried about losing their jobs cannot be expected to take such a lofty view, since they run the very real risk of being affected by the destructive aspect of increasing mechanization. The chances of their personally benefiting from the machine's job-creating faculty are nil, on the other hand.

Civil servants yield another example of the effect of position. They can hardly adopt a neo-liberal point of view, not only for the "communitarian" reasons discussed above, but also because the world, as they perceive it, is one in which the administration is the main mechanism capable of introducing some order in the jungle of differing interests and the myriad of individual initiatives. Max Weber has pointed out that this "theory," which characterizes state employees, has the status of a sort of historical constant. For the servants of the Roman state, like those of the Prussian state, an efficient political system was one based on a strictly hierarchical administration and subject to an all-powerful authority, which in turn was believed to be the embodiment of impersonal rules.

It is not true that machines always generate a net destruction of jobs, even at the local level. But the belief, by those social categories threatened with unemployment, that such is the case, is *understandable*. It is not true that the administration is the best social regulatory agency, but it is comprehensible that state employees believe in it.

Conversely, it should be stressed that although the biases resulting from the "Hardin" effects or from effects of position are powerful, they are definitely not unavoidable. The recent changes in the French trade union, the CFDT, are a most telling illustration of this. The new CFDT, led by Mrs. Notat, definitely gives the impression of making an attempt to transcend communitarian and localist viewpoints, and to consider the universals, in spite of the resistance encountered in some quarters, for comprehensible reasons, since it comes from people who are affected by the biases described above. Were any trade union to implement other strategically more astute forms of collective action in replacement of transportation strikes, so definitely contrary to the public interest, its popularity would immediately rise considerably. The same thing is true of the accommodating position of Robert Hue, secretary general of the French Communist Party, on the subject of privatizations. Viewed from the localist, communitarian viewpoint, it may be seen as a betrayal. But again, it may be an astute way of taking into account a truth, that is, as Tocqueville pointed out long ago, it is not in the general interest for the state to go into business.[6]

Collective beliefs are not necessarily automatically shaped by powerful biases, then. Public opinion is sensitive to innovative ideas and proposals. The crystallization of opinions is a complex and partially haphazard process. For many people, including those who formerly held nationalizations to be a dogma no less than a cure-all, perhaps the Crédit Lyonnais scandal was the necessary "shock of reality" that brought them at long last to the realization that Tocqueville was right. A further consideration is that for a political or trade union leader, a shrewd break with traditional practices in line with communitarian interests but contrary to the general interest may be a way of improving the image of his or her organization. A break of that sort is rarely risk-free.

7.5. Organizations and People

M. Douglas and S. Ney (1998) have developed an interesting theory of "cultural biases," which coincides with some specific aspects of the mechanisms discussed here. According to these writers, a person who is heavily involved in a hierarchical organization tends to have a bureaucratic, administrative conception of social order. On the other hand, a socially free-floating person such as those intellectuals referred to by Mannheim, will find it easier to pursue a romantic vision of the world. The combination of two dimensions–the degree of the individual's integration in his or her social environment and the more or less hierarchical nature of that environment–forms a valuable typology.[7]

7.6. Cognitive Effects

The "effects of position" discussed above are only one aspect of the "cognitive" factors affecting and perhaps even explaining opinions. Many opinions utilize veritable "theories": I believe in the validity of proposition "X" because "X" is a consequence of such and such theory, which I have good reason to consider trustworthy. This differs from "effects of position" inasmuch as social subjects find X attractive as a result of truly cognitive factors rather than of biases induced by their social affiliations.

One reason why public opinion widely approves the law on the thirty-five-hour work week is that it draws on an immediately comprehensible theory according to which if a restriction is placed on the amount of work each individual may be given, a greater number of individuals may, at least theoretically, receive a share. The validity of this theory is of course subject to a number of prerequisites. One is that all other factors remain constant: that the shift to the thirty-five-hour week would not cause any businesses to go bankrupt, thereby cutting down on jobs. Or again, no potential employer would be discouraged by the new work-time constraints, and so on. Since these prerequisites are all conjectural, the effect of the law is also hypothetical. But to anyone who lacks a clear perception of how *heroic* the hypothesis that employment is a "finite cake" actually is, the theory may seem quite credible. In point of fact, the difference between ordinary knowledge and scientific knowledge is one of degree rather than of their nature. After all, scientific theories are also based on the *ceteris paribus* clause. Hence, there is nothing surprising about its being so widely used in ordinary thinking. Beliefs pertaining to mechanization and unemployment involve effects of position, but they also draw on cognitive effects of this type. At the local level, the belief that gains in productivity cause losses of jobs is a valid one. To see that it is false at an overall level one must become cognizant of the fact that its generalization implies strong implicit underlying hypotheses, the validity of which is dubious.

These cognitive aspects of beliefs cannot be overemphasized: First of all, because they play a major role in shaping opinions; secondly, because questionable theories are often theories that would be right if the prerequisites they hypothesize, often unwittingly, materialized; and lastly, because their very importance leads us to an optimistic conclusion, which is that critical thinking can be learned, and consequently, that one of the main functions of education is to develop it.

In this respect, it is worthwhile meditating some findings yielded by Inglehart's study (1998): they point to variations, from one country to another, in the cognitive understanding of economic mechanisms, at least as measured by the facility with which the hypothesis of the "finite cake" is accepted (see table 7.4), since that is the hypothesis underlying the causal assertion that "if people were forced to retire earlier, there would be less unemployment."

Does this mean that in different countries the public is more or less well trained to analyze economic phenomena? That seems quite plausible to me, personally. If these percentages were simply a reflection of the extent to which "neo-liberal culture" has permeated these different countries it would be incomprehensible that Sweden, a country with a particularly long-standing, influential social-democratic tradition should have a higher score than the USA. Moreover, within each country, the variable "level of education" is more highly correlated than any other (sex, occupation, income, political sympathy, etc.,)

Table 7.4
Forced Retirement

When jobs are scarce, people should be forced to retire early: % "agree"

Spain	Germany (West)	France	England	USA	Sweden
62%	50%	49%	43%	16%	9%

Source: Inglehart, 1998.

with the frequency with which the simplistic answer is rejected: this suggests that training should be responsible for an increased awareness to systemic effects. With more training, people are more likely to see that lowering the age of retirement cannot have a mechanical effect on reducing unemployment.

If the "job cake" is finite, another way to reduce unemployment, one may think, would be to cut down the number of job candidates by excluding immigrants. Here we have a combination of two oversimplified prerequisites: the finite nature of the job cake and the infinite interchangeability of job candidates (see table 7.5).

Countries rank grossly similarly on these two questions. At the same time, comparison of the means shown in the two tables indicates an "axiological" effect. It is easier to refuse to let immigrants into one's country than to change the age of retirement. Indeed, the latter case involves a breach of contract, entailing social, economic, and ethical costs, under normal circumstances, whereas the former simply implies refusal of any contractual relationship. Now, axiologically speaking, the latter situation, that of a breach of contract, is less acceptable than the other (Kahneman et al., 1986b). It is this type of effect that I wish to discuss here. In passing, I would simply point out the value of a "judicatory" conception of opinion.

Table 7.5
Jobs Preference to Own Nationality

When jobs are scarce, employers should give priority to their own nationality over immigrants: % "agree"

Spain	Germany (West)	France	England	USA	Sweden
75%	62%	63%	51%	51%	35%

Source: Inglehart, 1998.

7.7. Axiological Effects

In their classical writings, both Scheler and Pareto demonstrate that all things being equal, a theory may be preferred to another for emotional or axiological rather than cognitive reasons. A theory, says Pareto, may be true without being useful, and vice versa; it may owe its influence to its *usefulness* rather than to its *truthfulness*.

Thus, many theories expounded by "specialists" influence people because they correspond to axiological beliefs rather than because of any intrinsic validity. Theories of "domination" or "dependency," for example, that were and often still are so popular in political and intellectual circles throughout the Western Hemisphere, come under this heading. According to them, "structural" mechanisms are the one and only cause of inequality between nations, and more specifically, the cause of the exploitation, by the Western countries, of the developing countries. This entirely ignores the obvious fact that the poverty reigning in some African and South American countries is due to the way they are governed. When Amin Dada expelled the Indians in Uganda, one of the most fertile countries in Africa, he ruined the country's agriculture in a matter of years (Revel, 1988). "Dependency" theories and their likes are as widely accepted as they are for one single reason: since they view Western nations as exclusively responsible for the effectively detestable state of affairs, they give the impression of respecting the dignity of the Third World nations. While the social *utility* of such theories is easy to grasp, it is more difficult to demonstrate why they are *erroneous*. Yet this is patently the case, as David Landes (1998) has so superbly shown. The wealth or poverty of any nation is only very marginally due the action of other nations. Other factors, including the attitudes of the population and of its governing elite as well as the contingencies of history and geography play a much greater role.

A second example may be borrowed from Tocqueville. He has suggested that the skepticism prevailing in modern societies is also the result of its congruency with egalitarianism.[8] He explains that in these societies all opinions must be treated with equal respect, although they may be seen to disagree on countless subjects. To solve this contradiction, it suffices to decree that truth is an illusion, and that only the "common opinions" are worthy of respect. This avoids the need to raise any individual opinion above any other one. There are clearly no grounds for this radical skepticism, but it enables the diversity of opinions to be reconciled with egalitarian values.

Third example: in a report produced in the early 1990s at the request of the French government, Legrand (1982), writes, "Thanks to Marxist criticism and the progress of its offshoots in sociology"[9] . . . we have at last come to the realization that the ideology of Science is none other than "the ideology of a specific social class, used by it for the mystification of the other classes it dominates." This type of analysis leads to the formation of a sort of official doctrine–"pedagogism"– apparently here to stay. The idea is that to combat unequal achievement at school, teachers should no longer mainly try to transmit some knowledge to pupils; their role, henceforth, is to "teach them to learn," or better yet, to think up and conduct "stimulating activities," and turn schools into "places for living." This theory, still in effect, is probably the cause of France's high illiteracy level. But while it has only minimal cognitive plausibility, it does have all sorts of functions from the "communitarian "and interest-group viewpoints. Above all, it glazes over the differences in pupils' performances and aptitudes, and feeds the hopes of achieving greater equality of educational opportunity. It has a "utility," then: that of satisfying an "axiological" demand.

7.8. Scheler Effects

Scheler (1978 [1912]) takes his inspiration from Nietzsche (1887), and through some useful amendments makes his theory of resentment operational for sociological analysis. He retains Nietzsche's idea that an evaluator may make a positive or negative evaluation of something that does not deserve that valence, when the value ascribed has a positive psychological effect on that person. A social actor who feels powerless with respect to an unpleasant situation may very well develop feelings of resentment, according to Scheler. The same situation becomes easier to accept when, prompted by that resentment, the actor modifies the value attributed to some aspects of the situation.[10] In addition, this value judgment will tend to be confirmed by all those individuals exposed to the same causes of resentment, and will derive a degree of "objectivity" from this agreement.

Weber pointed out the interest of a theory of this type, but warned against overgeneralization of its relevance. Scheler himself contended that Nietzsche's theory of resentment was not as valid as he would have it. Specifically, Scheler is just as skeptical as Simmel and Weber about ascribing the spread of Christianity and of socialist ideologies exclusively to feelings of resentment, as Nietzsche postulates. Conversely, he does view resentment as possibly explaining several major types of attitudes. Resentment accounts for the obsessions of renegades, for instance. Since he has a long history of acceptance of the ideas he now rejects, the renegade has deep feelings of impotence, since there is no way for him to rewrite his past. So he spends his time militating aggressively against the ideas he has repudiated, and in favor of others, whose main quality lies in their opposition to his former beliefs. The ease with which defrocked priests convert to materialist philosophies is an instance of the relevance of this elegant psychological analysis. Philosopher Louis Althusser, a former "tala prince,"[11] was to become the most "fundamentalist "of French Marxist thinkers. Resentment explains the bitterness of some social categories as well. Scheler mentions the case of retired civil servants: according to him, Bismarck himself suffered from rancor of this kind. It also accounts for what he calls "the romantic soul type" ("*der romantische Seelentypus*"). Someone who has the impression that there is no room for him in society attenuates his feelings of powerlessness by committing himself to "the ideology of the grand refusal" of society. There is no need to stress the importance of this mechanism for the understanding of "ideological" phenomena. Nozick (1997) has attempted to apply this theory to intellectuals, contending that they are proportionately more hostile to "capitalism" because society does not award them the prestige, power, influence, or material rewards they think they deserve, given the length of their studies, among other things. They rationalize the meager returns derived from their investment, and their powerlessness to do anything about that state of affairs, by producing an analysis of capitalism as inherently unfair and perverse. There may possibly be some truth in this theory, but other factors definitely should be considered as well, as shown by Bourricaud (1980) in particular. Be this as it may, it is clear that "Scheler effects" do also account for some biases.

7.9. Combined Effects

The application of a combination of these different models sheds light on countless enigmatic survey findings. I will confine my illustration of this point to two examples. First, as evidenced by Brulé (1999), surveys show the French to be highly critical of deficits in public spending, but relatively unconcerned about high taxes and not very interested in having taxes lowered; whence it may be inferred that they favor having the deficit absorbed by an increase in taxes rather than by cuts in expenditures. Given the fact that approximately one out of two French people does not pay income taxes while taking advantage of the collective assets financed by those taxes, it is easy to see why half of the people polled are hardly interested in tax cuts. Another factor is the invisible, and therefore "painless" character (according to Olson's theorem) of the taxes paid by all, indirect taxes, since they are attached to the individual purchasing of goods. Conversely, the notions of deficits in public spending and government indebtedness immediately conjure up a negative image. Why should the administration be allowed, any more than households, to "live beyond its means"? Understandably, then lower taxes are rarely a main point in French election programs, as opposed to other countries such as Germany, Great Britain, or the United States. This is because the weight of "visible" taxes falls on a minority. In all probability, then, it is only when the rest of Europe has engaged in a process of lowering taxes that this will become a real political objective in France, because French officials will no longer be able to avoid the issue. Julien Benda had identified the same mechanism as applying to warmongering (in a text written at a time when deafening sounds of saber-rattling were being heard): "One may in fact doubt that war will ever become so terrifying as to discourage those who love it, particularly since they are not necessarily the people who wage it." The example of opinions on taxes and deficits clearly shows that answers to this type of question are structured by the combined effects of several of the biases discussed above, namely biases "of position," "cognitive" biases, "affiliation" biases, and "commitment" biases.

Second example: the French media are periodically telling us how scandalized people are when the stock market value of a corporation rises following its announcement of a lay-off plan. "When unemployment mounts, the stock market rejoices" is the refrain constantly heard on the air then. There may be a dose of bad faith and demagogy in that reaction, but demagogy can only be effective, in this case, because it can play on powerful cognitive effects coming from the "postulate" that what is true *locally* and *in the short term* is true *in general* and *in the long term.* Now in fact, lay-offs here and now conserve jobs here, elsewhere, and tomorrow. But it is also true that the chances of having this lofty viewpoint adopted by the people who are being laid off or those who fear for their jobs are extremely slim, and their discontent makes them easy prey for demagogic politicians.[12]

These examples also clearly show that *depending on the issue*, the saying *Vox populi, vox Dei* may or may not apply. The fact that the French do not care about having taxes lowered is due to the fact that the majority has no interest in caring about that. In this case, the viewpoint of the "partial actor" rather than that of the "impartial spectator" prevails because of both the *nature of the issue* and the characteristics of French fiscal politics. On the basis of opinion surveys, politicians may then be tempted to treat lowering taxes as a subsidiary objective. And the leader of the National Assembly will be able to go on tranquilly spending 600,000 francs a year of the taxpayer's money on flowers.[13]

7.10. Tocqueville-Kuran Effects

Sociologists have developed still another important contribution to the theory of opinions and collective feelings, with respect to values in particular. A respondent who claims to believe "X" may really believe in that assertion, or have no opinion on the subject but believe that "X" is socially or intrinsically the right answer, or again, be afraid to give his or her true opinion. Tocqueville is probably the first writer to have forcibly drawn attention to this point, while using a most evocative example to illustrate it. It may very well happen that a majority of people believe white, and yet, black is thought to be the prevailing opinion. This occurs when it is thought illegitimate to proclaim that one believes white, and conversely, to state a belief in black is thought to be status-enhancing. In this case, only those who believe black express their opinion, and those who believe in white have the impression that everyone except themselves and their intimates believes black. In *The Ancien Régime and the Revolution* (1986 [1845]: book III, ch. 2), Tocqueville tells us that during the French Revolution public opinion was thought to be anticlerical, whereas a large majority of the population actually retained the "old faith." But that majority remained silent, and each believer had the impression of being unique in this respect. This "Tocqueville effect" explains why the majority of Russians were believed to have become communists in the 1920s, whereas only a minority had gone over to the new faith. But since it was difficult, and even dangerous, to express one's hesitations, each individual Russian tended to think he/she was the only one not to be a believer. The impression that most Germans were Nazis under Hitler or, as Henri Amouroux quipped, that there were forty million supporters of Pétain in Vichy-governed France and forty million supporters of de Gaulle at the Liberation, was able to prevail for the same reasons.

The fact that relativism–the doctrine according to which there is no truth, either theoretical or practical–has now become a sort of unofficial truth, although it contradicts private beliefs, all evidence and intimate convictions is ascribable to similar mechanisms. But such beliefs and evidence are scarcely expressed, whereas any theory that legitimizes relativism is socially valued and therefore status-enhancing for the person who conceives it, and normally approved by the media, acting, in one of their functions, as the resonance chamber of conformism. The opposite positions are rarely expressed, and when expressed, are hardly heard.

Kuran (1995) has thoroughly studied and formalized this "Tocqueville effect," and has given many examples of its application. For instance, the polls conducted in Nicaragua for the 1990 elections had all predicted that the Sandinists would win, whereas Violetta Chamorro came out fourteen points ahead of them. Why? Because the pollsters sent by the North American press were perceived by those polled as favoring the Sandinists. Many of those who planned to vote for V. Chamorro had therefore told the poll-takers that they were pro-Sandinist, which they were not.

Some of the curious findings of the monumental study on international values, conducted by Inglehart and collaborators, are probably ascribable to effects of the same type. A sampling of around one thousand individuals in forty-three countries were polled, using a questionnaire of several hundred items. The idea was to determine inter-country differences on a wide range of value judgments. A look at the results as to confidence in institutions shows China at or near the top of the list for most institutions. The Chinese claim to have great confidence in their educational system, their legal system, their parliament, their socialized medicine, and their political system, much more so than the Americans, Germans, or French, among others. It is hard to avoid seeing an illustration of the mechanisms evidenced by Tocqueville

Table 7.6
Confidence in Institutions

"A great deal" or "quite a lot" of confidence in	China	France	West Germany	USA
The education system	93%	66%	54%	55%
The legal system	76%	58%	65%	58%
Parliament	81%	48%	51%	46%
The social security system	81%	70%	70%	53%
The political system	80%	n.a.	n.a.	55%

Source: Inglehart, 1998.

and theorized by Kuran in these findings. The answers probably reflect "official" truths much more than the intimate beliefs of the individuals questioned (see table 7.6).

A similar explanation may be applied to other findings in the same study. Germans, for instance, do not feel it permissible to claim to be proud to be German, whereas the French are less inhibited in this respect, and Americans have no hesitations about proclaiming their pride in their national identity. There are official truths, and socially advisable beliefs (see table 7.7).

Tocqueville put his finger on another important mechanism, responsible for our faculty to reproduce other people's opinions without having any real, deep-down agreement with them. This aspect of opinion-forming, just as fundamental as the mechanism discussed above, accounts for some people's intellectual and moral impotence, according to the second *Democracy in America*. It is the outcome of our necessary dependency on others to distinguish truth from falsehood, on all sorts of subjects. "There is no philosopher in the world, however great, that does not believe a million things on the faith of others," Tocqueville writes (1986 [1845]: 445). Now with the increasing accumulation of knowledge and growing specialization, this dependency grows even greater. As society becomes more and more complicated, it generates more previously unheard-of situations, which raise new moral and intellectual dilemmas. And people most probably also tend increasingly to echo the prevailing opinion when asked to give their personal opinion. In other words, there are subjects on which individual opinions, by force of circumstances, reflect the position of

Table 7.7
Proud to be ...

% "very proud"	German (West)	French	Italian	English	American
	20%	35%	41%	54%	76%

Source: Inglehart, 1998.

"those in the know," who may very well not know at all. As Pareto tells us, the history of scientific thinking is the history of all of the errors that humankind swallowed on the faith of specialists given the name of scientists. The sally takes on an air of truth when applied to all those "specialists" on whom our contemporary world relies, and who are anything but scientists. We need only take all those "specialists," referred to above, who—with the blessing of political leaders, of course—have imposed methods for teaching reading, writing, languages, and mathematics, and not only teaching methods, but educational policies as well, the consequences of which seem to have been mostly catastrophic.

7.11. The Influence of the Impartial Spectator

Following his demonstration of the effects of "communitarian biases" on individual opinions and beliefs—to which we may add the other above-mentioned biases—Hardin, as I have mentioned, arrives at the conclusion that "universal values" and "unbiased" opinions are ineffectual. Only those universal values that seem to be functional in dyadic relations are socially forceful, according to him. For example, actor X has good reasons to keep the promise he made to Y if he wants to continue to maintain some cooperation with him. Here, Hardin reiterates Axelrod's solution (1984) to the famous dilemma of the prisoner: a universal value (keeping one's promise, not betraying someone, and so on) prevails when it coincides with the interest of the protagonists. There is no need to be as restrictive on this point as Hardin himself, since the prisoner's dilemma is not limited to dyads, and may involve any number of actors. It is nonetheless true that the "expected utility" model and game theory, on which Hardin bases his thinking, account for the positive valence attached to cooperation, but do not account for other values.

Hardin himself gives an answer to the all-important question of the origin and strength of universal values when he refers to the tragedy of Antigone. He does so unaware, however, since the answer he gives–or at least that may be deduced from his own examples–does not fit into the expected utility model on which his entire book is constructed. Indeed, unlike the Thebans, we *all* judge that Antigone did right in burying her brother, and that Creon acted despicably, not only because he was cruel, but because he flaunted universal values. Why this unanimous appreciation? How does today's spectator of *Antigone* differ from the Theban whose applause went to Creon? The explanation certainly does not reside in any "cultural" difference, in some *"ethos"* or *"habitus"* by which the Thebans were unlike us, but quite simply in the fact that their natural concern for the fate of Thebes prevented them from taking the "impartial spectator" position, whereas we ourselves are "impartial spectators" by dint of our total lack of care about the threats that weighed on Thebes at that time. Our opinion on a subject of that order is necessarily dictated by universal values. We are still waiting to meet a spectator of *Antigone* whose sympathies would go to Creon, as opposed to Antigone. Any sociologist who had the extravagant idea of polling spectators leaving the theater would unfailingly find a 100%-0% distribution, except for "random" errors.[14]

This is where the strength of universal values lies. They come to the actor's mind naturally, whenever that actor finds him or herself in a position close to that of the "impartial spectator." At the same time, the example of *Antigone* stresses an important point, which is that social subjects are susceptible to having very definite opinions on subjects that in no way touch on their interests. This in itself suffices to disqualify any purely utilitarian theory of values. The example of *Antigone* has the advantage of creating a "pure" situation, in which the spectators' distance necessarily makes them "impartial," and causes them to condemn Creon unanimously. In other cases, the proportion of partial and impartial spectators may be more complex and less easily predictable. In the poll on the aptitude of the special Court of Justice to deliver a fair judgment in the contaminated blood trial, the people who expressed their doubts were naturally dubious because they were in the impartial spectator position in this affair, and based their opinions on the argument: "why do we need a special court for political officials?" In this instance, *Vox populi, vox Dei.*

These remarks also yield an answer to the question that puzzled

Simmel: why do we perceive the behavior of actors in earlier times as strange and foreign? The answer is: mainly because, with respect to the past, we are necessarily in the "impartial spectator" position, since we are totally unable to modify past events, whereas, conversely, the people we are judging were actors with commitments at the time.

Here we clearly identify one of the mainsprings of moral progress or, to use Weber's more subtle vocabulary, of "diffuse moral rationalization" (*Durchrationalisierung*) visible in the course of history, since by definition, the past is judged by spectators who, collectively, are increasingly impartial as time goes by, and the lessons it teaches tend to clarify themselves. The notion of "clean warfare," over and beyond its superficial naïveté, is not only indicative of the new weapons performances, but also of the fact that the horrors of the twentieth-century wars have irreversibly modified our moral sensitivity to war as such, thanks to the increasing distance that has turned us into "impartial" spectators. War, previously viewed as a normal occurrence, is now perceived as abnormal and as only to be undertaken when it apparently cannot be avoided, and even then, only provided it is "clean." Similarly, the principle, inscribed in the United Nations Charter, which prohibits the violation of national sovereignty, is presently losing ground before our very eyes, to another principle, inscribed in the Universal Declaration of Human Rights, which guarantees the rights of individuals against oppressive States. The "war of the gods" between these two principles is arbitrated by the "impartial spectator," as shown by the fact that while global opinion seems to have been relatively critical of the strategy implemented by NATO in the war in Kosovo, and skeptical about the results achieved, there is widespread approval of the very fact of military intervention. The war in Kosovo and the pressures on British authorities to extradite Pinochet are striking examples of all of those occurrences that demonstrate the development–no doubt irrevocable–of a new "sensitivity." The "polytheism of values" does not prevent moral progress, it simply describes the conflicts that generally preside over the reshuffling of the hierarchies governing those values.

Just a word about Weber's famous "polytheism of values": the indefensible interpretation suggested by Leo Strauss has led scholars to interpret it as a relativist credo: I have my values, you have yours, and nothing can prove which of us is right.[15] The famous metaphors on the "polytheism of values" and the "war of the gods" cannot be isolated from two other notions, less famous, unquestionably, but just as crucial to Weber's thinking: "axiological rationality" and the "diffuse rationalization" of moral life. According to Weber, conflicts between values are the vector of progress–and of rationalization–in moral life, which is the outcome of "axiological rationality," a concept not very different from that of the "impartial spectator." A subject is guided by "axiological rationality" inasmuch as his behavior may lay claim to the approval of the "impartial spectator."

The case of striking transportation workers, alluded to above, may provide concrete illustration of this point. The right to strike is in conflict with the public interest here, and as a rule the public is not responsible for the situation that triggered the grievances and led to the strike. We have a "polytheism of values" here, with a "war of the gods" on two basic principles (the right to strike and the right of the public not to be "taken hostage"). Now the public is less and less willing to accept this sort of use of the right to strike, which is increasingly perceived as a "French exception." This trend is evidenced by the fact that the media increasingly tend to question the legitimacy of these practices, while the trade unions are developing and implementing innovative approaches aimed at limiting the inconveniences connected with the strike while maintaining the effectiveness of the protest movement. The way the public reacted to the long museum workers' strike in France in June 1999 is indicative of the same trend. The strike was generally disapproved, on the grounds that tourists were unfairly taken hostage, and that other ways of protesting could surely be found. In all of these examples, as in those mentioned above (the development of international law, the limitation of state sovereignty, and so on), "rationalization of moral life" occurs in a context of "polytheism of values." Understandably, this rationalization takes place in a context fraught with conflict. Trade unionists are easily led to use their power to cause inconvenience, when the right to strike makes it legitimate to do so. But the "impartial spectator" does not accept innocent victims being heavily taxed by that right, and wants to see more acceptable "solutions" explored. The evolution of the form taken by protest movements at the French electricity company yields another illustration of the "rationalization of moral life" prompted by the "impartial spectator": the unions have abandoned power cuts, which paralyze the economy and inconvenience individual consumers considerably.

Why is communism generally viewed as less horrendous and treated more leniently than national socialism, and why is it possible to proclaim oneself a communist without being downright ostracized? Not only may the "impartial spectator" himself perceive the goals of the communist "secular religion" as positive, however barbarous the means used may have been, whereas this is not the case for the national-socialist secular religion, but communism is closer to us, in time, than Nazism, as well. Also, the new elites of the ex-communist "block" are very much the same as the old ones, and again, Western communists may wash their hands of the horrors committed by the communist parties in power. As a consequence of these various factors, communism is protected by powerful "communitarian" effects.

Adam Smith's famous "impartial spectator" is therefore not simply a theoretical construct: it also identifies some crucial sociological and political mechanisms.

Had French public opinion been consulted, it probably would have rejected the idea of setting up a special court to judge political officials, and would also have taken issue with the assessment, by that court, of the responsibility of the ministers indicted in the contaminated blood case. In this case, the majority of the public would have taken the "impartial spectator" position. The poll findings mentioned above are sufficiently clear: the incidence of "communitarian" biases is slight in comparison with the effects of universal values.

But the "impartial spectator" has another influence as well. The "committed actor" anticipates that impartial judgment, more or less, and moves under the gaze of the "impartial spectator." Accordingly, some journalists, mostly anxious to court the politicians, at the onset of the contaminated blood affair (prompted by the henceforth familiar "communitarian biases"), reversed their attitudes in a matter of days. After the early comments, arguing that ministers have such extensive competencies that they should be exonerated from any penal responsibility–thus legitimizing recourse to a special court, a better solution for those political leaders–they proceeded to contend that in a complete democracy, there is no reason why a minister should not be judged by the same court as a company head or a school principal. Between the two comments, the "impartial spectator" had discretely made himself heard, through opinion polls in particular, but also through other channels such as "interactive" radio programs, to which he has inconspicuous but real access.

When J. Habermas speaks of a mysterious "communicative rationality," it is perhaps this set of micro-mechanisms that he has in mind, although he does not take pains to identify them. In any case, what is shown by the previous analysis is the absence of a guarantee, in a discussion within an ideal framework of pure, perfect social communication, that opinion will be in favor of the common weal. Even if we postulate an unfettered discussion, the chances are that the outcome will be determined *without regard* for the common weal if the majority of the opinion-givers are in the "partial actor" position (see the above examples of the thirty-five-hour work week and tax cuts) or *with regard* for the common weal if they are mostly in the "impartial spectator" position with respect to the question asked (see the example of the contaminated blood affair). In short, Habermas, unlike Kant, Weber, Durkheim, and Rawls,[16] does not understand that is impossible to construe a theory of collective values without introducing the notion of the "impartial spectator" in one way or another.

7.12. Public Opinion and the Rationalization of Social Life

The key role played by the "impartial spectator" has been stressed by all of the classical sociologists, as well as by Adam Smith (but the metaphor itself belongs to Smith exclusively). They apply it to the moral and political evolution of societies, and, correlatively, to how collective opinions and beliefs relative to values are generated. Tocqueville emphasizes the "tyranny of opinion," but his very choice of the word "tyranny" indicates that the impartial spectator may keep a critical eye on any collective opinion, however prevalent. In the same vein, Durkheim has shown that a collective belief cannot be sustained if people do not view it as grounded: "Concepts, originally taken to be true because they were collectively accepted, tend to be collectively accepted only on the condition that they are viewed as true. We demand their certification before giving them credence." Max Weber stresses the fact that moral life is pervaded by a process of "diffuse rationalization," over and beyond the "war of the gods" and the sound and fury of "historical forces," meaning by this that moral ideas are subjected to a selection process which retains those ideas preferred by the "impartial spectator" (Boudon 1997a). Max Scheler has shown that although "pharisaism" dominates social life, its very existence is revelatory of the fact that values prevail over interests, and that they determine the judgment of the "impartial spectator." Why, indeed, should the "pharisian" feel the need to convince people that his own interests coincide with the general interest, if not because he feels the gaze of the "impartial spectator" weighing down on him ? [17]

Many instances of "diffuse rationalization" of political life induced by the "impartial spectator" may be seen nowadays. It is he, in the last analysis, who is behind the resignation of the European Commission in March 1999, the challenging of the doings of the International Olympic Committee, or again, the laborious elimination of the oligarchic aspects of French democracy (one example of which is the wearing out of the rhetoric tending to justify the "French exception" governing multiple office-holding). It is thanks to him that, sometime in the future, the transportation workers' unions will perhaps devise some subtler, more acceptable kinds of collective action to replace strikes. There is even the possibility that the idea will gradually gain ground within the political community that public leaders owe their popularity and legitimacy above all to the attention they pay to the "impartial spectator": much more so, at any rate, than to the "image" fashioned by their "communications consultants" or to their efforts to cater to the interests of one "interest group" or "community" or another.

This conceptual framework accounts for the irrevocable changes in moral sensitivity reported by sociologists. Both Durkheim and Tocqueville resort to versions of the "impartial spectator" theory to explain them. Durkheim does think these irrevocable changes are facilitated by "extraneous" factors such as the increasing division of labor, which reinforces individualism, whence the notion of individual responsibility. But again, the notion of individual responsibility develops precisely because it is approved by the "impartial spectator." Durkheim never interprets the irreversibility of values as exclusively *functional*. The inadequacy of functional explanations of irrevocable changes in values is borne out—to take a contemporary example–by the fact that while the economic growth of the quarter-century Golden Age helped women to gain access to the labor market, thus contributing to the elimination of one aspect of social inequality between men and women, it is, concomitantly, the approval of "gender equality" as a value by the "impartial spectator" that has compelled its recognition. Similarly, it is because the "impartial spectator" rejects slavery outright, whenever a society proves capable of prospering without it, that in spite of the persistence of slavery in the facts, is condemned by all, and can only survive under cover, or at least illegally. Weber, too, defended the idea of a *Durchrationalisierung* of moral life, meaning that notwithstanding the conflicting action of "historical forces," some irrevocable changes in our moral sensitivity do occur. Like Tocqueville, he suggests that these irreversible changes are due to the "impartial spectator." In the same vein, Simmel has stressed the fact that when punishment for murder ceased to be indexed on the social importance of the victim, that change turned out to be irrevocable, for it is the nature of the act and the author's intentions in committing it that should determine the harshness of the sentence.

The micro-mechanisms that the most fertile schools of modern sociology discern, by various means, underlying data on opinions, also foreshadow a theory of opinions still to come. While avoiding any eclecticism, such a theory would at last move beyond that intellectually indolent model, full of preconceptions, patterned after *kinetics*, according to which correlations between opinions and socio-biographic data are necessarily explained by an occult "force," as well as the *economic* model, launched concurrently by Marxists, Nietzscheans, and proponents of the Rational Choice Model, according to which the opinions of social subjects are exclusively dictated by their individual and/or collective interests.

Perhaps, too, the theory of opinions whose outlines will be perceived through the identification of these mechanisms will put an end to the confused polemics on opinion polling. Some polls, those that place the respondent in the "impartial spectator" position, yield indications that should be taken into consideration by political leaders. To return to one of the examples discussed above, the fact that public opinion questions the legitimacy of the special court is not indifferent. Other polls, those that tend to place the respondent in the position of the "partial actor," may be—and in reality inevitably are— instrumentalized by politicians, but at their own risk.

The main conclusion to be drawn from these pages is, no doubt, that the answers of opinion-givers depend on the nature of the questions put in any real or mock consultation. They may tend toward the "partial actor" stance, as when the French are asked whether they care about tax cuts, or be more of the "impartial spectator" type, as when people are asked whether they sympathize more with Antigone or with Creon, or when they are consulted on the contaminated blood trial.

Be this as it may, one cannot, in my opinion, develop a theory of collective values without introducing the notion of the "impartial spectator" in one way or another. It is because, unlike Tocqueville, Durkheim, Simmel, and Weber, they do not recognize the latter as indispensable that some major schools of thought in the present-day social sciences are reduced to a paraleiptic treatment of the socially crucial subject of values.

Notes

1. This paper was written for the Conference on "The explanation of social norms. A comparison of sociological, economic and philosophic viewpoints based on the shared concepts of rationality and cognition" ("L'explication des normes sociales. Une comparaison des points de vue sociologique, économique et philosophique à partir de leurs concepts communs: rationalité et cognition"), organized by P. Demeulenaere and R. Viale at the Sorbonne on October 14–16, 1999. Translation into English by Helen Arnold.
2. Weber's "axiological rationality" is generally interpreted as indicating the simple coherency of the subject's acts with the values endorsed by him *for no reason*. This interpretation is incompatible with the basic postulate of "comprehensive" sociology, according to which an actor's actions and beliefs may be "understood" by the sociologist because they are meaningful to the actor: in other words, because the latter has reasons to partake of them.
3. Rawls's "veil of ignorance" is another version of Smith's "impartial spectator" as well.
4. There is an enormous amount of literature on "networks" that explores this theme, but networks are only one peculiar form of "community," in the broader sense of the term as employed by Hardin and used here as well.
5. This and the following section contain a very brief discussion of the cognitive mechanisms analyzed in Boudon (1986, 1994b, 1999d).
6. It is against the will of a great many French politicians, and thanks to the European Union, that the Colbertian model of the state is gradually fading out in contemporary France. The policy of privatization presently pursued by the government is mostly the outcome of a combination of international pressure and of the requirements for building the new Europe.
7. Douglas and Ney (1998) contend that their analysis founds a theory of cultural biases because it rests on a typology. However, their typology only accounts for some rather specific biases and does not uncover the mechanisms underlying biases in general. A typology is a *descriptive* tool rather than an *explanatory* one and for that reason does not in itself constitute a theory.
8. "I have pointed out how in times of enlightenment and democracy the human spirit is loath to accept dogmatic beliefs" (Tocqueville, 1986 [1845]: 445), which beliefs are defined by Tocqueville as "those that men receive trustfully, without discussing them" (ibid).
9. Legrand is apparently referring to the school of sociology led by P. Bourdieu.
10. These hypotheses are also found in the "cognitive dissonance" model, according to which the subject attempts, in a minimalist way, to modify his belief system so as to eliminate contradictions. Insufficient attention has been paid to the fact that this model implies that ordinary thought processes follow the same rules as scientific thinking.

214   The Origin of Values

11. In the slang of the *Ecole normale supérieure,* a college for the intellectual elite, the term "talas" designates people who "vonT-A-LA messe" (who go to mass). See Peyrefitte (1998).
12. A perfectly classical version of this script was played out, for example, from mid-September 1999 on, when the Michelin corporation announced its lay-offs.
13. Information given by Canal+ TV, October 13, 1999.
14. The habit of polling has reinforced the idea that individual opinions are random, ungrounded, or again, socially determined, since people are of course only questioned about issues on which opinions are divided.
15. This interpretation has been legitimized both by conservatives such as Leo Strauss and Carl Schmitt and by postmodernists, all too happy to turn Weber into a post-Nietzschean. One need only refer to Coser (1984), however, to realize that there is nothing new about the rejection of an interpretation of this sort ("Many commentators have contended, for example, that Strauss completely misunderstood Max Weber ; but this seems never to have disturbed him or his followers"). This is an excellent example of the application of "Hamilton's law" (1996), according to which some hackneyed errors may be endlessly repeated in both scholarly and non-specialized circles. In France, R. Aron's preface to a popular edition of Max Weber's lectures, *Le savant et le politique,* helped to keep Strauss' interpretation in circulation.
16. There is also Rousseau (the "general will").
17. In itself, this remark suffices to disqualify the allegations of all those neo-Marxists, neo-Nietzscheans, and "Rational Choice Model" neo-Benthamians who proclaim the universality of their explanations, of the utilitarian value type.

References

Abel, T. 1964. "The Operation Called Verstehen." In H. Albert, ed., *Theorie und Realität. Ausgewählte Aufsätze zur Wissenschaftslehre der Sozialwissenschaften*, pp. 177–188. Tübingen: Mohr.

Albert, H. 1990. "Der Mythos des Rahmens am Pranger." *Zeitschrift für philosophische Forschung* Band 44, 1: 85–97.

Allais, M. 1953. "Le comportement de l'homme rationnel devant le risque: critique des postulats de l'école américaine." *Econometrica* 21, 4: 503–46.

Axelrod, R. 1984. *The Evolution of Cooperation*. New York: Basic Books.

Bazerman, M. 1985. "Norms of Distributive Justice in Interest Arbitration." *Industrial and Labor Relations Review* 38, 4, July: 558–70.

Bell, D. 1997. *La fin de l'idéologie*. Paris: PUF.

Bergeron, H. 1999. *Soigner ou prendre soin des toxicomanes: anatomie d'une croyance collective*. Paris: PUF.

Bloom, A. 1987. *The Closing of the American Mind*. Simon & Schuster: New York.

Bloor, D. 1980, *Knowledge and Social Imagery*. London: Routledge & Kegan Paul.

Bodin, J. 1986 [1576]. *Les six livres de la République*. Paris: Fayard.

Boudon, R. 1974. *Education, Opportunity and Social Inequality*. New York: Wiley.

Boudon, R. 1981. *Logic of social action*. London/Boston: Routledge & Kegan Paul.

Boudon, R. 1982. *The Unintended Consequences of Social Action*. London: Macmillan.

Boudon, R. 1986. *L'idéologie ou l'origine des idées reçues*. Paris: Fayard/Seuil, Collection "Points." Eng. trans.: *The Analysis of ideology*. London: Polity Press. 1989.

Boudon, R. 1989. Subjective Rationality and the Explanation of Social Behavior. *Rationality and Society* 1, 2, oct.: 171–196.

Boudon, R. 1992. Sentiments of Justice and Social Inequalities. *Social Justice Research* 5, 2, June: 113–135.

Boudon, R. 1993. "European Sociology: The Identity Lost?" In B. Nedelmann and P. Sztompka, eds., *Sociology in Europe. In search of identity,* pp. 27–44. New York/ Berlin: De Gruyter.

Boudon, R. 1994a. "La logique des sentiments moraux." *L'Année sociologique* 44: 19–51.

Boudon, R. 1994b. *The Art of Self-Persuasion*. London: Polity Press.

Boudon, R. 1995a. "A propos des sentiments de justice: nouvelles remarques sur la théorie de Rawls." *L'Année sociologique* 45, 2: 273–296.

Boudon, R. 1995b. *Le juste et le vrai; essais sur l'objectivité des valeurs et de la connaissance*. Paris: Fayard.

Boudon, R. 1997a. "La rationalité axiologique." In S. Mesure, ed., *La rationalité des valeurs*, pp. 15–57. Paris: PUF, and in R. Boudon, *Le sens des valeurs*, pp. 137–203. Paris: PUF, "Quadrige," 1999.

215

Boudon, R. 1997b. "Le 'paradoxe du vote' et la théorie de la rationalité." *Revue française de sociologie* 38, 2: 217–227.

Boudon, R. 1997c. "Peut-on être positiviste aujourd'hui?" In C.H. Cuin, ed., *Durkheim d'un siècle à l'autre*, pp. 265–288. Paris: PUF.

Boudon, R. 1998. "Social mechanisms without black boxes." Conference on "Social Mechanisms." In R. Swedberg and P. Thedstrom, eds., *Social Mechanisms: An Analytical Approach to Social Theory*, pp. 172–203. Cambridge: Cambridge University Press.

Boudon, R. 1999a. "Les Formes Elementaires de la Vie Religieuse: une théorie toujours vivante." *L'Année Sociologique* 49, 1: 149–198.

Boudon, R. 1999b. "La théorie des valeurs de Max Scheler vue depuis la théorie des valeurs de la sociologie classique." *Cahier du Gemas*, 6.

Boudon, R. 1999c. *Le sens des valeurs*. Paris: PUF, "Quadrige."

Boudon, R. 1999d. "Local vs. general ideologies: a normal ingredient of modern political life." *Journal of Political Ideologies* 4, June, 2: 141–161.

Bourricaud, F. 1980. *Le bricolage idéologique*. Paris: PUF.

Brickman, Ph., Folger, R., Goode, E., Schul, Y. 1981. "Microjustice and Macrojustice." In M. J. Lerner and S. C. Lerner, eds., *The Justice Motive in Social Behavior, Adapting to Times of Scarcity and Change*, pp. 173–208. New York: Plenum Press.

Brulé, M. 1999. "Pourquoi notre dépense publique a la vie dure?" *Sociétal* 24, March: 4–6.

Brym, A.J. 1980. *Intellectuals and politics*. London: Allen & Unwin.

Bunge, M. 1996. *Finding philosophy in social science*. New Haven, CT: Yale University Press.

Caplovitz, D. 1967. *The Poor Pay More*. London: Macmillan/New York: Free Press.

Coleman, J. S. 1986. *Individual Interests and Collective Action: Selected Essays*. Cambridge: Cambridge University Press.

Coleman, J. S. 1990. *Foundations of Social Theory*. Cambridge/London: The Belknap Press of Harvard University Press.

Coser, L. 1956. *The Functions of Social Conflict*. Glencoe, IL: The Free Press.

Coser, L. 1984. *Refugee Scholars in America*. Newhaven: Yale University Press.

dal Lago, A. 1988. "Le nouveau polythéisme." In G. Vattimo, ed., *La sécularisation de la pensée*. Paris: Seuil.

Damon, C. 1988. *The Moral Child, Nurturing Children's Natural Moral Growth*. New York: Free Press.

Davidson, D. 1980. "Actions, Reasons and Causes." In *Essays on action and events*. Oxford: Oxford University Press.

Deliège, R. 1993. *Le système des castes*. Paris: PUF.

Deutsch, M. 1975. "Equity, Equality, and Need, What Determines Which Value Will be Used as the Basis of Distributive Justice? *The Journal of Social Issues* 31, 3: 137–151.

Deutsch, M. 1986. "Cooperation, Conflict, and Justice." In H. W. Bierhoff, R. L. Cohen, J. Greenberg, eds., *Justice in Social Relations*, pp. 3–17. New York: Plenum Press.

Douglas, M., Ney, S. 1998. *Missing Persons: A Critique of Personhood in the Social Sciences*. Berkeley: University of California Press and London: Russell Sage Foundation.

Downs, A. 1972. "Up and Down with Ecology—the 'Issue-attention Cycle'" *The Public Interest* 28, summer: 38–50.

Duhem, P.,1954. *Le système du monde*. Paris: Hermann & Cie.

Durkheim, E. 1979 [1912]. *Les formes élémentaires de la vie religieuse. Le système totémique en Australie*. Paris: PUF.

Elster, J. 1985. *Making Sense of Marx. Studies in Marxism and Social Theory*. Cambridge: Cambridge University Press.

Elster, J. 1992. *Local Justice. How Institutions Allocate Scarce Goods and Necessary Burdens*. New York: Russell Sage Foundation.

Ferry, L., Renaut, A. 1985. *La Pensée 68: Essai sur l'Antihumanisme Contemporain*. Paris: Gallimard.

Fleischmann, E. 1964. "De Weber à Nietzsche." *Archives européennes de sociologie* 5, 2: 190–238.

Frey, B. S. 1997. *Not Just for the Money: An Economic Theory of Personnal Motivation*. Cheltenham: Edward Elgar.

Frohlich, N., Oppenheimer, J. A. 1992. *Choosing Justice, an Experimental Approach to Ethical Theory*. Oxford: University of California Press.

Geertz, C. 1984. "Distinguished Lecture: Anti anti-relativism." *American Anthropologist* 86, 2: 263–278.

Glendon, M.-A. 1996. *A Nation under Lawyers*. Cambridge, MA: Harvard University Press.

Goffman, E. 1974. *Frame Analysis. An Essay on the Organization of Experience*. New York: Harper & Row.

Goldthorpe, J. 1996. "Class Analysis and the Reorientation of Class Theory: The Case of the Persisting Differentials in Educational Attainment." In *Gn Sociology: Numbers, Narratives, and the Integration of Research and Theory*, Oxford: Oxford University Press

Habermas, J. 1981, *Theorie des kommunikativen Handelns*. Frankfurt: Suhrkamp.

Hamilton, R. F. 1996. *The Social Misconstruction of Reality*. New Haven/London: Yale University Press.

Hardin, R. 1995. *One for All: The Logic of Group Conflict*. Princeton, NJ: Princeton University Press.

Harsanyi, J. C. 1955. "Cardinal Welfare, Individualistic Ethics, and Interpersonal Comparisons of Utility." *The Journal of Political Economy* 63, 4, August: 309–21.

Harsanyi, J. C. 1961. "On the Rationality Postulates Underlying the Theory of Cooperative Game." *Journal of Conflict Resolution* 5.

Harsanyi, J. C. 1977. *Rational Behaviour and Bargaining Equilibrium in Games and Social Situations*. Cambridge: Cambridge University Press.

Heath, A. 1971. "Review Article: Exchange Theory." *British Journal of Political Science* 1, 1, January: 91–119.

Hechter, M. 1992. "Should Values Be Written Out of the Social Scientist's Lexicon ?" *Sociological Theory* 10, 2, fall: 214–230.

Hennis, W. 1987. *Max Webers Fragestellung*. Tübingen: J. C. B. Mohr [Paul Siebeck].

Hochschild, J. L. 1981. *What's Fair? American Beliefs about Distributive Justice*. Cambridge, Massachusetts/London, England: Harvard University Press.

Hollis, M. 1977. *Models of Man: Philosophical Thoughts on Social Action*. Cambridge: Cambridge University Press.

Homans, G. C. 1958. "Social Behavior as Exchange." *American Journal of Sociology* 63, 6: 597–606.

Hübner, K. 1985. *Die Wahrheit der Mythen*. Munich: Beck.

Inglehart, R., Basañez, M., Moreno, A. 1998. *Human Values and Beliefs, a Cross-Cultural Sourcebook*. Ann Arbor: The University of Michigan Press.

Janicaud, D. 1996. "Partage technique et intelligence éthique." In P. Livet, ed., *L'éthique à la croisée des savoirs*, pp. 89–100. Paris: Vrin.

Kahneman, D., Knetsch, J., Thaler, R. 1986a. "Fairness and the Assumption of Economics." *Journal of Business* 59: 285–300.

Kahneman, D., Knetsch, J. L., Thaler, R. 1986b. "Fairness as a Constraint on Profit Seeking." *The American Economical Review* 76, 4: 728–41.

Kant, I. 1785. *Grundlegung zur Metaphysik der Sitten*, in Kant's *gesammelte Schriften*. Hrsg von der Königlich Preussischen Akademie der Wissenschaften, Berlin: G. Reimer, W. De Gruyter, 1910, Tome IV, 1911.

Kant, I. 1787. *Kritik der reinen Vernunf.* Bibliographisches Institüt, Leipzig/Vienna: Meyers Volksbücher, 2nd ed., no date.

Kant, I. 1797. "Über ein vermeintes Recht aus Menschenliebe zu lügen." *Berlinische Blätter* 1: 301–314.

Kellerhals, J., Modak, M., Sardi, M. 1995. "Justice, sens de la responsabilité et relations sociales." *L'Année sociologique* 45, 2: 317–349.

Knies, K. G. A. 1883. *Die politische Oekonomie vom geschichtlichen Standpunkte*. Neue, durch abgesonderte Zusätze verm. Aufl. der *"politischen Oekonomie vom Standpunkte der geschichtlichen Methode*," Braunschweig: Schwetschke & Sohn, 1853.

Kuran, T. 1995. *Private Truths, Public Lies. The Social Consequences of Preference Falsification*. Cambridge, MA: Harvard University Press.

Landes, D. S. 1998. *The Wealth and Poverty of Nations: Why Some Are So Rich and Some So Poor*. London : Little Brown.

Legrand, L. 1982. *Pour un collège démocratique*. Rapport au ministre de l'éducation nationale. La Documentation française.

Lukes, S. 1967. "Some Problems about Rationality." *Archives européennes de sociologie* 8, 2: 247–264.

MacIntyre, A. 1981. *After Virtue*. London: Dockworth.

Marx, K. 1968. "Matériaux pour l' 'économie.'" In *Oeuvres: Economie*. T. II, Paris: Gallimard.

Mead, G. H. 1934. *Mind, Self and Society. From the Standpoint of a Social Behaviorist*. Chicago: The University of Chicago Press.

Mills, C. W. 1951. *White Collars. The American Middle Classes*. New York: Oxford University Press.

Mitchell, G., Tetlock, P. E., Mellers, B. A., Ordonez, L. D. 1993. "Judgements of Social Justice: Compromise Between Equality and Efficiency." *Journal of Personality and Social Psychology* 65, 4: 629–639.

Mommsen, W. 1965. "Max Weber's Political Sociology and His Philosophy of World History." *International Social Science Journal* 17, 1: 23–45.

Mommsen, W.J. 1959. *Max Weber und die deutsche Politik, 1890–1920*. Tübingen: J. C. B. Mohr.

Nietzsche, F. 1887. *Zur Genealogie der Moral*. T.3. In *Werke*. Hrsg. von Karl Schlechta, Frankfurt am Main/Wien: Ullstein Verl., 1972.

Nisbet, R. A. 1966. *The Sociological Tradition*. Glencoe, IL: The Free Press.

Nisbett, R., Ross, L. 1980. *Human Inference*. Englewood Cliffs, NJ: Prentice Hall.

Nozick, R. 1997. "Why Do Intellectuals Oppose Capitalism?" In *Socratic Puzzles*, Cambridge, MA: Harvard University Press.

Oberschall, A. 1994. "Règles, normes, morale: émergence et sanction." *L'Année sociologique* 44, "Argumentation et Sciences Sociales": 357–384.

Olson, M. 1993. "Dictatorship, Democracy and Development." *American Political Science Review* 87, 3, September: 567–576.

Opp, K. D. 1983. *Die Entstehung sozialer Normen*. Tübingen: J. C. B. Mohr.

Overbye, E. 1995. "Making a Case for the Rational, Self-regarding, 'Ethical' Voter—

and Solving the 'Paradox of Not Voting' in the Process." *European Journal of Political Research* 27: 369–96.

Pareto, V. 1935. *The Mind and Society*. New York: Harcourt Brace.

Pascal, B. 1977 [1670]. *Pensées*. Paris: Gallimard.

Peyrefitte, A. 1998. *Rue d'Ulm: chroniques de la vie normalienne*. Paris: Fayard. 5th ed.

Piaget, J. 1985. *Le jugement moral chez l'enfant*. Paris: P.U.F. 6th ed.

Popkin, R. H. 1964. *The History of Scepticism from Erasmus to Descartes*. Assen: Van Gorcum.

Popper, K. 1967. "La rationalité et le statut du principe de rationalité." In E. M. Claasen, ed., *Les fondements philosophiques des systèmes économiques*, pp. 142–150. Paris: Payot.

Popper, K. 1976. "The Myth of the Framework." In E. Freeman, ed., *The Abdication of Philosophy: Philosophy and the Public Good*, pp. 23–48. La Salle, IL: Open Court.

Popper, K. R. 1968. *The Logic of Scientific Discovery*. London: Hutchinson.

Radnitzky, G. 1987. "La perspective économique sur le progrès scientifique: application en philosophie de la science de l''analyse coût-bénéfice." *Archives de philosophie* 50, April-June: 177–198.

Rawls, J. 1971. *A Theory of Justice*. Cambridge, MA: The Belknap Press of Harvard University Press.

Rawls, J. 1993. *Political Liberalism*. New York: Columbia University Press.

Revel, J. F. 1988. *La connaissance inutile*. Paris: Grasset.

Root, H. L. 1994. *The Fountain of Privilege: Political Foundations of Economic Markets in Old Regime France and England*. Berkeley: University of California Press.

Rorty, R. 1989. *Contingency, Irony and Solidarity*. Cambridge/New York: Cambridge University Press.

Ruse, M. 1993. "Une défense de l'éthique évolutionniste." In J. P. Changeux, ed., *Fondements naturels de l'éthique*, pp. 35–64. Paris: Odile Jacob.

Ryle, G. 1966 [1949]. *The Concept of Mind*. London: Hutchinson.

Scheler, M. 1954 [1916]. *Der Formalismus in der Ethik und die materiale Wertethik*. [*Jahrbuch für Philosophie und phänomenologische Forschung*, January 1913 and July 1916]. 1st Germ. ed. 1916, reprinted in *Gesammelte Werke*. V. 2, Bern/München: Francke.

Scheler, M. 1978 [1912]. *Das Ressentiment im Aufbau der Moralen*. Frankfurt: Klostermann.

Schmidt, V. 1994. "Bounded Justice." *Social Science Information* 33: 305–333.

Schweisguth, E., Grunberg, G. 1996. "Bourdieu et la misère: une approche réductionniste." *Revue française de science politique*, 46, 1: 134–155.

Shweder, R. A. 1977. "Likeliness and Likelihood in Everyday Thought: Magical Thinking in Judgments about Personality." *Current Anthropology* 18, 4, December: 637–659.

Simmel, G. 1892. *Die Probleme der Geschichtsphilosophie*. Munchen: Duncker & Humblot.

Simmel, G. 1989. *Gesammelte Schriften zur Religionssoziologie*. Berlin: Duncker & Humblot.

Smith, A. 1976[1776]. *An Inquiry into the Nature and Causes of the Wealth of Nations*. London: W. Strahen and T. Cadell/ Oxford: Clarendon Press.

Sperber, D. 1996. *La contagion des idées*. Paris: Odile Jacob.

Strauss, L. 1953. *Natural Right and History*. Chicago: Chicago University Press.

220   **The Origin of Values**

Sukale, S. 1995. "Introduction to Max Weber." *Schriften zur Soziologie.* Stuttgart: Reclam.
Tarski, A. 1936. "Der Wahreitsbegriff in den formalisierten Sprache." *Studia Philosophica* 1.
Taylor, C. 1997. *La liberté des modernes.* Selected essays presented by Ph. De Lara. Paris: PUF.
Tocqueville, A. de. 1986 [1845]. *De La démocratie en Amérique II.* In *Tocqueville. De la démocratie en Amérique, Souvenirs, l'Ancien Régime et la Révolution,* pp. 427–659. Paris: Laffont.
Tocqueville, A. de. 1986 [1856]. *L'Ancien Régime et la Révolution.* In *Tocqueville. De la démocratie en Amérique, Souvenirs, l'Ancien Régime et la Révolution,* pp. 893–1121. Paris: Laffont.
Trevelyan, G. M. 1993. *Histoire sociale de l'Angleterre.* Paris: Laffont.
Turner, B. S. 1992. *Max Weber: from History to Modernity.* London: Routledge.
Tversky, A., Slovic, P., Kahneman, D., eds. 1982. *Judgement under Uncertainty.* Cambridge: Cambridge University Press.
Tyler, T., Lind, E. A. 1992. "A Relational Model of Authority in Groups." In M. P. Zanna, ed., *Advances in Experimental Social Psychology,* 25, pp. 115–191. San Diego: Academic Press.
Voegelin, E. 1952. *The New Science of Politics.* Chicago, IL: The University of Chicago Press.
Walzer, M. 1983. *Spheres of Justice. A Defense of Pluralism and Equality.* Oxford: Martin Robertson.
Weber, M. 1922. *Wirtschaft und Gesellschaft.* Tübingen: Mohr.
Weber, M. 1978 [1921]. *Gesammelte Aufsätze zur Religionssoziologie.* II. Die Wirtschaftsethik der Weltreligionen. Hinduismus und Buddhismus. Munich: Beck.
Weber, M. 1986 [1920]. *Gesammelte Aufsätze zur Religionssoziologie.* I. Tübingen: Mohr.
Weber, M. 1988 [1922]. *Gesammelte Aufsätze zur Wjissenschaftslehre.* Tübingen: Mohr.
Wilson, J. Q. 1993. *The Moral Sense.* New York: Macmillan/The Free Press.

Index

values and, 6–7
See also Axiological rationality;
    Polytheism of values
Wills, C. W.
    rational choice model, 139–141

value sociology examples, 139–141
Wilson, James, 8, 37, 75
Women, gender equality, 212

Zero hypothesis, 99–100